German In 32 Lessons

The Gimmick Series

German In 32 Lessons

Adrienne

adapted by Alfred Schemmer

W · W · NORTON & COMPANY

New York · London

W. W. Norton & Company, Inc., 500 Fifth Avenue, New York, N.Y. 10110
W. W. Norton & Company Ltd., 37 Great Russell Street, London WC1B 3NU
Copyright © 1978 by Adrienne Penner
Printed in the United States of America.
All Rights Reserved

Adapted from the French edition published by Flammarion 1977
© Flammarion 1977.
First published in Great Britain 1978

Library of Congress Cataloging in Publication Data

Adrienne.
    German in 32 lessons.

    1. German language—Grammar—1950–
2. German language—Conversation and phrase books.
3. German language—Self-instruction.
I. Schemmer, Alfred.   II. Title.
PF3112.5.A3 1978   438'.3'421   78–23496

ISBN 0-393-04533-1

For Carolyn and Jimmy McGown
and their grandfather

Contents/Inhaltsverzeichnis

Preface/Vorwort

The Gimmicks for the more advanced student have been found so useful by so many — in French, German, Spanish and English — throughout Europe and America — that I have prepared a method to meet the needs of students at an earlier stage of language learning. There is much to criticise in present methods.

Beginners aren't imbeciles!

The boring repetition of inane exercises in 'modern' methods is an insult to the intelligence. To repeat, endlessly, structured sentences is a sure way to kill the discovery of one's own style. Without the freedom to make mistakes, the student will never learn to 'feel' the language. This is why, after a year or more of study, the student, often, can barely get a sentence out on his own. Emphasis on constant structuring discourages creativity, and speaking a language is a creative process.

Forced feeding

It's no good having perfect grammar if your vocabulary is limited to a few words. This is THE problem in language learning, for a language IS ITS VOCABULARY. Grammar and writing exercises over and over should not be dwelt on ridiculously. It will come automatically if vocabulary is learned properly. It doesn't matter if the beginner is lost . . . confused. Beginners are not fragile. They won't break. I don't ask mine to understand. I ask them to learn . . . hundred of words. The theorist may need high grammar. Mr and Ms John Q. Public need words in order to understand and be understood. Vocabulary should be programmed and progressive — and gobbled up.

Tests

TESTS ARE ABSOLUTELY INDISPENSABLE FOR THOSE WHO WANT TO LEARN A LANGUAGE IN LESS THAN TEN YEARS! You can be tested by the teacher or by a friend. Each lesson should be well tested, written if possible, to make sure the words are 'in the head' and not just in the book. And, as learning is rarely 'solid' the first time, the same test should be repeated throughout the year. You must memorize hundreds, thousands of words. There is no way to communicate without words. I don't care how perfect your grammar is.

Mistakes are an asset!

Making mistakes is one of the principal ways the student learns a language . . . when it really sinks in. For verbs there is nothing better. Written resumés are excellent for this reason, and the student should write them for homework as of the first lessons: at first a small paragraph about his house, job, family, etc., and then a page summary of a movie, etc. This is the way he will find his style.

Homework
Homework is always a good thing — if only studying for constant vocabulary tests. Written summaries are an excellent way to ensure that verbs and vocabulary are being assimilated.

Pace
A very good glass can assimilate one lesson a week (a once- or twice-a-week class). Those with less time might need two to three weeks for each lesson.

Not strictly kosher!
When necessary to facilitate learning, I have sacrificed strict grammatical explanations. The purist may frown on this, but the student will understand more easily. As it is easier to learn a group of works rather than the classic one-to-one translation, the vocabulary is taught by association.

Institut audio-visuel
Those who want to contact me personally should write to: Adrienne, IAV, 40 rue de Berri, 75008 Paris, France.

The ideal lesson
An ideal lesson might include:
— 15 minutes: the student asks each other questions to begin the class — using the verbs and vocabulary they have learned.
— 20 minutes: oral summary of a story, film, etc.
— 15 minutes: test (written and corrected).
— 15 minutes: grammar drills and vocabulary explanation from book, etc.
— 20 minutes: read story or article — they give quick summaries.

Optional
— 10 minutes: dictation.
— 20 minutes: debate.
— 20 minutes: scene playing.

BOXED IN!

The 'boxes' are there to concentrate your attention on the vital basic skeleton of language. Read and assimilate each well. Then learn the vocabulary by heart, always testing yourself by writing it down. Next do the exercises, correcting your work with the key at the end of the book. Each lesson represents about one week's work. After years and years of teaching executives, journalists, actors, ministers and diplomats — this method works! This is the best class text or 'self-learner' in town!!

LEKTION 1

IST DAS EIN SCHWARZER STUHL?	Is it a black chair?
Ja, das ist ein schwarzer Stuhl.	Yes, it's a black chair.

WAS IST DAS?	What is it?
Das ist ein schwarzer Stuhl.	It's a black chair.

note: All nouns have capital letters.

1 = **eins**   2 = **zwei**   3 = **drei**   4 = **vier**   5 = **fünf**

translate:

1) The mouse is white.
2) Is the chair big?
3) See you soon!
4) The book's red.
5) Is the pen black or white?
6) It's a pink telephone.
7) The watch is small, but the clock's big.
8) Is it a white wall?
9) Is it a cat or a dog?
10) Darn it!
11) Is it a blue alarm-clock?
12) Good-bye!

note: Words in German are either masculine, feminine or neuter — with no logic to guide you!

ADJECTIVES

ein grosser Mann (masculine)
ein grosses Haus (neuter)   **eine grosse Frau** (feminine)

fill in the right adjective ending:

1) Das ist eine dick . Katze.
2) Das ist ein schwarz . . Stuhl.
3) Das ist eine gross . Mauer.
4) Das ist ein rot . . Buch.
5) Das ist ein weiss . . Telefon.
6) Das ist eine blau . Tür.
7) Das ist ein gross . . Wecker.
8) Ist das ein blau . . Buch?
9) Ist das eine klein . Armbanduhr?
10) Ist das ein schwarz . . Tisch?
11) Ist das eine rot . Tür?
12) Ist das ein gross . . Haus?

2

DER — DIE — DAS	=	THE
der **Mann** (masculine)	→	the man
die **Tür** (feminine)	→	the door
das **Kind** (neuter)	→	the child
die **Wagen** (plural)	→	the cars

note: — die is the plural of der, die das.
   — One of the major problems in German are the 'little words'.

add the article, then put into the interrogative:

1) ____ Tür ist weiss.
2) ____ Tisch ist gross.
3) ____ Haus ist klein.
4) ____ Kugelschreiber ist blau.
5) ____ Maus ist weiss.
6) ____ Buch ist marineblau.
7) ____ Telefon ist rosa.
8) ____ Wecker ist schwarz.
9) ____ Frau ist blau.
10) ____ Katze ist klein.
11) ____ Buchhandlung ist klein.
12) ____ Armbanduhr ist blau.
13) ____ Kuli ist rot.
14) ____ Katze ist dick.
15) ____ Bleistift ist gross.

answer in the affirmative:

1) Ist das ein schwarzer Stuhl?
2) Ist das ein rotes Telefon?
3) Ist das ein Kugelschreiber?
4) Ist das ein grosser Tisch?
5) Ist der Wecker rosa?
6) Ist das ein grosses Haus?
7) Ist die Frau dick?
8) Ist das ein Hund?
9) Ist die Maus schwarz?
10) Ist die Buchhandlung klein?
11) Ist das eine weisse Maus?
12) Ist die Armbanduhr marineblau?

translate, then put into the interrogative:

1) It's a big car.
2) The car's big and white.
3) The woman's drunk.
4) The door's red and blue.
5) The table's small.
6) It's a big house.
7) The bookstore's big.
8) It's a big chair.
9) The mouse is black.
10) It's a big alarm-clock.
11) It's a black pen.
12) The man's big.
13) The wall's white.
14) It's a big bookstore.

VOKABELN = VOCABULARY

	Übersetzung = translation	Sinnverwandte Wörter = synonyms	Gegenteil = opposite
1. (die) Katze	cat	(die) Maus	(der) Hund = dog
2. (der) Tisch	table ≠ chair		(der) Stuhl
3. ja	yes		nein = no
4. guten Tag	hello ≠ good-bye	hallo	auf Wiedersehen, tschüss = bye
5. noch einmal	again	wieder	
6. (die) Mauer	wall	(die) Wand	
7. (das) Telefon	telephone, phone		
8. (der) Kugelschreiber	pen (ballpoint)	(der) Kuli	(der) Bleistift = pencil
9. /(die) Armbanduhr /(die) Uhr	/watch/clock	(der) Wecker = alarm-clock	
10. (die) Tür	door		
11. /und/oder	/and/or	aber = but	
12. schwarz	black		weiss = white
13. Mist!	darn it!	Scheisse! = shit!	
14. klein	little ≠ big		gross, dick
15. /der, die, das /ein, eine	/the/a, an		
16. rot	red	rosa = pink	
17. blau	/blue/drunk	marineblau = navy blue	
18. (das) Buch	book	(die) Buchhandlung = bookstore	
19. (die) Hausaufgabe	homework		
20. bis bald!	see you soon!		

LEKTION 2

NICHT = NOT

IST DIE FRAU SCHÖN?   Is the woman beautiful?

Ja, die Frau ist schön.   Yes, the woman's beautiful.
Nein, die Frau ist <u>nicht</u> schön.   No, the woman is<u>n't</u> beautiful.

KEIN(E) = NOT A

IST DAS EIN WAGEN?   Is it a car?

Ja, das ist ein Wagen.   Yes, it's a car.
Nein, das ist <u>kein</u> Wagen.   No, it <u>isn't a</u> car.

---

6 = **sechs**   7 = **sieben**   8 = **acht**   9 = **neun**   10 = **zehn**

translate:

1) Could you repeat it, please?
2) The girl isn't old and neither am I/me neither.
3) How are you? — Fine, thank you and you?
4) Peter's strong and me too.
5) Is it a boy or a girl?
6) The old man's fat.
7) Peter's rich, but John's poor.
8) It isn't an easy lesson.
9) But the homework isn't difficult.
10) It's wrong.

6

put into the negative, then into the interrogative:

1) Das ist ein Aschenbecher.
2) Es ist so spät.
3) Das ist ein brauner Regenmantel.
4) Die Musik ist laut.
5) Das ist ein alter Wagen.
6) Das ist eine lange Pfeife.
7) Das ist ein schwarzer Schuh.
8) Das Kind ist jung.
9) Die Tür ist weiss.
10) Das ist eine schwere Hausaufgabe.
11) Der reiche Mann ist gut.
12) Das ist eine breite Strasse.
13) Die Musik ist gut.
14) Das ist ein kleiner Schlüssel.
15) Die Lektion ist leicht.
16) Das ist Lektion 3.
17) Das ist ein grosses Zimmer.
18) Das dicke Papier ist weiss.
19) Das ist richtig.
20) Das kleine Kind ist ein Mädchen.
21) Der alte Mann ist reich.
22) Der braune Aschenbecher ist schwer.
23) Die dicke Frau ist alt.
24) Das ist eine blaue Schachtel.
25) Das ist ein guter Mann.
26) Das ist eine schöne Pfeife.
27) Die junge Frau ist schön.
28) Das ist eine enge Strasse.

add the adjective ending, then put in the negative, and then into the interrogative:

1) Das ist eine lang ____ Strasse.
2) Das ist ein braun ____ Hut.
3) Das ist ein gross ____ , neu ____ Wagen.
4) Das ist ein klein ____ Kind.
5) Das ist ein dick ____ Mann.
6) Das ist eine schön ____ Pfeife.
7) Das ist ein braun ____ Schuh.
8) Das ist ein lang ____ , schwarz ____ Regenmantel.
9) Das ist ein stark ____ Mann.
10) Peter ist stark ____
11) Maria ist ein klein ____ Mädchen.
12) Das ist eine gross ____ Uhr.
13) Das ist ein schwer ____ Tisch.
14) Das ist eine weiss ____ Mauer.
15) Frau Schmidt ist jung ____
16) Das ist eine schwer ____ Lektion.
17) Das ist eine leicht ____ Hausaufgabe.
18) Das Buch ist rot ____ .
19) Das ist eine gross ____ Buchhandlung.
20) Der Tisch ist klein ____
21) Das ist ein laut ____ Wecker.
22) Das ist eine weiss ____ Maus.
23) Das ist ein arm ____ Mann.
24) Das ist ein neu ____ Feuerzeug.
25) Das ist eine alt ____ Schachtel.
26) Brigitte ist ein jung ____ Mädchen.
27) Das ist ein stark ____ , dick ____ Mann.
28) Peter ist ein klein ____ Junge.

learn by heart, then ask someone to give you a test

1) **das Mädchen ist jung**   ≠   **alt**
   the girl's young   old

2) **die Frau ist dick**   ≠   **dünn**
   the woman's fat   thin

3) **der Tisch ist schwer**   ≠   **leicht**
   the table's heavy   light

4) **die Musik ist laut**   ≠   **leise**
   the music's loud   soft

5) **die Strasse ist breit**   ≠   **eng**
   the street's wide   narrow

6) **Michael ist reich**   ≠   **arm**
   Mike's rich   poor

7) **der Mann ist stark**   ≠   **schwach**
   the man's strong   weak

8) **das Papier ist dick**   ≠   **dünn**
   the paper's thick   thin

9) **das Zimmer ist gross**   ≠   **klein**
   the room's big   small

10) **der Mensch ist gut**   ≠   **schlecht**
    the man's good   bad

11) **die Lektion ist schwer**   ≠   **leicht**
    the lesson's difficult   easy

12) **der Wagen ist alt**   ≠   **new**
    the car's old   new

9

VOKABELN

	Übersetzung	Sinnverwandte Wörter	Gegenteil
1. auch	also ≠ neither	ich auch = me too	auch nicht, ich auch nicht = me neither
2. Wie geht es Ihnen?	How are you? ≠ Fine thank you, and you?	Wie geht's?	Danke gut und Ihnen?
3. (der) Mann	man ≠ woman	(der) Kerl = guy, (der) Typ = fellow	(die) Frau, (die) Biene = broad
4. (der) Junge	boy ≠ girl		(das) Mädchen
5. /(das) Kind /(das) Blag	/child/kid	(das) Baby = baby	
6. guten Morgen	good morning	guten Abend = good evening, gute Nacht = good night	
7. (die) Schachtel	/box/old hag		
8. das ist richtig	that's right ≠ it's wrong	genau = that's it, das stimmt = that's correct	das ist falsch
9. (der) Schlüssel	key		
10. /(der) Schuh /(die) Socke	/shoe/sock	(der) Hausschuh = slipper	
11. Können Sie wiederholen, bitte?	Could you repeat, please?		
12. /(der) Aschenbecher/(das) Streichholz/(das) Feuerzeug	/ashtray/match /lighter	Feuer = a light, (die) Pfeife = pipe	
13. /grün/braun	/green/brown	gelb = yellow	
14. kurz	short ≠ long		lang
15. /(der) Hut /(der) Mantel	/hat/coat	(der) Regenmantel = raincoat	
16. Es tut mir leid.	I'm sorry.	entschuldigen Sie = excuse me, ich entschuldige mich = I apologize	
17. Es ist so spät!	Time's up!		

LEKTION 3

SIND DAS LANGE ZIGARETTEN?   Are they long cigarettes?

Ja, das sind lange Zigaretten.   Yes, they're long cigarettes.
Nein, das sind keine langen   No, they aren't long cigarettes.
Zigaretten.

note: — Feminine nouns form their plurals by adding —n.
       — Adjectives take —e if they aren't preceded by an article; after an
         article they take —en.
       — keine is feminine as well as plural.
       — das at the beginning of the sentence doesn't change in the plural:
         das ist eine Zigarette → das sind zwei Zigaretten.
       — For the other forms of the plural, see the list at the end of the
         lesson.

WAS IST DAS?   What is it?

Das sind lange Zigaretten.   They're long cigarettes.

---

11 = **elf**   16 = **sechzehn**
12 = **zwölf**   17 = **siebzehn**
13 = **dreizehn**   18 = **achtzehn**
14 = **vierzehn**   19 = **neunzehn**
15 = **fünfzehn**   20 = **zwanzig**

11

answer in the negative, then put into the singular:

1) Sind die Autos neu?
2) Sind das lange Strassen?
3) Sind das starke Männer?
4) Sind das kleine Kinder?
5) Sind das schwarze Schuhe?
6) Sind das blaue Taschentücher?
7) Sind das moderne Kleider?
8) Sind das weisse Hüte?
9) Sind das leichte Hausaufgaben?
10) Sind das kurze Hosen?
11) Sind das grüne Handschuhe?
12) Sind das grosse Zimmer?
*13) Sind die Röcke lang?
14) Sind das schwarze Anzüge?
15) Sind die Schlipse breit?
16) Sind das braune Jacken?
17) Sind das lange Zigaretten?
18) Sind die Lektionen schwer?
19) Sind das gute Lehrerinnen?
20) Sind die Strassen breit?
21) Sind das weisse Wände?
22) Sind das grosse Häuser?
23) Sind das alte Uhren?
24) Sind die Parks grün?
25) Sind das schöne Bilder?
26) Sind die Abende lang?
27) Sind das junge Töchter?
28) Sind das schlechte Menschen?

```
┌─────────────────────────────────────────────────────────────────┐
│ ADJECTIVES                                                        │
│                                                                   │
│ Der        Wagen                        car                       │
│ Die grosse Uhr      ist neu.   The big clock   is new.            │
│ Das        Haus                         house                     │
│                                                                   │
│            Wagen                        cars                      │
│ Die grossen Uhren   sind neu.  The big clocks  are new.          │
│            Häuser                       houses                    │
└─────────────────────────────────────────────────────────────────┘
```

note: Adjectives take –e in the singular and –en in the plural if preceded by
(the definite article) DER, DIE, or DAS.

add the adjective ending:

1) Das ist ein klein _____ Kind.
2) Das sind klein _____ Kinder.
3) Das sind keine schwach_____ Frauen.
4) Das sind keine braun _____ Schuhe.
5) Die neu _____ Handschuhe sind braun.
6) Das ist ein alt _____ Wagen.
7) Kurz_____ Röcke sind nicht modern.
8) Das ist kein schön _____ Anzug.
9) Das sind keine schwer _____ Lektionen.
10) Reich _____ Menschen sind nicht arm.
11) Das ist kein arm _____ Mann.
12) Das ist ein rot _____ Telefon.
13) Das sind grün _____ Parks.
14) Das ist ein gross _____ Baum.
15) Das sind gut _____ Lehrerinnen.
16) Das ist ein schlecht _____ Mensch.

```
PLURALS

der grosse WAGEN (the big car)    →   die grossen WAGEN (the big cars)
die junge FRAU (the young         →   die jungen FRAUEN (the young
woman)                                women)
der schwarze STUHL (the black     →   die schwarzen STUHLE (the black
chair)                                chairs)
das alte HAUS (the old house)     →   die alten HÄUSER (the old houses)
```

note: — Words ending in —el, —er, —en don't have a special plural form,
but often add the 'umlaut' (two dots on the vowel): der Vater (the
father) → die Väter (the fathers).
— If one of the last two letters is —e, feminine nouns add —n, other-
wise —en; if they end in —in they add —nen.
— Nouns of only one syllable mostly take —e if they're masculine and
—er if they're neuter, both take the Umlaut (a—ä, o—ö, u—ü).
— Look at the list at the end of this lesson (page 16).

put into the plural:

1) der neue Hut   16) der kleine Bruder
2) die alte Frau   17) das blaue Meer
3) der grosse Baum   18) der gute Mensch
4) das kleine Kind   19) die kleine Schwester
5) das neue Auto   20) ein blaues Auge
6) die junge Mutter   21) ein schwarzes Taxi
7) die kleine Schwester   22) das neue Kino
8) der reiche Mann   23) die schöne Tochter
9) der blaue See   24) ein schlechtes Bild
10) das rote Taxi   25) ein weisses Hemd
11) der grüne Park   26) ein breiter Schlips
12) der rote Apfel   27) der schwarze Anzug
13) ein langer Abend   28) der kurze Tag
14) der junge Vater   29) die weisse Hose
15) ein grüner Apfel   30) der grosse Zoo
```
```

translate:

1) How are you?
2) Time's up.
3) They're new clothes.
4) His young sisters are small.
5) The old man's fat.
6) They're green trees.
7) The red books are big.
8) The new gloves are white.
9) What's the matter?
10) Nothing special.
11) Is that all?
12) They're wide streets.
13) You're welcome.
14) The homeworks are long, but easy.

translate, then put into the interrogative:

1) Big cars are loud.
2) They're white shirts.
3) They're big trees.
4) Big men are strong.
5) They're black stockings.
6) The book and the picture are blue.
7) They're black taxis.
8) The lessons are easy.
9) The homework's difficult.
10) The white paper's thin.
11) The new sweater's blue.
12) They're narrow streets.

LIST OF SOME PLURALS

1. WORDS ENDING IN —EL, —ER, —EN

der Apfel (apple)	→ die Äpfel
der Nagel (nail)	→ die Nägel
der Vater (father)	→ die Väter

die Mutter (mother)	→ die Mütter
die Tochter (daughter)	→ die Töchter
der Bruder (brother)	→ die Brüder
der Wagen (car)	→ die Wagen

2. FEMININE NOUNS

die Uhr (clock)	→ die Uhren
die Tür (door)	→ die Türen
die Frau (woman)	→ die Frauen
die Schwester (sister)	→ die Schwestern

die Tafel (blackboard)	→ die Tafeln
die Freundin (girl-friend)	→ die Freundinnen
die Lehrerin (teacher)	→ die Lehrerinnen

3. MASCULINE MONOSYLLABIC WORDS

der Abend (evening)	→ die Abende
der Baum (tree)	→ die Bäume
der Hund (dog)	→ die Hunde

der Mann (man)	→ die Männer
der Mensch (man, human)	→ die Menschen
der See (lake)	→ die Seen

4. MONOSYLLABIC NEUTER NOUNS

das Buch (book)	→ die Bücher
das Kind (child)	→ die Kinder
das Bild (picture)	→ die Bilder

das Jahr (year)	→ die Jahre
das Meer (sea)	→ die Meere
das Auge (eye)	→ die Augen

5. SOME FOREIGN WORDS

das Auto (car)	→ die Autos
das Kino (cinema)	→ die Kinos
der Park (park)	→ die Parks

das Taxi (taxi)	→ die Taxis
der Zoo (zoo)	→ die Zoos

note: The rules given on page 13 have many exceptions!!!

VOKABELN

	Übersetzung	Sinnverwandte Wörter	Gegenteil
1. (das) Kleid	dress	(der) Rock = skirt	
2. /(das)Hemd /(der) Schlips /(der) Anzug	/shirt/tie/suit	(die) Weste = vest (die) Jacke = jacket	
3. (der) Strumpf	stockings		
4. (die) Hose	slacks	(der) Stiefel = boot	
5. /(die) Tasche /(der) Handschuh	/bag/glove	(die) Handtasche = handbag (US purse)	
6. Wie heissen Sie?	What's your name?		
7. (der) Pullover	sweater	(der) Rollkragen = turtleneck	
8. (der) Schal	scarf	(das) Taschentuch = handkerchief	
9. Welch Farbe ist das?	What colour is it?		
10. danke sehr	many thanks ≠ you're welcome	bitte = please	bitte, nichts zu danken = don't mention it
11. Was gibt's Neues?	What's new?		nichts Besonderes = nothing special
12. (die) Kleidung	clothes	(das) Kleidungsstück = clothing	
13) ansehen	to watch		
14. (die) Tafel	/blackboard/bar /chart	(die) Kreide = chalk	
15. Was ist los?	What's the matter?	Was geht nicht? = what's wrong	es geht = it's O.K.
16. das macht nichts	it doesn't matter	es macht nichts = never mind	
17. das ist alles	that's all		
18. Verstehen Sie?	Do you understand?	Kapiert? = get it?	ich bin verwirrt = I'm mixed up

LEKTION 4

POSSESSIVE ADJECTIVES AND PRONOUNS

mein(e)	= my	**meiner, e, es**	= mine
dein(e) **euer, eure** **Ihr(e)**	= your	**deiner, e, es** **eurer, eure, eures** **Ihr, e, es**	= yours
sein(e)	= his, its	**seiner, e, es**	= his, its
ihr(e)	= her	**ihrer, e, es**	= hers
unser, unsre·	= our	**unserer, unsre, es**	= ours
ihr(e)	= their	**ihrer, e, es**	= theirs

note: — mein, dein, etc. are used for masculine and neuter nouns.
— meine, deine, etc. are for the feminine and the plural.
— Be careful with the translations of 'your': dein(e) is used for family, friends and lovers! (The plural is euer, eure.)

IST DAS DEIN BUCH?	Is it your book?
Ja, das ist mein Buch.	Yes, it's my book.
Ja, das ist mein(e)s.	Yes, it's mine.
Nein, das ist nicht mein Buch.	No, it isn't my book.
Nein, das ist nicht mein(e)s.	No, it isn't mine.

note: No difference between meines and meins.

21 = **einundzwanzig**	60 = **sechzig**
22 = **zweiundzwanzig**	70 = **siebzig**
23 = **dreiundzwanzig**	80 = **achtzig**
etc.	90 = **neunzig**
30 = **dreissig**	100 = **hundert**
40 = **vierzig**	1000 = **tausend**
50 = **fünfzig**	

translate in the negative form:

1) Her homework's difficult.
2) Your eyes are blue.
3) His ears are big and red.
4) The book's your book. It's yours. (3 translations)
5) Paris is near London.
6) His blue slacks are short.
7) Their child's in Paris.
8) It's our car.
9) It's her dress. It's hers.
10) The bookshop's far from here.
11) His broad's rich.
12) Your car's there. (3 translations)
13) Her guy's weak.
14) My new house is near Hamburg.
15) My old friend's here.
16) My coat's red and so is yours.
17) His wife's fat.
18) Our new lesson's difficult.
19) The little lake's over there.
20) Her nails are red.
21) My brown umbrella's new.
22) His nose is big.

use the possessive adjective instead of the noun:

e.g. Das ist mein Pullover.

     — Das ist meiner.

1) Das sind deine Bücher. Das sind _____ .
2) Das ist mein Hemd. Das ist _____ .
3) Das ist unser Haus. Das ist _____ .
4) Das ist seine Biene. Das ist _____ .
5) Das sind ihre Kinder. Das sind _____ .
6) Das ist ihr Wagen. Das ist _____ .
7) Diese sexy Hose ist ihre Hose. Das ist _____ .
8) Diese jungen Männer sind ihre Brüder. Das sind _____ .
9) Dieses rote Feuerzeug ist mein Feuerzeug. Das ist _____ .
10) Dieser schwarze Anzug ist sein Anzug. Das ist _____ .
11) Das sind unsre Hausaufgaben. Das sind _____ .
12) Das ist euer Regenschirm. Das ist _____ .
13) Der lange Schal ist ihr Schal. Das ist _____ .
14) Die schwarzen Strümpfe sind ihre Strümpfe. Das sind _____ .
15) Das sind eure Jacken. Das sind _____ .
16) Das ist seine Tasche. Das ist _____ .
17) Das ist unsre Tafel. Das ist _____ .
18) Das ist deine Kreide. Das ist _____ .
19) Das ist mein Wecker. Das ist _____ .
20) Das ist ihre Armbanduhr. Das ist _____ .
21) Das ist mein Rock. Das ist _____ .
22) Das ist unsre Kleidung. Das ist _____ .
23) Das ist sein Pullover. Das ist _____ .
24) Das neue Auto ist mein Auto. Das ist _____ .
25) Das neue Wagen ist dein Wagen. Das ist _____ .

ADJECTIVES

DER NEUE FREUND
the new friend

(M)EIN NEUER FREUND
my, a new friend

DIE NEUE FREUNDIN
the new friend

(M)EINE NEUE FREUNDIN
my, a new friend

DAS NEUE HAUS
the new house

(M)EIN NEUES HAUS
my, a new house

DIE NEUEN FREUNDE
the new friends

NEUE FREUNDE, MEINE NEUEN FREUNDE
new friends, my new friends

note: — Since ein and mein don't show if the noun's masculine or neuter, the adjective has to:

der Freund — der gute Freund — ein guter Freund
das Haus   — das schöne Haus — ein schönes Haus

— If there isn't any article in the plural, the adjective adds —e.
— Nouns add —in for the feminine (boyfriend = Freund; girlfriend = Freundin).
— Don't get uptight — even Germans make mistakes with the adjective endings!

add the correct adjective endings:

1) Ihr neu ____ Freund ist reich.
2) Wo sind meine braun ____ Handschuhe?
3) Mein neu ____ Hemd ist eng.
4) Ist das euer neu ____ Haus?
5) Neu ____ Lektionen sind schwer.
6) Die breit ____ Strasse ist weit von hier.
7) Ist ihr rot ____ Kleid modern?
8) Wo sind die grün ____ Bäume?
9) Wo sind die gross ____ Parks.
10) Ihre klein ____ Kinder sind in Florida.
11) Der alt ____ Mann ist arm.
12) Das neu ____ Kino ist gross.

translate:

1)	a white cat	31)	a brown box
2)	the black mouse	32)	the big key
3)	big dogs	33)	her black shoes
4)	a heavy table	34)	white socks
5)	the black chairs	35)	the green slippers
6)	a white wall	36)	a heavy ashtray
7)	my new telephone	37)	new lighters
8)	her blue pen	38)	the long pipe
9)	your short pencil	39)	a green hat
10)	her old alarm clock	40)	a white raincoat
11)	my new watch	41)	long coats
12)	big clocks	42)	a narrow shirt
13)	a small door	43)	the blue tie
14)	the little red book	44)	his new jackets
15)	our new bookstore	45)	her black stockings
16)	my difficult homework	46)	wide slacks
17)	beautiful women	47)	the new boots
18)	soft music	48)	a long scarf
19)	the wide roads	49)	white handkerchiefs
20)	a strong man	50)	the old blackboard
21)	the thick paper	51)	white chalk
22)	a thin girl	52)	a short nail
23)	an easy lesson	53)	the old father
24)	her old car	54)	red pictures
25)	the rich men	55)	the green park
26)	poor guys	56)	the big windows
27)	his new broad	57)	her green eyes
28)	a rich fellow	58)	his red ears
29)	little children	59)	a red mouth
30)	the fat girl	60)	their long legs

VOKABELN

	Übersetzung	Sinnverwandte Wörter	Gegenteil
1. los!	go on! ≠ wait a minute	weiter	Warten Sie eine Minute
2. (das) Fenster	window		
3. (der) Regenschirm	umbrella	(der) Regen = rain	
4. (der) Tag	day	(die) Woche = week	
5. /(das) Jahr /(der) Monat	/year/month	(das Jahrhundert = century	
6. Sonntag	Sunday	Montag, Dienstag, Mittwoch, Donnerstag, Freitag, Samstag=Sonnabend, Sonntag	
7. /wo/mit/in /wann	/where/with/in /when		
8. hier	here ≠ there		dort, dort drüben = over there
9. vor	in front of ≠ behind	gegenüber = across from	hinter
10. in der Nähe von	near ≠ far from		weit von
11. auf	on ≠ under	über = above	unter
12. neben	next to		
13. (der) Kopf	head	(das) Gesicht, (die) Schnauze (slang) = face	
14. /(das) Auge /(die) Nase	/eye/nose	sehen = to see	
15. (das) Ohr	ear	hören = to hear	
16. /(die) Hand /(der) Arm	/hand/arm		(der) Fuss = foot, (das) Bein = leg
17. (der) Mund	mouth	(der) Zahn = tooth	
18. Wie buchstabiert man es?	How do you spell it?		
19. (der) Finger	finger	(der) Nagel = nail	(die) Zehe = toe
20. vor allem	above all		

LEKTION 5

WIE SPÄT IST ES?	What time is it?
Es ist zehn Uhr.	It's ten o'clock.
Es ist viertel vor zehn.	It's a quarter to ten.
Es ist viertel nach zehn.	It's a quarter past ten.
Es ist halb elf.	It's half past ten.

note: Instead of 'half past' Germans say 'half the next hour'.

translate:

1) It's ten to four.
2) It's a quarter to three.
3) It's six o'clock in New York and noon in Bonn.
4) Half past four? All right!
5) Saturday at midnight? No dice!
6) It isn't a quarter to one, it's a quarter past one.
7) Is the lesson at half past one?
8) Five to six or five past six, it's all the same to me.
9) Is it half past seven or half past eight?
10) Four o'clock in the morning or in the afternoon?

```
DIESER — JENER = THIS — THAT

DIESER  (masc.)                      DIESER WAGEN              car
DIESE   (fem.)    this, this one     DIESE FRAU        this    woman
DIESES  (neut.)                      DIESES HAUS               house

DIESE   (plural)  these              DIESE BÜCHER      these   books

JENER   (masc.)                      JENER WAGEN               car
JENE    (fem.)    that, that one     JENE FRAU         that    woman
JENES   (neut.)                      JENES HAUS                house

JENE    (plural)  those              JENE BÜCHER       those   books
```

note: — But very often the article's used instead:
Der ist gut = This one's good.
— If there isn't the comparison between 'this' and 'that', Germans
tend to say 'dieser' all the time.

```
IST DIESES BUCH GUT?            Is this a good book?

Ja, dieses Buch ist gut.        Yes, this book's good.
Nein, dieses Buch ist nicht gut, No, this book is no good,
aber jenes Buch ist gut.        but that book's good.
Nein, dieses ist nicht gut,     No, this one is no good.
aber jenes ist gut.             but that one's good.
```

put into the interrogative plural:
e.g. Dieser Mantel ist meiner.
      — Sind diese Mäntel deine?

1) Jenes Haus ist nicht weit von Berlin.
2) Jenes Flugzeug ist deins.
3) Dieses Zimmer ist gross.
4) Jenes Hemd ist eng.
5) Diese Uhr ist meine, und jene ist ihre.
6) Jenes Kleid ist sexy.

insert the correct forms of **dieser** and **jener**:

e.g. _____ Haus ist schön, aber _____ ist hässlich.

— Dieses Haus ist schön, aber jenes ist hässlich.

1) _____ Regenmantel ist meiner, aber _____ ist deiner.
2) _____ Hemd ist schmutzig, aber _____ ist sauber.
3) _____ Lehrer hat recht, aber _____ hat unrecht.
4) _____ Lektionen sind leicht, aber _____ sind schwer.
5) _____ Auto ist schnell, aber _____ ist langsam.
6) _____ Flasche ist voll, aber _____ ist leer.
7) _____ Kurs ist interessant, aber _____ ist langweilig.
8) _____ Tisch ist hoch, aber _____ ist niedrig.
9) _____ Haus ist hier, aber _____ ist dort.
10) _____ Jahreszeit ist kalt, aber _____ ist heiss.
11) _____ Pullover ist schwarz, aber _____ ist braun.
12) _____ Mädchen ist alt, aber _____ ist jung.
13) _____ Kinder sind klein, aber _____ sind gross.
14) _____ Bleistift ist lang, aber _____ ist kurz.
15) _____ Mensch ist gut, aber _____ ist schlecht.
16) _____ Frau ist schön, aber _____ ist hässlich.
17) _____ Zimmer ist kalt, aber _____ ist warm.
18) _____ Bonbon ist süss, aber _____ ist sauer.
19) _____ Häuser sind hoch, aber _____ sind niedrig.
20) _____ Buch ist interessant, aber _____ ist langweilig.
21) _____ Mantel ist weiss, aber _____ ist grün.
22) _____ Park ist in der Nähe, aber _____ ist weit von hier.
23) _____ Flugzeug ist schnell, aber _____ ist langsam.
24) _____ Taxi ist meins, aber _____ ist deins.

WELCHER = WHICH, WHICH ONE

masc. **WELCHER Wagen?** = which car?   **WELCHER?**
fem.   **WELCHE Frau?**   = which woman? **WELCHE?**   = which one?
neut. **WELCHES Haus?** = which house? **WELCHES?**

plural **WELCHE Bücher?** = which books? **WELCHE?** = which ones?

insert the correct form of **welcher**:

1) _____ Kurs?
2) _____ Freund?
3) _____ Haus?
4) _____ Mantel?
5) _____ Strasse?
6) _____ Jahreszeit?
7) _____ Flasche?
8) _____ Monat?
9) _____ Biene?
10) _____ Mann?
11) _____ Buch?
12) _____ Auto?
13) _____ Flugzeug?
14) _____ Bus?
15) _____ Taxi?
16) _____ See?
17) _____ Schiff?
18) _____ Frage
19) _____ Kinder?
20) _____ Bahnhof?

21) _____ Lektionen?
22) _____ Zimmer?
23) _____ Fahrräder?
24) _____ Lineal?
25) _____ Zigarette?
26) _____ Zigaretten?
27) _____ Bonbon?
28) _____ Regenmantel?
29) _____ Kerl?
30) _____ Biene?
31) _____ Typ?
32) _____ Park?
33) _____ Kinder?
34) _____ Tafel?
35) _____ Anzug?
36) _____ Zug?
37) _____ Lehrerinnen?
38) _____ Schwester?
39) _____ Bruder?
40) _____ Woche?

translate:

1) Which book is mine? This one or that one?
2) January's a cold month, of course.
3) Which season's hot: winter or summer?
4) What time is it? It's midnight.
5) This car's white, but that one's black.
6) Is tomorrow Tuesday?
7) Is that your taxi or mine?
8) This underground(subway) is full but that one's empty.
9) This station isn't far from here.
10) A quarter to ten? It's a deal!

put into the singular, then into the negative, and then into the interrogative:

1) Diese Frauen sind dünn, aber jene sind dick.
2) Weisse Wagen sind schön.
3) Die kleinen Kinder sind hier.
4) Jene Hemden sind weiss, aber diese sind schwarz.
5) Diese Bücher sind neu, aber jene sind alt.
6) Grüne Parks sind in der Nähe.
7) Diese neuen Bücher sind interessant.
8) Meine braunen Pullover sind schmutzig.
9) Jene Rocke sind eng, aber diese sind weit.
10) Diese Tage sind kurz.
11) Meine alten Freunde sind hier.
12) Diese warmen Monate sind schön.
13) Diese Kerle sind interessant.
14) Diese U-Bahnen sind voll.
15) Diese Lektionen sind langweilig.
16) Diese Strassen sind gefährlich, aber jene sind sicher.
17) Jene Flaschen sind leer.
18) Diese Lehrer sind gut, aber jene sind schlecht.

GEGENTEIL 2

learn by heart, then ask someone to give you a test

1) **die Katze ist hübsch**   ≠   **hässlich**
   the cat's pretty   ugly

2) **der Mantel ist schmutzig**   ≠   **sauber**
   the coat's dirty   clean

3) **der Lehrer hat recht**   ≠   **unrecht**
   the teacher's right   wrong

4) **die Strasse ist gefährlich**   ≠   **sicher**
   the road's dangerous   safe

5) **die Lektionen sind leicht/einfach**   ≠   **schwer, schwierig**
   the lessons are easy/simple   hard, difficult

6) **das Lineal ist lang**   ≠   **kurz**
   the ruler's long   short

7) **mein Fahrrad ist schnell**   ≠   **langsam**
   my bike's fast   slow

8) **das Zimmer ist kalt**   ≠   **heiss**
   the room's cold   hot

9) **die Flasche ist leer**   ≠   **voll**
   the bottle's empty   full

10) **das Bonbon ist süss**   ≠   **sauer/bitter**
    the candy's sweet   sour/bitter

11) **die Decke ist hoch**   ≠   **niedrig**
    the ceiling's high   low

12) **unser Kurs ist interessant**   ≠   **langweilig**
    our lesson's interesting   boring

VOKABELN

	Übersetzung	Sinnverwandte Wörter	Gegenteil
1. am Mittag	at noon		um Mitternacht = at midnight
2. am Morgen	in the morning	am Nachmittag = the afternoon	in der Nacht = at night, am Abend = in the evening
3. /(der) Sommer /(der) Frühling /(die) Jahreszeit	/summer/spring /season	(der) Winter = winter, (der) Herbst = fall	
4. wieviel(e)?	how much (many)?		
5. /(die) Art/(die) Weise	/kind/way	(die) Sorte = sort	
6. heute	today	morgen = tomorrow	gestern = yesterday
7. das ist mir gleich	I don't care	es ist mir einerlei = it's all the same to me	
8. gehen	to go ≠ to come	weggehen = to go away, ausgehen = to go out	kommen, bleiben = to stay
9. /(die) Stunde /(die) Sekunde	/hour/second	(die) halbe Stunde = half hour, (die) Minute = minute	(der) Moment = while
10. Januar	January	Februar, März, April, Mai, Juni, Juli, August, September, Oktober, November, Dezember	
11. /(das) Auto /(das) Flugzeug /(das) Schiff /(der) Zug/(das) Taxi	/car/plane/boat /train/taxi	(der) Wagen, (der) Bus = bus, (die) U-Bahn = subway, (der) Bahnhof = station	
12. fragen	ask ≠ answer	eine Frage stellen = to ask a question	antworten, (die) Antwort = answer
13. einverstanden	all right ≠ no dice	das geht klar = it's a deal	auf keinen Fall
14. natürlich, selbstverständlich	of course ≠ of course not	sicher(lich) = certainly	natürlich nicht
15. verrückt	crazy	bescheuert, bekloppt	

LEKTION 6

SEIN = TO BE

ich <u>bin</u>	I am	**ich <u>bin</u> nicht**	I'm not
du <u>bist</u>	you are	**du <u>bist</u> nicht**	you aren't
er	he	**er**	he
sie <u>ist</u>		**sie <u>ist</u> nicht**	
es	she is	**es**	she isn't
das	it	**das**	it
wir <u>sind</u>	we are	**wir <u>sind</u> nicht**	we aren't
ihr <u>seid</u>	you are	**ihr <u>seid</u> nicht**	you aren't
sie	they are	**sie**	they aren't
Sie <u>sind</u>	you	**Sie <u>sind</u> nicht**	you

note: — The present in German can also be translated by our present
perfect. e.g. I ve been here since May = Ich bin seit Mai hier.
— DU is for friends and lovers (the plural is IHR).
— Sie, sind is singular and plural; this polite form is always
conjugated like the third(!) form of the plural, the only difference
being its capital letter.

SIND SIE AMERIKANER?   Are you American?

Ja, ich bin Amerikaner.   Yes, I'm American.
Nein, ich bin kein Amerikaner.   No, I'm not American.

insert the correct form of **sein**:

1) Die Decke _____ hoch.
2) Ich _____ kein Bulle.
3) Der Film _____ langweilig.
4) Die Sekretärin _____ hübsch.
5) Wir _____ keine Doktoren.
6) Peter und Helga, _____ ihr Schüler?
7) Herr Müller, _____ Sie Rechtsanwalt?
8) _____ das Kino weit von hier?
9) _____ ich Student?
10) Welcher Student _____ gut?

put into the negative, and then into the interrogative:
e.g. Sie ist ein hübsches Mädchen.
     — Sie ist kein hübsches Mädchen.
     — Ist sie ein hübsches Mädchen.

1) Er ist ein langsamer Schüler.
2) Dezember ist ein kalter Monat.
3) Wir sind reiche Geschäftsmänner.
4) Sie sind gefährliche Bullen.
5) Sie sind eine hübsche Lehrerin.
6) Das ist eine langweilige Arbeit.
7) Sie sind schwierige Direktoren.
8) Wir sind glückliche Leute.
9) Er ist ein starker Kerl.
10) Sie haben recht.

AUCH — AUCH NICHT	=	ALSO, EITHER, NEITHER
Sie ist sehr hübsch und ich auch.		She's very pretty and so am I.
Sie ist nicht sehr hübsch und ich auch nicht.		She isn't very pretty and I'm not either

DAS IST	=	IT'S
DAS IST interessant.	=	It's interesting.
DAS IST langweilig.	=	It's boring.
DAS IST klasse.	=	It's great.
DAS IST hübsch.	=	It's pretty.
DAS IST früh.	=	It's early.

translate:

1) He's a good teacher and so am I.
2) He isn't very tall and she isn't either.
3) Our school isn't very big and your's isn't either.
4) You're a student and so am I.
5) We aren't in Frankfurt and neither are you.
6) She's a good student and so are you.
7) You're American and so am I.
8) They aren't good friends and neither are you.
9) They're right and so are we.
10) We aren't sad and neither are you.
11) These fellows aren't interesting and neither are those.
12) This tube's (subway's) empty and so is that.
13) January isn't a hot month and February isn't either.
14) My broad's pretty and yours is too.
15) This street isn't safe and that one isn't either.

put into the negative plural:

1) Ich bin ein schlechter Sekretär.
2) Er ist ein glücklicher Kerl.
3) Du bist eine gute Krankenschwester.
4) Sie sind mein guter Freund.
5) Das neue Krankenhaus ist in der Nähe.
6) Diese Arbeit ist schmutzig.
7) Welche Lektion ist schwierig, diese oder jene?
8) Dieser braune Stuhl ist meiner.
9) Dieses Problem ist einfach.
10) Bin ich eine Studentin?
11) Du bist ein guter Student.
12) Das kleine Kind ist sehr hübsch.

translate:

1) I'd like you to meet Peter.
2) Which car's slow? That one!
3) Is he a good student?
4) Yes, I think so.
5) Are these films interesting?
6) Is this too much work?
7) Thank you, it's enough.
8) This book's boring, but that one's interesting.
9) Thank heavens! This lesson's easy.
10) Excuse me! What does it mean?
11) Which shirts are dirty? Those ones over there!
12) He's a cop! It's a pity.

VOKABELN

	Übersetzung	Sinnverwandte Wörter	Gegenteil
1. Ich möchte Ihnen ... vorstellen	I'd like you to meet ...		angenehm = pleased to meet you
2. /wer?/welcher?	/who?/which?	dass = that	
3. /(der) Doktor /(der) Rechtsanwalt	/doctor/lawyer	(das) Krankenhaus = hospital, (die) Krankenschwester = nurse	
4. /(der) Geschäftsmann/die Geschäfte	/businessman /business	(die) Geschäftsfrau = businesswoman	
5. /(der) Student /(die) Schule	/student/school	(die) Studentin, (der) Schüler = pupil	(der) Lehrer = teacher
6. (der) Bulle	cop	(der) Polizist, (der) Schutzmann	
7. /(der) Boss /(das) Büro	/boss/office	(der) Chef = chief, (der) Direktor = director	
8. zu viel	too much ≠ not enough	genug = enough	nicht genug
9. (die) Schwierigkeit	difficulty	(das) Problem = problem, (die) Sorge = worry	
10. (die) Arbeit	work	(der) Job, (die) Maloche = job	
11. ich denke	I think so	ich glaube, ich finde = I believe so	ich hoffe = I hope so, finden Sie? = do you think so?
12. einer von beiden	either (one)		keiner von beiden = neither (one)
13. das ist schade	it's a pity ≠ thank heavens		Gott sei Dank
14. was bedeutet das?	what does it mean?	(der) Sinn, (die) Bedeutung = meaning	
15. (das) Kino	cinema (US movies)	(der) Film = film	
16. (die) Sekretärin	secretary	(die) Schreibkraft = typist = Tippse (slang)	

LEKTION 7

HABEN = TO HAVE

ich habe	I have	**ich habe nicht**	I haven't
du hast	you have	**du hast nicht**	you haven't
er	he	**er**	he
sie **hat**	**she** has	**sie** **hat nicht**	**she** hasn't
es	it	**es**	it
man	one	**man**	one
wir haben	we have	**wir haben nicht**	we haven't
ihr habt	you have	**ihr habt nicht**	you haven't
sie **haben**	**they** have	**sie** **haben nicht**	**they** haven't
Sie	**you**	**Sie**	**you**

note: — Remember the German present can also be our present perfect:
I've had my car since January = Ich habe mein Auto seit Januar.
— MAN is a general pronoun and can be translated by 'one, you, we'.

HABEN SIE EIN AUTO?   Do you have a car?

Ja, ich habe ein Auto.   Yes, I have a car.
Nein, ich habe kein Auto.   No, I don't have a car.

---

note: Remember: <u>kein</u> = not a; Germans say, 'I have not a car.'

insert the correct form of **haben**:

1) Ich _____ viele Studenten.
2) Der Boss _____ eine gute Sekretärin.
3) Ihr _____ ein schönes Haus.
4) _____ Sie viele Freunde?
5) Der Doktor _____ ein schnelles Auto.
6) Dieser Freund _____ eine hübsche Biene.
7) Wieviele Kinder _____ Sie?
8) Wir _____ ein grosses Problem.
9) _____ der Schüler recht?
10) _____ das Haus eine Garage?

MASCULINE ARTICLE

Subject (nominative)   direct object (accusative)

der Wagen (the car)   **den** Wagen
ein Wagen (a car)   **einen** Wagen
mein Wagen (my car)   **meinen** Wagen

note: — This is very important! If a masculine noun is used as a direct
      object (in English the noun comes after the verb; I see <u>the car</u>), the
      articles, the possessives and the adjectives take —en. This case is
      called 'accusative'; the case of the subject is called 'nominative'.
      — Nouns in the feminine, neuter and plural don't change.

SUBJECT — DIRECT OBJECT

Der Wagen ist hier.   =   The car's here. (subject)
Ich habe den Wagen.   =   I have <u>the car</u>. (direct object)

HAST DU EINEN WAGEN?   Do you have a car?

Ja, ich habe einen Wagen.   Yes, I have a car.
Nein, ich habe keinen Wagen. No, I don't have a car.

note: KEIN also adds —en when direct object!

```
NEGATIONS

NICHTS = NOTHING, NOT ANYTHING

Ich habe nichts = I don't have anything.


NICHT MEHR = NOT ANY MORE, NOT ANY LONGER

Ich bin nicht mehr in New York = I'm no longer in New York.

KEIN MEHR = NOT A . . . ANY LONGER, ANY MORE

Ich habe kein Auto mehr = I don't have a car any more.


NIEMAND = NOBODY, NOT ANYBODY

Es ist niemand da = There isn't anybody.


NIE = NEVER/EVER

Er ist nie hier = He's never here/he isn't ever here.


NOCH NICHT = NOT YET

Er ist noch nicht hier = He isn't here yet.


NOCH KEIN(E) = NOT A . . . YET

Ich habe noch kein Haus = I haven't a house yet.
```

translate:

1) She hasn't anything.
2) He still has a car.
3) I'm no longer in Berlin.
4) It isn't midnight yet.
5) He isn't at work any more.
6) There isn't anybody at school.
7) We're never at home.
8) We don't have problems any more.
9) I'm not a child any longer.
10) She isn't ever at work.
11) He isn't a doctor yet.
12) You're no longer sad.

put into the interrogative, then answer in the negative:
e.g. Ich habe Geld.
    — Hast du Geld?
    — Ich habe kein Geld.

1) Ich habe etwas.
2) Er hat noch einen Wagen.
3) Ich bin noch in Berlin.
4) Jemand ist zu Hause.
5) Er hat schon eine neue Biene.
6) Es ist schon Mitternacht.
7) Wir haben immer Schwierigkeiten.
8) Ich habe noch eine Arbeit.
9) Er ist immer bei der Arbeit.
10) Jemand ist in der Schule.

use in sentences beginning with **ich habe**:
e.g. ein guter Freund
    — ich habe einen guten Freund

1) eine schwarze Katze
2) ein schwerer Tisch
3) ein neues Telefon
4) ein neuer Kugelschreiber
5) ein starker Mann
6) mein alter Wagen
7) ein reicher Typ
8) eine braune Schachtel
9) der kleine Schlüssel
10) der grüne Aschenbecher

11) ein schwarzer Schuh
12) rote Schuhe
13) ein enges Hemd
14) ein brauner Stiefel
15) ein weisser Regenmantel
16) der grüne Hut
17) ein interessanter Freund
18) ein langweiliger Bruder
19) blaue Augen
20) ein roter Mund

answer first in the affirmative, and then in the negative:
e.g. Hast du einen Wagen?
- Ja, ich habe einen Wagen.
- Nein, ich habe keinen Wagen.

1) Hat der Schüler einen guten Lehrer?
2) Haben Sie Schwierigkeiten?
3) Hast du einen guten Job?
4) Hat das Zimmer eine niedrige Decke?
5) Hat die Woche acht Tage?
6) Haben wir einen kalten Sommer?
7) Hat der Park einen grossen See?
8) Haben Sie eine schwarze Katze?
9) Hat Frau Schmidt einen neuen Hund?
10) Habe ich eine schönen Hut?

insert the correct endings, then put into the plural:

1) Das Zimmer hat ein ____ gross ____ Fenster.
2) Der Direktor hat ein ____ neu ____ Wagen.
3) Die Kinder haben ein ____ schön ____ Katze und ein ___ schön ____ Hund.
4) Der Park hat ein ___ klein ____ See und gross ____ Bäume.
5) Ich habe kein ____ Wagen und kein ____ Fahrrad.
6) Meine Biene hat ein ____ neu ____ Freund.
7) Ich habe ein ___ schwer ____ Kopf.
8) Der Casanova hat ein schwarz ____ Hemd, ein ____ weiss ____ Schlips, und ein ____ rot ____Anzug.

ADVERBEN UND SÄTZE (ADVERBS AND PHRASES) 1

1. **wegen**	because of	15. **viel**	a lot of, much ≠
2. **selten**	rarely	≠ **ein wenig,**	a little, a bit
3. **oft**	often	**ein bisschen**	
4. **− fast**	− almost	16. **im Falle, dass**	in case
− ungefähr	− nearly	17. **wenigstens**	at least
5. **− auf jeden**	− at any rate	18. **− sehr**	− very
Fall	− in any case	**− ziemlich**	− pretty (rich)
− in jedem		19. **vor . . .**	. . . ago
Fall		20. **− einmal**	− once
6. **− kaum**	− scarcely	**− einmal**	− once a week
− schwerlich	− hardly	**pro Woche**	
7. **bis**	until, till	21. **schon**	already
8. **− gewöhnlich**	− usually	22. **nicht mehr**	not . . . anymore
− sonst		23. **ohne**	without
9. **am Tage, als**	the day when	24. **ausser**	without
10. **nie**	never, ever	25. **beide**	both
11. **immer**	always	26. **zusammen,**	together
12. **mehr oder**	more or less	**gemeinsam**	
weniger		27. **etwas**	something
13. **warum**	why	28. **noch**	still
14. **weil**	because	29. **jemand**	somebody, someone

VOKABELN

	Übersetzung	Sinnverwandte Wörter	Gegenteil
1. und Sie?	what about you?		
2. /regnen/(der) Regen	/to rain/rain	giessen = to pour	
3. schneien	to snow	(der) Schnee = snow	
4. (das) Wetter	weather	es ist schön = it's nice out	
5. einmal	once (zweimal = twice)	ein einziges Mal = only once	
6. studieren	to study ≠ to teach	lernen = to learn	lehren
7. (die) Sonne	sun	es ist sonnig = it's sunny	(die) Wolke = cloud
8. viel	much ≠ a little, a bit	viele = many, die meisten = most of	ein wenig, ein bisschen
9. /(der) Sturm /(der) Wind	/storm/wind		
10. sich anziehen	to get dressed		sich ausziehen = to get undressed
11. schlafen gehen	to go to bed ≠ to get up		aufstehen, aufwachen = to wake up
12. (die) Sache	thing	(das) Ding = (das) Zeug	
13. ich bin in Eile	I'm in a hurry		
14. rauchen	to smoke	(die) Zigarette = cigarette	
15. sich waschen	to get washed		
16. /essen/trinken	/to eat/to drink	(das) Getränk = drink	
17. einkaufen gehen	to go shopping	(der) Einkauf = shopping	
18. /um 8 Uhr/in der Schule/bei der Arbeit/zu Hause	/at 8 o'clock/at school/at work/at home		

LEKTION 8

PRESENT TENSE, REGULAR VERBS:

KOMMEN = TO COME

ich komme	I come/am coming	**ich komme nicht**	I don't come/ I'm not coming
du kommst	you come	**du kommst nicht**	you don't come
er **sie** **kommt** **es** **man**	he she comes it	**er** **sie** **kommt nicht** **es** **man**	he she doesn't come it
wir kommen	we come	**wir kommen nicht**	we don't come
ihr kommt	you come	**ihr kommt nicht**	you don't come
sie **kommen** **Sie**	they you come	**sie** **kommen nicht** **Sie**	they you don't come

note: — —EN is the infinitive of all verbs.
   — The German present is used for an action one is doing now, for a
      repeated action, and a past which continues (our present perfect).
         Ich spreche jetzt   = I'm speaking now.
         Ich spreche oft   = I often speak.
         Ich spreche seit zwei Stunden = I've been speaking for two hours.
   — Very often Germans use the present, when we use the future.

SPRECHEN SIE OFT DEUTSCH?   Do you often speak German?

Ja, ich spreche oft deutsch.   Yes, I often speak German.
Nein, ich spreche nicht oft deutsch.   No, I don't often speak German.

```
ARBEITEN = TO WORK

Ich arbeite                          I work/am working

du arbeitest                         you work

er                                   he
sie                                  she   works
     arbeitet
es                                   it
man

wir arbeiten                         we work

ihr arbeitet                         you work

sie                                  they
     arbeiten                              work
Sie                                  you
```

note: If the root of the verb ends in —t or —d you have to add an —e if the present ending is —t or —st.

conjugate the verb, then put the sentence into the interrogative:
e.g. Ich (arbeiten).
   — Ich arbeite.
   — Arbeitest du?

1) Du (warten) auf den Bus.
2) Es (schneien) und (regnen).
3) Sie (bedeuten) mir sehr viel.
4) Ich (finden) es.
5) Er (antworten) immer falsch.
6) Wir (hören) die Musik.
7) Dieser Film (bedeuten) nichts.
8) Ihr (arbeiten) immer noch.
9) Sie (finden) ihren Typ klasse.
10) Er (antworten) richtig.
11) Wir (antworten) falsch.
12) Ihr (finden) es schön.
13) Sie (warten) auf ihren Freund.
14) Du (arbeiten) viel.

44

conjugate the verb, then put the sentence into the interrogative:

e.g. Er (arbeiten) heute.

    — Er arbeitet heute.

    — Arbeitet er heute?

1) Ich (wiederholen) die Lektion.
2) Es (tun) mir leid.
3) Das (machen) nichts.
4) Ich (verstehen) nichts.
5) Ihr (sprechen) deutsch.
6) Du (gehen) in die Schule.
7) Ihr (fragen), wir (antworten).
8) Sie (kommen) morgen.
9) Ich (bleiben) eine Stunde.
10) Ich (glauben), er (sein) ein Bulle.
11) Ihr (studieren) deutsch.
12) Wir (gehen) um 8 Uhr schlafen.
13) Es (gehen) nicht.
14) Ich (hassen) Polizisten.
15) Er (malochen) am Morgen.
16) Du (haben) viel Zeit.
17) Das Kino (zeigen) einen guten Film.
18) Der Lehrer (lehren) und die Schüler (lernen).
19) Du (kommen) immer spät.
20) Gewöhnlich (rauchen) ich Pfeife.
21) Ihr (kommen) immer am Morgen.
22) Es (schneien) im Januar.
23) Ich (zeigen) mein Büro.
24) Er (glauben) nichts.
25) Sie (bleiben) eine Woche.

IRREGULAR VERBS:

SPRECHEN = TO SPEAK

ich spreche	I speak	**ich spreche nicht**	I don't speak
du sprichst	you speak	**du sprichst nicht**	you don't speak
er	he	**er**	he
sie spricht	she speaks	**sie spricht nicht**	she doesn't speak
es	it	**es**	it
man		**man**	
wir sprechen	we speak	**wir sprechen nicht**	we don't speak
ihr sprecht	you speak	**ihr sprecht nicht**	you don't speak
sie	they	**sie**	they
Sie sprechen	you speak	**Sie sprechen nicht**	you don't speak

note: If a verb's irregular, it has a vowel change in the second and third person of the singular; all the other forms are regular.

insert the correct form of the verb:

1) ich breche, du _____
2) wir sehen, er _____
3) du liest, ihr _____
4) wir können, er _____
5) ich schlafe, du _____
6) ich treffe, du _____
7) Sie tragen, du _____
8) ihr fangt, sie _____
9) ich fahre, du _____
10) sie nehmen, du _____
11) er gibt, sie _____
12) wir stehlen, du _____
13) Sie schlagen, es _____
14) ihr ratet, du _____
15) sie essen, du _____
16) ich sterbe, er _____
17) du fängst, wir _____
18) ich empfehle, sie _____
19) wir wollen, ich _____
20) sie helfen, sie _____
21) ich befehle, er _____
22) sie werden, sie _____
23) wir braten, du _____
24) er wäscht, sie _____
25) wir entlassen, er _____
26) ich bin, er _____
27) wir tun, ich _____
28) ihr werft, er _____

translate:

1) I've been learning German since May.
2) He works hard every day.
3) Are you coming tomorrow?
4) They're reading now.
5) She's been talking for two hours.
6) Is she studying?
7) It's raining and snowing.
8) We're eating, but these things are bad.
9) Are you learning English?
10) I only work in the morning.
11) Whose turn is it?
12) Does she know where she is?
13) Does she love that bastard?
14) Thank heavens, I don't work on Saturday.
15) I've been waiting for you since noon.
16) I don't understand: he's crazy about that broad.
17) She only reads good books.
18) Do I ask too many questions?
19) I'm working a lot, but you're doing nothing.
20) He takes the tube (subway) every day.
21) Do you know my little sister?
22) I begin every day at noon.
23) Why don't you help?
24) Do you speak German?
25) He always talks so slowly.

IRREGULAR VERBS — (present tense)

		ICH bin	ER ist	SIE sind
1. sein	to be	ICH bin	ER ist	SIE sind
2. haben	to have	habe	hat	haben
3. brechen	to break	breche	bricht	brechen
4. tun	to do	tue	tut	tun
5. essen	to eat	esse	isst	essen
6. fallen	to fall	falle	fällt	fallen
7. geben	to give	gebe	gibt	geben
8. wissen	to know	weiss	weiss	wissen
9. sehen	to see	sehe	sieht	sehen
10. sprechen	to speak	spreche	spricht	sprechen
11. fangen	to catch	fange	fängt	fangen
12. nehmen	to take	nehme	nimmt	nehmen
13. werfen	to throw	werfe	wirft	werfen
14. behalten	to keep	behalte	behält	behalten
15. tragen	to wear, carry	trage	trägt	tragen
16. können	can, to be able	kann	kann	können
17. müssen	must, to have to	muss	muss	müssen
18. lesen	to read	lese	liest	lesen
19. fahren	to drive	fahre	fährt	fahren
20. schlafen	to sleep	schlafe	schläft	schlafen
21. lassen	to let	lasse	lässt	lassen
22. stehlen	to steal	stehle	stiehlt	stehlen
23. sterben	to die	sterbe	stirbt	sterben
24. schlagen	to beat, hit	schlage	schlägt	schlagen
25. raten	to guess, to advise	rate	rät	raten
26. empfehlen	to suggest	empfehle	empfiehlt	empfehlen
27. treffen	to meet	treffe	trifft	treffen
28. wollen	to want	will	will	wollen
29. helfen	to help	helfe	hilft	helfen
30. befehlen	to command	befehle	befiehlt	befehlen
31. geschehen	to happen		geschieht	
32. werden	to become	werde	wird	werden
33. entlassen	to lay off	entlasse	entlässt	entlassen
34. braten	to roast	brate	brät	braten
35. waschen	to wash	wasche	wäscht	waschen

VOKABELN

	Übersetzung	Sinnverwandte Wörter	Gegenteil
1. jeden (Tag)	every (day)	jeder = everyone, each one	alle = all
2. – in Paris **– in meinem Büro** **– in meinem Zimmer**	– in Paris – in my office – in my room	in einer Stunde = in an hour	
3. gewisse	certain, sure	sicher	zweifelhaft = doubtful
4. nicht mehr	not . . . any more		immer noch = still
5. wollen	to want (ich möchte = I'd like)	wünschen = to wish	
6. mögen	to like ≠ to hate	gernhaben, lieben = to love, verrückt sein nach = to be crazy about	hassen, nicht ausstehen können = can't stand
7. zeigen	to show		
8. zuhören + **dative**	to listen to		
9. warten auf + **acc.**	to wait for	ich warte auf Sie = I'm waiting for you	
10. arbeiten	to work ≠ to do nothing	malochen	nichts tun, faulenzen
11. pünktlich	on time	früh = early	(zu) spät = late
12. glücklich	happy ≠ sad	froh = glad	traurig
13. (das) Ende	end ≠ beginning	(der) Schluss	(der) Anfang
14. (der) Schuft	bastard ≠ bitch	(das) Schwein	(die) Zicke
15. interessant	interesting ≠ boring	spannend = exciting	langweilig
16. Wer ist an der Reihe?	whose turn is it?	Wer ist dran?	ich bin dran, an der Reihe = it's my turn
17. helfen	to help		

LEKTION 9

note: WER? is the subject, WEN? the direct object of the question.

put into the interrogative, changing first person to second, and second to third, where appropriate:

e.g. Ich sehe meinen freund.
— Wen siehst du?

1) Ich frage meine Schwester.
2) Mein Bruder ist zu Hause.
3) Wir essen Steak.
4) Das Fleisch ist gut.
5) Ich sehe einen Amerikaner.
6) Niemand ist im Büro.
7) Im Moment sehe ich Peter nicht.
8) Ich bestelle eine Flasche Bier.
9) Er schläft den ganzen Tag.
10) Der Toast schmeckt sehr gut.
11) Ich treffe eine Freundin.
12) Sie liest ein Buch.
13) Meine Schwester hat einen neuen Wagen.
14) Ich sehe meine Mutter.
15) Ich warte auf meine Biene.

```
NOCH — NICHT MEHR = STILL — NOT . . . ANY MORE

LEBT ER NOCH IN NEW YORK?    Does he still live in New York?

Ja, er lebt noch in New York.      Yes, he still lives in New York.
Nein, er lebt nicht mehr in New    No, he doesn't live in New
York.                              York any more.
```

```
DASS = THAT

Ich denke, dass er morgen kommt.   I think (that) he'll come
tomorrow.                          tomorrow.

Er sagt, dass er noch in Berlin    He says (that) he still lives in
wohnt.                             Berlin.
```

note: — After dass and most other conjunctions the verb goes to the end of
the sentence.
— Germans very often use the present when we'd use the future.

begin the sentences with **ich denke, dass**:
e.g. Er kommt heute Nachmittag.
    — Ich denke, dass er heute Nachmittag kommt.

1)   Sie arbeitet jeden Tag.
2)   Meine Schwester ist zu Hause.
3)   Er liest das Buch.
4)   Niemand bleibt zu Hause.
5)   Der Bahnhof ist in der Nähe.

translate:

1) I don't know who's coming.
2) He's fat because he loves bread.
3) I think that he's at work.
4) It's a pity that you're late.
5) I hope that he'll come on time.
6) I can't wait, because I'm in a hurry.
7) Do you think that he's American.
8) I'm asking what you're reading.
9) Of course I know that you've been here since March.
10) Are you tired because you work a lot?
11) I sleep all day because I'm on vacation.
12) Can you tell Peter that his broad's waiting?
13) He drives a fast car, because he's always in a hurry.
14) He hopes that you won't be late.
15) I'm learning German because I'd like to go to Munich.
16) I'm not buying that raincoat because it's expensive.
17) I'm sorry, I don't know where the station is.
18) It's my turn.
19) He's late because he's coming on foot.
20) I know more or less who he is.
21) Do you think that he's a bastard?
22) That's the restaurant where we always eat.
23) Do you know how many children she has?
24) I'd like to know when she's at home.
25) I must say that I'm crazy about music.

```
WAS FÜR EIN? = WHAT KIND OF?

WAS FÜR EINEN WAGEN HAST        What kind of car do you have?
DU?
Ich habe einen Mercedes.         I have a Mercedes.

WAS FÜR TEE TRINKST DU?         What kind of tea do you drink?
Ich trinke Ceylontee.            I drink Ceylon tea.
```

note: No article in front of a collective noun (Tee, Geld, Fleisch, etc.)!

```
HERR → HERRN

WEN SIEHST DU?                   Whom do you see?

Ich sehe Herrn Müller.           I see Mr Miller.
Ich sehe einen Jungen.           I see a boy.
```

note: If <u>Herr</u> and <u>Junge</u> aren't the subjects of their sentences you have to add −n.

insert the article where necessary:

1) Was für _____ Arbeit hat er?
2) Was für _____ Wagen fährt er?
3) Was für _____ Geld hat man in Amerika?
4) Was für _____ Frauen lieben Sie?
5) Was für _____ Fleisch nehmen wir heute?
6) Was für _____ Lehrer haben Sie?
7) Was für _____ Lektion ist das?
8) Was für _____ Probleme haben Sie?
9) Was für _____ Doktor empfiehlst du?
10) Was für _____ Bücher nehmen wir?
11) Was für _____ Park ist das?
12) Was für _____ Schwierigkeiten haben Sie?
13) Was für _____ Brot essen Sie?
14) Was für _____ Haus haben wir?

note: — Both sentences are in the present in German.
　　　 — After wenn the verb's at the end.
　　　 — The second sentence starts with the verb!

link the pairs of sentences using **wenn**:
e.g. Ich habe Geld. Ich kaufe einen Wagen.
　　 — Wenn ich Geld habe, kaufe ich einen Wagen.

1) 　Ich habe viel Zeit. Ich komme.
2) 　Der Direktor ist nicht im Büro. Ich arbeite nicht.
3) 　Ich habe kein Geld. Ich bleibe zu Hause.
4) 　Der Lehrer ist gut. Ich lerne viel.
5) 　Das Wetter ist schön. Ich gehe spazieren.
6) 　Ich komme pünktlich. Ich fahre mit der U-Bahn.
7) 　Ich habe Ferien. Ich lese viel.
8) 　Mein Hemd ist schmutzig. Ich wasche es.

translate:

1) If I'm tired, I'll go to bed.
2) If the weather's bad, I'll stay at home.
3) If the doctor has time, he'll come.
4) If the dress is expensive, will you buy it?
5) If the room's big, I'll take it.

answer in the affirmative and then in the negative:
e.g. Wenn sie Geld haben, kaufen sie einen Wagen?
     — Ja, wenn ich Geld habe, kaufe ich einen Wagen.
     — Nein, wenn ich Geld habe, kaufe ich keinen Wagen.

1) Wenn der Kellner kommt, bestellst du ein Steak?
2) Wenn das Kleid billig ist, kauft sie es?
3) Wenn du Zeit hast, gehst du zu Fuss?
4) Wenn die Sekretärin im Büro ist, arbeitet sie?
5) Wenn du Geld hast, gehen wir einkaufen?
6) Wenn wir reich sind, fahren wir nach Hawaii?
7) Wenn ich in Eile bin, nehme ich den Bus?
8) Wenn sie viel trinkt, ist sie blau?
9) Wenn du einen Bullen siehst, bist cu glücklich?
10) Wenn einer von beiden gehen muss, geht er?
11) Wenn die Flasche leer ist, kaufen Sie eine neue?
12) Wenn der Kurs interessant ist, lernen wir viel?
13) Wenn es Sommer ist, nimmt er Ferien?
14) Wenn es mir gleich ist, sage ich etwas?
15) Wenn sie einen schweren Kopf hat, nimmt sie ein Aspirin?

VOKABELN

	Übersetzung	Sinnverwandte Wörter	Gegenteil
1. teuer	expensive ≠ cheap		billig
2. sprechen mit	to speak to		
3. /zu Fuss/am Radio/mit der U-Bahn/in Ferien	/on foot/on the radio/on the subway/on vacation		
4. jetzt	now (vorläufig = for the time being)	im Moment = gegenwärtig = at present	
5. für + acc.	for		
6. (zu Fuss) gehen	to walk	spazierengehen = to go for a walk	
7. (die) Mahlzeit	meal	(das) Butterbrot = sandwich	
8. /(das) Frühstück /(das) Mittagessen	/breakfast/lunch	(das) Abendessen = dinner	
9. schmecken	to taste	bedienen Sie sich = help yourself	
10. /(das) Messer /(die) Gabel /(der) Löffel /(die) Serviette	/knife/fork/spoon /napkin	(der Kaffeelöffel = coffee-spoon	
11. ich muss . . .	I have to . . . , I must	ich habe zu . . .	
12. sagen	to say	erzählen = tell	
13. (das) Restaurant	restaurant	(die) Speisekarte = menu	
14. /bestellen/(der) Kellner	/to order/waiter	(der) Ober, (die) Kellnerin = waitress	
15. /(die) Tasse /(das) Glas/(das) Wasser	/cup/glass/water	(die) Untertasse = saucer, (die) Flasche = bottle	
16. /(das) Brot /(die) Butter	/bread/butter	(der) Toast = toast	
17. (das) Fleisch	meat	(das) Steak = steak	
18. (der) Teller	plate	(das) Gericht = dish	

LEKTION 10

THE ARTICLE

	subject (nominative)	*direct object (accusative)*	*indirect object (dative)*
(masc.)	**DER** Man	**DEN** Mann	**DEM** Mann
	the man	the man	to the man
(fem.)	**DIE** Frau	**DIE** Frau	**DER** Frau
	the woman	the woman	to the woman
(neut.)	**DAS** Kind	**DAS** Kind	**DEM** Kind
	the child	the child	to the child
(plural)	**DIE** Kinder	**DIE** Kinder	**DEN** Kindern
	the children	the children	to the children

note: — If a noun is used as an indirect object, you have to put it into the dative. In English the indirect object, or the dative, is often translated by 'to': Ich gebe dem Schüler ein Buch = I'm giving a book to the student.

— Remember: the nominative is the subject of the sentence: the accusative is the direct object.

put into the dative:

1) Ich gebe (das Kind) ein Bonbon.
2) Ich helfe (die Frau).
3) Wir sprechen mit (die Freunde).
4) Der Kellner gibt (der Mann und die Frau) die Rechnung.
5) Sie geben (der Kellner) ein Trinkgeld.
6) Sie sagt (der Freund), dass sie morgen kommt.
7) Die Mutter hilft (die Kinder).
8) Das Kleid gefällt (die Freundin).
9) Wir antworten (der Lehrer oder die Lehrerin).
10) Sie dankt (der Doktor und die Krankenschwester).

WEM? = WHOM, TO WHOM?

WEM GIBST DU DAS BUCH?   Who are you giving the book to?

Ich gebe dem Lehrer das Buch.   I'm giving the book <u>to the teacher</u>.
Ich gebe der Lehrerin das Buch.   I'm giving the book <u>to the teacher</u>.
Ich gebe dem Mädchen das Buch.   I'm giving the book <u>to the girl</u>.
Ich gebe den Schülern das Buch.   I'm giving the book <u>to the pupils</u>.

note: — What the position of the words! You <u>can't</u> say, 'Ich gebe das Buch
dem Lehrer'.
— In the dative plural all nouns add —<u>n</u>.
— All articles and the possessive adjectives take the same endings.

insert the correct article:

1)   Erzählen Sie _____ Lehrer den Film?
2)   Er hilft _____ Direktor.
3)   Es tut _____ Kind leid.
4)   Er gibt _ _ Kindern ein Glas Limonade.
5)   Sie dankt _____ Rechtsanwalt.
6)   Die Lehrerin stellt _____ Schüler eine Frage.
7)   Die Studenten antworten _____ Professorin.
8)   Sie zeigt _____ Freund einen Film.
9)   Was empfehlen Sie _____ Schuft.
10)   Helfen Sie bitte _____ Mädchen.
11)   Er begegnet _____ Freund.
12)   Die Polizisten folgen _____ Wagen.
13)   Er sagt _____ Lehrerin, dass er morgen nicht kommt.
14)   Es tut _____ Jungen und _____ Mädchen leid.

POSITION OF WORDS IN A SENTENCE

ER   **TRINKT**   **OFT**   **EINEN KAFFEE**   **AM ABEND**
subject   verb   adverb   object   time

IM RESTAURANT.
place

note: — The position of the verb is most important: it always comes second.
           The subject can be in front of or after the verb:
           Er trinkt oft Kaffee or Oft trinkt er Kaffee.
      — The adverb of time's always before the adverb of place.
      — In a subordinate clause the verb goes to the end:
           Er kommt morgen = He's coming tomorrow (main clause).
           Ich weiss, dass er morgen kommt = I know he'll come tomorrow
           (subordinate clause).
      — The dative's before the accusative: Ich dem Vater das Buch.
                                (dative)   (accusative).

re-arrange the words in the correct order:

1)   Ich will sprechen deutsch gut.
2)   Sie essen im Restaurant am Abend oft.
3)   Er selten kommt pünktlich.
4)   Wir trinken Kaffee manchmal bei der Arbeit.
5)   Der Lehrer stellt Fragen den Schülern von Zeit zu Zeit.
6)   Ich gebe ein Buch meinem Freund.
7)   Sie immer alles sagen ihren Eltern.
8)   Ich möchte zuhören der Musik.
9)   Wir zeigen einen Disney-Film den Kindern Sonntag.
10)   Er endlich kommt.
11)   Ich zeige mein neues Haus den Freunden.
12)   Wir fahren nach Berlin im Januar.
13)   Heute ich komme mit der U-Bahn.
14)   Manchmal er hilft seiner Mutter.

translate:

1) That big yellow car belongs to my rich boss.
2) If you order lamb, I'll order fish.
3) I feel like having a cold drink.
4) Do you want your steak well done or rare?
5) How much is a coffee here?
6) If the restaurant's expensive, I'll only have French fries.
7) Does this grey cat belong to your little sister?
8) They've been eating fish since Monday.
9) I'm about to go out.
10) He's alone, therefore he's sad.
11) I hope that this bad salad's free.
12) I can't eat any more because I'm full.
13) I must say that your dessert tastes very good.
14) If you have time, you can help your brother.
15) My car doesn't work, I must walk.
16) What kind of car do you drive?
17) If you want, I'll wash the car.
18) If you take the bus, you'll be late.
19) If he beats his girl, she'll leave.
20) I'm going to bed, because I'm tired.
21) What would you care for?
22) At the moment I'm not hungry.
23) If I haven't got my new car yet, you'll go alone.
24) Do you suggest this book or that one?
25) If it rains, I won't go.

SOME VERBS FOLLOWED BY THE DATIVE

1. **begegnen**	to meet	13. **fehlen an**	to lack
2. **danken**	to thank	14. **leiden an**	to suffer from
3. **drohen**	to threaten	15. **zweifeln an**	to doubt
4. **folgen**	to follow	16. **bestehen aus**	to consist of
5. **gehören**	to belong to	17. **gratulieren**	to congratulate
6. **gehorchen**	to obey	18. **nahen**	to approach
7. **gefallen**	to please	19. **leidtun**	to be sorry
8. **helfen**	to help	20. **empfehlen**	to suggest (to)
9. **schaden**	to harm	21. **geben**	to give to
10. **trauen**	to trust	22. **antworten**	to answer (s.o.)
11. **zuhören**	to listen to	23. **erzählen**	to tell (s.o.)
12. **sagen**	to say to	24. **zeigen**	to show (to)

insert the correct endings:

1) Ich helfe mein ____ klein ____ Bruder.
2) Sie antwortet ihr____ neu ____ Freund.
3) Ihr zeigt d ____ alt ____ Herr ____ den Weg.
4) Er folgt d ____ hübsch ____ Mädchen.
5) Ein Walt Disney-Film gefällt d ____ klein ____ Kinder ____ .
6) Sie gratuliert d____ jung ____ Vater.
7) Er tut mein ____ gut ____ Freund leid.
8) Traut er sein ____ neu ____ Biene?
9) Was empfiehlt der Lehrer sein ____schlecht ____Schüler____ .
10) Was gibt sie ihr____ Vater und ihr ____ Mutter?
11) Sie folgt ihr____ neu ____Freund.
12) Er dankt d____ alt ____Professor.
13) Ich drohe d ____ Schuft.
14) Sie gehorcht ihr____ Vater nicht mehr.

ADVERBEN UND SÄTZE 2

1. **allein**	alone	14. — **zu**	— to
2. **ungefähr**	about, around	— **um zu**	— in order to
3. **zwischen**	between	15. **im Begriff zu**	about to
4. **endlich**	at last	16. **sogar vorher**	even before
5. **inzwischen**	in the meantime	17. — **ganz plötzlich**	all of a sudden
6. **vielleicht**	perhaps	— **plötzlich**	— suddenly
7. **trotz**	in spite of	18. — **auf der anderen Seite**	— on the other hand
8. **anstatt**	instead of	— **im Gegenteil**	— on the contrary
9. — **von Zeit zu Zeit**	— from time to time	19. — **sofort**	— at once
— **manchmal**	— sometimes	— **gleich**	— immediately
10. — **so**	— thus, so	20. **sonst**	if not
— **deshalb**	— therefore	21. **auf . . . zu**	towards
11. **jedoch**	however	22. **damit**	so that
12. **obwohl**	although	23. **zuerst**	at first
13. **genau**	exactly	24. **noch nicht**	not yet

62

VOKABELN

	Übersetzung	Sinnverwandte Wörter	Gegenteil
1. ich bin satt	I'm full ≠ I'm hungry	ich bin voll	ich bin hungrig, ich sterbe vor Hunger = I'm starving
2. (das) Salz	salt	(das) Gewürz = spice	(der) Pfeffer = pepper
3. /(das) Huhn/(das) Kalbfleisch	/chicken/veal		
4. blutig	rare ≠ well done	mittel = medium	durchbraten
5. /(das) Lamm /(der) Fisch	/lamb/fish		
6. (die) Kartoffel	potato	die Pommes frites = French fries	
7. (die) Suppe	soup	(der) Eintopf	
8. /(der) Salat /(die) Tomate	lettuce, salad/ tomato		
9. /wieviel macht das? /(der) Preis	/how much is it? /price	wieviel kostet das? = how much does it cost?	kostenlos = free
10. /(der) Kuchen /(der) Nachtisch	/cake/dessert	(das) Eis = ice-cream, (der) Geschmack = flavour	
11. /(die) Rechnung /(das) Trinkgeld	/bill/tip	Bedienung enthalten = tip included	
12. /(der) Tee/(der) Kaffee	/tea/coffee	(die) Milch = milk	
13. mit Eis	with ice		straight = pur
14. Eier mit Speck	eggs and bacon	(der) Schinken = ham	
15. (der) Käse	cheese	(der) Wein = wine	
16. /(das) Gemüse /(die) Erbse	/vegetables /pea	(die) Karotte = carrot, grüne Bohnen = runner (string) beans	
17. was möchten Sie gern?	what would you care for?	worauf haben Sie Lust?	ich habe Lust auf einen Kaffee = I feel like a coffee

LEKTION 11

SEPARABLE VERBS:

AUFSTEHEN = TO GET UP

ich stehe <u>auf</u>	I get up	**ich stehe nicht <u>auf</u>**	I don't get up
du stehst <u>auf</u>	you get up	**du stehst nicht <u>auf</u>**	you don't get up
er **sie steht <u>auf</u>** **es**	he she gets up it	**er** **sie steht nicht <u>auf</u>** **es**	he she doesn't get up it
wir stehen <u>auf</u>	we get up	**wir stehen nicht <u>auf</u>**	we don't get up
ihr steht <u>auf</u>	you get up	**ihr steht nicht <u>auf</u>**	you don't get up
sie **Sie stehen <u>auf</u>**	they you get up	**sie** **Sie stehen nicht <u>auf</u>**	they you don't get up

note: — The prefix always goes to the end of the sentence.
— In the infinitive and at the end of a subordinate clause the prefix isn't separated from the verb: Ich bin müde, weil ich früh <u>aufstehe</u> = I'm tired because I get up early.

STEHST DU SONNTAGS FRÜH AUF?   Do you get up early on Sundays?

Ja, ich stehe sonntags früh <u>auf</u>.   Yes. I get up early on Sundays.
Nein, ich stehe sonntags nicht früh <u>auf</u>.   No, I don't get up early on Sundays.

re-arrange the words in the correct order:

1) Morgen ich früh aufstehe.
2) Sie nicht zunimmt, obwohl sie isst viel.
3) Ich aufhöre, weil die Arbeit ist schmutzig.
4) Sie ausgibt viel Geld.
5) Wir ausgehen am Freitagabend.
6) Der Bus kommt an um zehn Uhr.
7) Aufstehen Sie früh?
8) Sie immer gut aussieht.
9) Fortsetzen Sie die Arbeiten?
10) Wenn du weggehst, ich traurig bin.
11) Was vorschlägst du für das Wochenende?
12) Er nachprüft immer sein Geld.

complete the verbs and translate the sentence:

1) Es ist spät, ich gehe ____.
2) Das kommt auf meine Freundin ____.
3) Das hängt von meinem Freund ____.
4) Dieses Haus ist zu alt, ich ziehe ____.
5) Ich stehe nicht früh ____.
6) Du hörst nicht ____.
7) Sie gibt ____, dass ich recht habe.
8) Was schlagen Sie ____?
9) Wenn Sie zu viel essen, nehmen Sie ____.
10) Wann fängt der Film ____?
11) Ich höre ____, weil ich müde bin.
12) Er gibt viel Geld ____.
13) Wen stellen Sie ____?
14) Sie legt ihn immer ____.
15) Wir ziehen unseren Pullover ____, weil es heiss ist.
16) Sie lassen den Schuft ____.
17) Wenn er nicht lernt, fällt er ____.
18) Ich rufe Sie morgen ____.
19) Die Sonne geht um fünf Uhr ____.
20) Wann setzen wir die Lektion ____?
21) Sie sieht ihren Freund lange ____.
22) Er zündet seine Pfeife ____.
23) Wenn es regnet, ziehe ich meinen Regenmantel ____.
24) Mein Zahn tut ____.
25) Ein Glas Whisky tut immer ____.
26) Er bringt nichts ____.
27) Ich ziehe Kaffee ____.
28) Er prüft die Rechnung ____.

translate:

1) When are you going away?
2) He spends a lot of money.
3) He's lighting his pipe.
4) He starts at eight and stops at half past five.
5) He's taking off his suit.
6) He's moving out.
7) That depends on my father. (two translations)
8) Does your head hurt?
9) I'll phone you tonight.
10) I hope the police will arrest the bastard.
11) You have to admit that she's cute.
12) He always takes his broad in.
13) I think they'll hire my friend.
14) How long has she been losing weight?
15) Do you prefer coffee or tea?
16) He's packing his clothes.
17) He doesn't manage anything.
18) What are you planning for the weekend?
19) Who does it depend on? (two translations)
20) Who are they going to hire?
21) I'm going out tomorrow night.
22) Why are you hanging up?
23) I'd like to continue the lesson.
24) She looks happy.
25) Why are you taking her in?
26) When does the dinner start?
27) She's putting on her sexy dress.
28) I always wake up at noon.

LIST OF SEPARABLE VERBS (the bar separates the prefix from the verb)

1. **weg/gehen**	= to go away	31. **fest/nehmen**	= to arrest
2. **auf/hören**	= to stop, to quit	32. **frei/lassen**	= to release
3. **aus/geben**	= to spend (money)	33. **aus/brechen**	= to escape
4. **an/zünden**	= to light	34. **vor/schlagen**	= to propose
5. **an/sehen**	= to watch/to look at	35. **zu/nehmen**	= to gain weight
6. **fort/setzen**	= to continue	36. **ein/ziehen**	= to move in
7. **an/fangen**	= to begin	37. **aus/ziehen**	= to move out
8. **aus/gehen**	= to go out	38. **an/nehmen**	= to accept/to think
9. **an/ziehen**	= to put on (clothes)	39. **zurück/weisen**	= to refuse
10. **aus/ziehen**	= to take off (clothes)	40. **zu/geben**	= to admit
11. **um/ziehen**	= to change (clothes), to move	41. **ab/machen**	= to arrange, settle
12. **auf/stehen**	= to get up	42. **fest/setzen**	= to settle, to fix
13. **auf/gehen**	= to rise (sun)	43. **fest/legen**	= to fix
14. **auf/wachen**	= to wake up	44. **aus/sehen**	= to look
15. **zu/hören**	= to listen	45. **aus/lösen**	= to bring on
16. **an/kommen**	= to arrive	46. **vor/stellen**	= to imagine
17. **auf/nehmen**	= to pick up	47. **herein/legen**	= to take some-one in
18. **ab/hängen von** an/kommen auf	= to depend on	48. **vor/geben**	= to pretend
19. **aus/suchen**	= to select	49. **ein/stellen**	= to hire
20. **weh/tun**	= to hurt	50. **zustande/ bringen**	= to manage
21. **gut/tun** ·	= to be a relief	51. **fertig/werden**	= to swing
22. **aus/ruhen**	= to rest	52. **wahr/werden**	= to come true
23. **vor/kommen**	= to occur	53. **her/stellen**	= to manufac-ture
24. **sich auf/regen**	= to get excited	54. **an/deuten**	= to hint
25. **an/rufen**	= to phone, call up	55. **ein/steigen**	= to get on (bus)
26. **auf/legen**	= to hang up	56. **aus/steigen**	= to get off (bus)
27. **ab/nehmen**	= to pick up (phone) to lose weight	57. **um/steigen**	= to change (bus)
		58. **vor/haben**	= to plan
		59. **aus/packen**	= to unpack
		60. **ein/packen**	= to pack
28. **übrig/bleiben**	= to be left	61. **sich fertig/ machen**	= to get ready
29. **durch/fallen**	= to fail (exam)	62. **vor/ziehen**	= to prefer
30. **sich an/hören**	= to sound	63. **nach/prüfen**	= to check

67

VOKABELN

	Übersetzung	Sinnverwandte Wörter	Gegenteil
1. nächste (Woche)	next (week)	die folgende Woche = the following week	
2. bekommen	to get	erhalten	
3. brauchen	to need		fehlen = to lack
4. /scherzen/(der) Spass	/to kid/joke	hänseln = to tease	
5. es sieht so aus	apparently so	es scheint so = so it seems	
6. wunderbar	wonderful ≠ horrible	herrlich, klasse = swell, toll = cool, reizend = charming, echt gut = great	schrecklich, mies = seedy, lausig = lousy, beschissen = shitty, wertlos = worthless
7. /(die) Zeitung /(das) Papier	/newspaper/paper	(die) Zeitschrift = magazine	
8. /spielen/(das) Spiel	/to play/play, game	(das) Spielzeug = toy, (die) Puppe = doll	
9. dumm	stupid ≠ intelligent, bright	blöde = dumb, (das) Arschloch = ass	klug, intelligent, =helle
10. alles	everything, all ≠ nothing	etwas = something, irgendetwas = anything	nichts, kein(er,e,es) = none
11. fallen	to fall	fallen lassen = to drop	aufheben = to pick up = aufsammeln
12. einige	some	mehrere = several	kein = not any
13. /wie oft? /seit wann?	/how often? /how long?		
14. /schön/nett	/beautiful/cute		hässlich = ugly
15. heute abend	tonight ≠ last night	(der) Abend	gestern abend, morgen abend = tomorrow night

LEKTION 12

PREPOSITIONS + DATIVE

AUS	=	FROM (place)
Ich komme aus dem Büro.		I'm coming from the office.
BEI	=	AT (somebody's place)
Er wohnt bei seiner Mutter.		He lives at his mother's.
MIT	=	WITH, BY (transport)
Ich komme mit dem Wagen.		I'm coming by car.
NACH	=	AFTER
Nach dem Film gehe ich weg.		I'm going to leave after the film.
SEIT	=	FOR, SINCE
Ich warte seit einer Woche.		I've been waiting for a week.
VON	=	FROM (person)
Der Brief ist von meiner Biene.		The letter's from my broad.
ZU	=	TO (place)
Er geht zum Bahnhof.		He's going to the station.

note: — All these prepositions are followed by the dative!
  — Remember that the German present translates the English present
    perfect: Ich warte seit einer Woche = I've been waiting for a week.
  — The following contractions aren't compulsory, but frequently used:
    in dem = im; zu dem = zum; zu der = zur; an dem = am; bei dem =
    beim.

insert the correct case:

1) Ich komme aus _____ Restaurant. (das)
2) Seit _____ Jahr kommt er nicht mehr. (ein)
3) Nach _____ Abendessen gehen wir aus. (das)
4) Geht sie allein zu _____ Bahnhof? (der)
5) Hängst das von _____ Arbeit ab. (die)
6) Kommt er mit _____ Bus? (der)
7) Wohnt er bei _____ neuen Freundin? (die)
8) Sie sind seit _____ Monat verheiratet. (ein)
9) Nach _____ Lektion gehe ich schlafen. (die)
10) Von _____ ist der Brief? (wer?)

PREPOSITIONS + ACCUSATIVE

DURCH = THROUGH
Er geht durch den Park. He's going through the park.

FÜR = FOR
Das Buch ist für den Lehrer. The book's for the teacher.

GEGEN = AGAINST
Ich bin gegen diese Idee. I'm against this idea.

OHNE = WITHOUT
Sie kommt ohne ihren Freund. She's coming without her friend.

UM = AROUND
Er geht um die Ecke. He's walking around the corner.

note: Always the accusative after these prepositions!

insert the correct case:

1) Ist das Trinkgeld für ____ Kellner? (der)
2) Warten Sie auf ____ Freund oder auf ____ Freundin? (ein, eine)
3) Für ____ ist die Zeitung? (wer?)
4) Diese schöne Uhr ist für ____ Mutter. (meine)
5) Um zum Bahnhof zu kommen, müssen Sie durch ____ Park gehen. (der)
6) Ist die Universität um ____ Ecke? (die)
7) Ich bin gegen ____ Ding. (das)
8) Ist dein neuer Anzug für ____ Sommer oder für ____ Herbst?
9) Er kommt nie ohne ____ Mutter. (seine)
10) Warum ist seine Familie gegen ____ Ehefrau? (seine)
11) Er geht mit dem Kopt durch ____ Wand. (die)
12) Ohne ____ Sekretärin kann ich nicht kommen. (meine)
13) Wir schwimmen durch ____ See. (der)
14) Gegen ____ sind Sie? (wer?)

MÜSSEN	= MUST, TO HAVE TO
MUSS ICH ES MACHEN?	Must I do it?
Ja, Sie müssen es machen.	Yes, you must/have to do it.
Nein, Sie brauchen es nicht zu machen.	No, you don't have to do it.
Nein, Sie dürfen es nicht machen.	No, you mustn't do it.
Nein, Sie müssen es nicht machen.	

note:— The infinitive goes to the end of the sentence.
    — There are three negative forms of müssen:
       a. **nicht brauchen zu** is used if something isn't necessary.
       b. **nicht dürfen** is used if something's forbidden.
       c. **nicht müssen** isn't used very much.

KÖNNEN	= CAN, TO BE ABLE TO
KÖNNEN SIE DEUTSCH SPRECHEN?	Can you speak German?
Ja, ich kann deutsch sprechen.	Yes, I can speak German.
Nein, ich kann nicht deutsch sprechen.	No, I can't speak German.

note: You can even drop the infinitive if the sentence remains understandable: Ich kann deutsch = I can (speak) German.

```
MÜSSEN/KÖNNEN (present tense)

ich muss        I must/have to    ich kann        I can

du musst        you must          du kannst       you can

er              he                er              he
sie muss        she must          sie kann        she can
es              it                es              it

wir müssen      we must           wir können      we can

ihr müsst       you must          ihr könnt       you can

sie müssen      they    must      sie können      they    can
Sie             you               Sie             you
```

put into the affirmative, and then into the negative:

1) Muss er so viel Geld ausgeben?
2) Können Sie morgen abend kommen?
3) Muss er mit seiner Freundin sprechen?
4) Kann ich mit deinem Wagen fahren?
5) Kann sie englisch sprechen?
6) Muss ich früh aufstehen?
7) Muss man hier Trinkfeld geben?
8) Kann das vorkommen?
9) Kann man so dumm sein?
10) Musst du hier aussteigen?
11) Kann ich die Lektion fortsetzen?
12) Muss ich sofort einziehen?
13) Könnt ihr hören?
14) Müssen die Bullen den Mann freilassen?
15) Kann ich die Arbeit zurückweisen?

translate:

1) I must speak to the secretary, she doesn't often come on time.
2) You have to (one has to) understand that irregular verbs aren't easy to learn.
3) I can't help you because I'm doing my homework.
4) We can go to the restaurant on foot.
5) We must go for a walk at midnight.
6) You don't have to do it now.
7) Can you speak German?
8) I don't have to go.
9) Are you able to do it?
10) I have to go to my office on the tube (subway).
11) She can speak English very well.
12) I must ask my father.
13) We have to speak with the teacher this afternoon.
14) I don't know whether he loves his wife or not.
15) She's married to a stupid man.
16) I think he's single because he lives with his mother.
17) You can give it to a relative, your aunt for instance.
18) I don't understand why he's against her brothers and sisters.
19) My mother-in-law's leaving at four, thank heavens!
20) I'm against this idea, although it's fair.
21) She always goes out without her husband.
22) He always calls at midnight, that's too late.
23) It's a relief to be at home again.
24) When do we arrive at his parents' place?
25) Can you pick up the newspaper, please?
26) She always selects beautiful clothes.

VOKABELN

	Übersetzung	Sinnverwandte Wörter	Gegenteil
1. sogar	even	sogar ich = even me	
2. wenn, ob	if	ob . . . oder nicht = whether or not	
3. (die) Mutter	mother ≠ father		(der) Vater
4. (die) Schwester	sister ≠ brother		(der) Bruder
5. (die) Schwieger-mutter	mother-in-law ≠ father-in-law	(die) Schwiegereltern = parents-in-law	(der) Schwieger-vater
6. (die) Nichte	niece ≠ nephew	(die) Tante = aunt, (der) Onkel = uncle	(der) Neffe
7. (der) Sohn	son ≠ daughter	(die) Eltern = parents, (die) Geschwister = brothers and sisters	(die) Tochter
8. (der) Ehemann	husband ≠ wife		(die) Ehefrau
9. /(der) Grossvater /(der) Enkel	/grandfather /grandson	(die) Grossmutter = grandmother, (das) Enkelkind = grandchild	
10. ledig	single ≠ married	verlobt = engaged	verheiratet
11. (die) Familie	family	(der) Verwandte = relative	
12. (die) Person	person	(die) Leute = people	
13. zum Beispiel	for instance	z.B.	
14. nett	nice ≠ mean	gerecht = fair	gemein, böse
15. die Hausarbeit machen	to do the housework	(die) Hausfrau = housewife	
16. während	for, during		
17. fremd	strange	komisch	
18. glücklicherweise	fortunately ≠ unfortunately	zum Glück = luckily	unglücklicherweise, leider
19. (das) Dienst-mädchen	maid	(die) Putzfrau = cleaning lady	

LEKTION 13

PERSONAL PRONOUNS

subject		direct object (Akkusative)
ICH I	→	**MICH** me
DU you	→	**DICH** you
ER he	→	**IHN** him
SIE she	→	**SIE** her
ES it	→	**ES** it
MAN you, one, we		
WIR we	→	**UNS** us
IHR you	→	**EUCH** you
SIE they, you	→	**SIE** they, you

This answers the questions
WHO(M)? = WEN?

note: — This is really easy, exactly like English!
— man can be tricky to translate, sometimes its 'you', sometimes 'we' or 'one'.

SEHEN SIE MICH?	Do you see me?
Ja, ich sehe Sie.	Yes, I see you.
Nein, ich sehe Sie nicht.	No, I don't see you.

75

Ich sehe mich	= I see me	**Ich sehe mich nicht**	= I don't see me
Ich sehe dich	= I see you	**Ich sehe dich nicht**	= I don't see you
Ich sehe ihn	= I see him	**Ich sehe ihn nicht**	= I don't see him
Ich sehe sie	= I see her	**Ich sehe sie nicht**	= I don't see her
Ich sehe es	= I see it	**Ich sehe es nicht**	= I don't see it
Ich sehe uns	= I see us	**Ich sehe uns nicht**	= I don't see us
Ich sehe euch	= I see you	**Ich sehe euch nicht**	= I don't see you
Ich sehe sie	= I see them	**Ich sehe sie nicht**	= I don't see them
Ich sehe Sie	= I see you	**Ich sehe Sie nicht**	= I don't see you

answer the questions using the pronoun instead of the noun:
e.g. Hast du den Wagen schon lange?
　　 — Ja, ich habe ihn schon lange.

1) Kennt sie ihren Freund seit Januar?
2) Bekommt er seinen Job durch seinen Vater?
3) Ist der Whisky für deine Eltern?
4) Kommt sie heute ohne ihren Bruder?
5) Bekommt Peter seinen neuen Wagen morgen?
6) Ist diese Zeitung für dich?
7) Verstehen Sie mich?
8) Ist dieses Buch für uns?
9) Können wir euch morgen anrufen?
10) Könnt ihr uns hören?

insert the correct pronoun instead of the noun:

e.g. Ich sehe den Stuhl.

     — Ich sehe ihn.

1)   Ich kenne den Mann.
2)   Peter liebt seine Frau.
3)   Wir lesen das Buch.
4)   Er sieht den Film heute.
5)   Ich höre die Musik gut.
6)   Wir treffen Peter und Maria.
7)   Ihr schreibt den Brief.
8)   Ist das Buch für meinen Vater.
9)   Meine Mutter kennt diese Frau.
10)   Können wir diesen alten Tisch kaufen?
11)   Ich möchte den Kaffee mit Milch.
12)   Sie wartet immer auf Peter und mich nach der Lektion.
13)   Ich frage dich und deinen Bruder.
14)   Ich schreibe meinen Eltern den Brief.
15)   Ist das Buch für meine Schwester und mich?
16)   Sie sind gegen diesen Kerl.
17)   Die Bonbons sind für Peter, Maria und dich.
18)   Fragt ihr meinen Bruder und mich?
19)   Kennen Sie Herrn und Frau Schmidt?
20)   Ich ziehe den Pullover an.
21)   Sie wäscht ihr Kleid.
22)   Ich kenne die Lektion gut.
23)   Er gibt seinem Bruder die Armbanduhr.
24)   Ich zeige meinem Freund mein Büro.
25)   Der Student nimmt die Kreide.
26)   Ich möchte diesen schlechten Film nicht sehen.

translate:

1) You have to make your bed every morning.
2) The crowd's waiting for the directors.
3) Is your bedroom upstairs or downstairs?
4) Your answer's right, but his is wrong.
5) Are you sure that his story's true?
6) I don't think this story's true.
7) Is it for him?
8) She works full-time although she has five children.
9) It's different from mine.
10) You can take the elevator if you're in a hurry.
11) You have to admit that that fur coat's very expensive.
12) It's too bad but her dress is the same as mine.
13) When does the sun rise in summer?
14) Why don't you ever listen to your friends, when they suggest something?
15) She's dumb. She thinks her diamond's real.
16) If your mother-in-law lives here, I'll move out.
17) It doesn't cost much, it's really cheap.
18) I've been here for about a week.
19) Do you eat eggs and bacon every morning?
20) Help yourself if you can't wait for the maid.
21) If the film isn't exciting, I'll leave before.
22) Take your time, I'm not in a hurry.
23) If his work is careless, we'll lay him off.
24) Can you lend me ten marks?
25) I'm sorry but we're closing now.
26) I like your living-room. (translate with "gefallen")
27) I can't see you well and they can't either.
28) Who knows her?

learn by heart, then ask someone to give you a test

1. **ich bin glücklich**   ≠   **traurig**
   I'm happy   sad

2. **Klaus ist gross**   ≠   **klein**
   Klaus is tall   small

3. **es ist das gleiche wie meins**   ≠   **verschieden von**
   it's the same as mine   different from

4. **der Kuchen ist hart**   ≠   **weich**
   the cake's hard   soft

5. **die Wäsche ist trocken**   ≠   **nass**
   the laundry's dry   wet

6. **ein Pelzmantel ist teuer**   ≠   **billig, preiswert**
   a furcoat's expensive   cheap

7. **das Wasser ist tief**   ≠   **seicht**
   the water's deep   shallow

8. **ich gehe vorher weg**   ≠   **nachher**
   I'm leaving before   after

9. **die Zimmer oben**   ≠   **unten**
   the rooms on top   down below

10. **ich gehe hinauf**   ≠   **hinunter**
    I'm going upstairs   downstairs

11. **die Antwort ist richtig**   ≠   **falsch**
    the answer's right   wrong

12. **mein Diamant ist echt**   ≠   **unecht**
    my diamond's real   fake, phony

13. **ich arbeite halbtags**   ≠   **ganztags**
    I work part-time   full-time

14. **diese Geschichte stimmt**   ≠   **stimmt nicht**
    this story's true   false, untrue

GEGENTEIL 3 (fortsetzung = continued)

15. **seien Sie nicht so unhöflich/grob** ≠ **höflich**
    don't be so impolite/rude   polite

16. **seine Arbeit ist sorgfältig** ≠ **nachlässig**
    his work is careful   careless

17. **mein Bruder ist lieb** ≠ **böse**
    my brother's kind   mean

18. **er ist intelligent/klug** ≠ **dumm/dämlich**
    he's intelligent/clever   stupid/dumb

19. **mein Zimmer ist unordentlich** ≠ **aufgeräumt**
    my room's sloppy   neat

20. **das Kino ist voll** ≠ **leer/keine Menschenseele**
    the cinema's crowded   empty/not a soul

21. **anfangen, beginnen** ≠ **beenden, aufhören**
    to start, to begin   to finish, to stop

22. **lehren, unterrichten** ≠ **lernen**
    to teach   learn

23. **borgen, pumpen** ≠ **leihen**
    to borrow   to lend

24. **schliessen, zumachen** ≠ **öffnen, aufmachen**
    to close, to shut   to open

80

VOKABELN

	Übersetzung	Sinnverwandte Wörter	Gegenteil
1. (das) Schlaf-zimmer	bedroom	das Bett machen = to make the bed	
2. /(das) Wohn-zimmer/(das) Esszimmer	/living room /dining room	(der) Raum = room, place	
3. (die) Küche	kitchen	(die) Pfanne = pan, (der) Topf = pot	
4. /(das) Bad (ezimmer)/(das) Waschbecken	/bath(room)/sink	(die) Toilette = (das) Klo = the John, the loo	
5. /(der) Vorhang /(der) Teppich	/curtain/rug, carpet		
6. unten	downstairs		oben = upstairs
7. /(die) Wohnung /(das) Haus	flat (US apartment) /house	(die) Möbel = furniture	
8. (die) Lampe	lamp	(die) Birne = bulb (das) Licht = light	
9. fühlen	to feel		
10. (die) Strasse	street, road		
11. (der) Fahrstuhl	lift (US elevator)		(die) Treppe = stairs
12. bequem	comfortable ≠ uncomfortable		unbequem
13. (der) Stock	floor	auf dem Boden = on the floor, (der) Fussboden = ground	(die) Decke = ceiling
14. zu dumm	too bad ≠ all the better		um so besser
15. das hängt von Ihnen ab	it depends on you	das kommt auf Sie an	
16. Beeilen Sie sich!	Hurry up! ≠ Take your time!		Nehmen Sie sich Zeit!
17. (der) Schrank	closet	(das) Regal = shelf	
18. (die) Menge	crowd		

LEKTION 14

PERSONAL PRONOUNS *(AKKUSATIV)* *(DATIV)*

subject	direct object	indirect object
ICH I	**MICH** me	**MIR** (to) me
DU you	**DICH** you	**DIR** (to) you
ER he	**IHN** him	**IHM** (to) him
SIE she	**SIE** her	**IHR** (to) her
ES it	**ES** it	**IHM** (to) it
MAN one, we, you		
WIR we	**UNS** us	**UNS** (to) us
IHR you	**EUCH** you	**EUCH** (to) you
SIE they, you	**SIE** them, you	**IHNEN** (to them, (to) you

note: — Indirect pronouns don't exist in English and are a true problem!
— Whenever 'to' is said or implied in English, you must use these forms in German.
— But: wie ich = like me;
ich bin's = it's me.

SAGEN SIE IHM ALLES?	Do you tell him everything?
Ja, ich sage ihm alles. **Nein, ich sage ihm nicht alles.**	Yes, I tell him everything. No, I don't tell him everything.

note: Revise list on page 61 of verbs which are followed by the dative.

GEHÖREN = to belong to

WEM GEHÖRT DIESER HUND? Who does this dog belong to?

Er gehört meinem Freund. It belongs to my friend.
Er gehört ihm. It belongs to him.

GEFALLEN = to please, to like

GEFÄLLT IHNEN MEIN WAGEN? Do you like my car? (Does my car please you?)

Ja, er gefällt mir. Yes, I like it.
Nein, er gefällt mir nicht. No, I don't like it.

---

note: This construction is very frequent in German, especially for 'to like something'.

GUT GEHEN = to be well

WIE GEHT ES IHNEN? How are you?

Es geht mir gut? I'm well/fine.

LEIDTUN = to be sorry

WEM TUT ES LEID? Who's sorry?

Es tut meiner Freundin leid. My friend's sorry.
Es tut ihr leid. She's sorry.

---

insert pronouns instead of nouns:

e.g. Geben sie ihrem Freund das Buch?
— Geben sie es ihm?

1) Die Schüler sprechen oft mit ihrem Lehrer.
2) Dieser Wagen gehört meinem Vater.
3) Ich erzähle meinen Freunden diese Geschichte.
4) Er zeigt seinen Eltern die Universität.
5) Sie zeigen ihren Lehrern die Bücher.
6) Ich leihe meinem Bruder meinen Wagen.
7) Ich habe meinen Wagen noch nicht lange.
8) Es tut Peter leid.
9) Es geht Maria gut.
10) Wir schreiben Maria und dir den Brief.
11) Er hilft seinen Eltern nie.
12) Gefällt dir die Tasche?
13) Die Lehrer erklären den Schülern die Lektion.
14) Das Haus gehört meiner Mutter.
15) Mein Freund zeigt mir den Film von den Ferien.
16) Ich komme mit meiner Freundin und ohne meinen Freund.
17) Können Sie der alten Dame helfen?
18) Die Schüler fragen den Lehrer, und der Lehrer antwortet den Schülern.
19) Die Bullen folgen dem roten Auto.
20) Geht es Peter gut?
21) Es tut meiner Sekretärin leid, dass sie nicht kommen kann.
22) Er spricht mit seinem Freund und mit seiner Freundin.
23) Er erzählt von seinen Brüdern und Schwestern.
24) Ich fahre mit meiner Biene in die Stadt.
25) Er arbeitet mit seinen Brüdern.
26) Diese Bücher gefallen dem Kind.

translate:

1) When do you need the car? I need it on Monday.
2) Who does that lighter belong to? It belongs to her.
3) With whom are you coming? I'm coming with him.
4) I'd like to give it to him.
5) The boss is travelling all month.
6) How much is a round-trip?
7) Give me a cheque and I'll give you the money.
8) I'm sure that bicycle belongs to you.
9) We can only see her once a week.
10) You must tell me everything.
11) You mustn't tell him anything.
12) Can you lend me some money?
13) Perhaps you know him better.
14) Is the dough for me? Yes, it's for you. (singular and plural)
15) I don't have any cash on (bei) me.
16) Any film with that actor is excellent.
17) From time to time she writes me a letter.
18) For whom is he reserving the room?
19) This doll belongs to my little sister.
20) Have you been waiting for me since one o'clock?
21) If the water's shallow one can't swim.
22) I think that the restaurant closes at midnight.
23) My brother's kind but not very bright.
24) Does it depend on you? No, it doesn't depend only on me.
25) Are you taking the apartment? Yes, I'm taking it.
26) Why are you against him?
27) Do you like this book? (Does this book please you?)
28) You must buy a new bathing suit.

VOKABELN

	Übersetzung	Sinnverwandte Wörter	Gegenteil
1. /gut/besser am besten	/good/better/the best ≠ bad, worse worst		schlecht, schlechter, am schlechtesten
2. /verreisen/(die) Reise/(das) Reisebüro	/to travel/a trip /travel agent	(der) Aufenthalt = stay	
3. (die) Hinfahrkarte	one way ticket ≠ round trip		(die) Hin- und Rückfahrkarte
4. /(die) Stadt/(das) Dorf/(das) Land	/city/village /country(-side)	(der) Staat = state	
5. reservieren	reserve ≠ cancel	voll = booked	annulieren
6. in Ferien	on vacation	auf Urlaub	
7. (das) Hotel	hotel	(das) Zimmer = room	
8. /(der) Strand /(der) Badeanzug	/beach/bathing suit	(die) Küste = coast, (der) Sand = sand, schwimmen = to swim	
9. (der) Berg	mountain	skifahren = to ski	(das) Tal = valley
10. ich bin dafür	I'm for ≠ against		dagegen
11. (das) Geld	money (change = (das) Kleingeld)	(die) Moneten = (der) Kies = dough, (das) Bargeld = cash	
12. /(der) Scheck /(die) Bank	/cheque/bank		
13. /(das) Stück /(der) Schauspieler/(das) Theater	/play/actor /theatre	spielen = to act	
14. (der) Photoapparat	camera	(der) Film = film	
15. ein netter Ort	a nice place (note: der Platz = square)	(der) Flecken = spot	
16. (die) Dusche	shower	(das) Bad = bath, (die) Badewanne = bathtub	
17. (der) Sonnenbrand	sunburn	braunwerden = to tan	

LEKTION 15

SOLLEN = TO BE SUPPOSED TO/SOMEONE WANTS SOMEONE TO

SOLL ICH MORGEN KOMMEN?	Am I supposed to come tomorrow? Do you want me to come tomorrow?
Ja, Sie sollen morgen kommen.	Yes, you're supposed to come tomorrow. Yes, I want you to come tomorrow.
Nein, Sie sollen nicht morgen kommen.	No, you aren't supposed to come tomorrow. No, I don't want you to come tomorrow.

DÜRFEN = MAY, TO BE ALLOWED

DARF ICH HIER RAUCHEN?	May I smoke here?
Ja, Sie dürfen hier rauchen.	Yes, you may smoke here. Yes, you're allowed to smoke here.
Nein, Sie dürfen hier nicht rauchen.	No, you aren't allowed to smoke here. No, you mustn't smoke here.

note: Remember that <u>nicht dürfen</u> means 'mustn't'.

WOLLEN = TO WANT (TO)

WILLST DU DIESEN FILM SEHEN?	Do you want to see this film?
Ja, ich will diesen Film sehen. **Nein, ich will diesen Film nicht sehen.**	Yes, I want to see this film. No, I don't want to see this film.

MÖCHTE = WOULD LIKE (TO)

MÖCHTEN SIE MIT MIR GEHEN?	Would you like to go with me?
Ja, ich möchte mit Ihnen gehen. **Nein, ich möchte nicht mit Ihnen gehen.**	Yes, I'd like to go with you. No, I wouldn't like to go with you.

SOLLEN, DÜRFEN, WOLLEN, MÖCHTE (present tense)

ich soll	I'm supposed to	**ich darf**	I may
du sollst	you're supposed to	**du darfst**	you may
er **sie soll** **es**	he she 's supposed to it	**er** **sie darf** **es**	he she may it
wir sollen	we're supposed to	**wir dürfen**	we may
ihr sollt	you're supposed to	**ihr dürft**	you may
sie **Sie** sollen	they you 're supposed to	**sie** **Sie** dürfen	they you may
ich möchte	I'd like	**ich will**	I want
du möchtest	you'd like	**du willst**	you want
er **sie möchte** **es**	he she 'd like it	**er** **sie will** **es**	he she wants it
wir möchten	we'd like	**wir wollen**	we want
ihr möchtet	you'd like	**ihr wollt**	you want
sie **Sie** möchten	they you 'd like	**sie** **Sie** wollen	they you want

---

IMPERATIVE

GEHT!   Go!

GEHE!   Go!

GEHEN SIE! Go!

GEHEN WIR! Let's go!

note: — To get the imperative singular you drop the ending of the second
person: Du gibst = you're giving; Gib! = Give!
— The imperative plural's exactly like the second form of the plural.
— For the polite form you put the verb first, the same for 'let's'.
— exception: Sei! = Seien Sie! = Be!

conjugate the verb:

1) _____ ich morgen kommen? (sollen)
2) Ich _____ ein Glas Bier. (möchte)
3) Was _____ du essen? (wollen)
4) Du _____ hier nicht rauchen. (dürfen)
5) Was _____ sie? (wollen)
6) Wir _____ Ihnen helfen. (möchte)
7) _____ ihr den Film sehen? (wollen)
8) _____ er auch helfen? (sollen)
9) Du _____ nicht so schnell sprechen. (sollen)
10) Er _____ es machen, aber er _____ nicht. (wollen, dürfen)
11) Ihr _____ euer Bett machen, bevor ihr ausgeht. (müssen)
12) _____ er dich anrufen? (sollen)
13) _____ ihr eine Tasse Kaffee trinken? (möchte)
14) Du kannst mir helfen, wen du _____. (wollen)
15) Ich _____ morgen nicht arbeiten. (möchte)
16) Die Kinder _____ den Film nicht sehen, aber der Vater _____ ihn sehen. (dürfen)
17) Er _____ es nicht machen? (wollen)
18) _____ du die Musik hören? (möchte)

translate in the negative form:

1) You may come tomorrow.
2) I'd like a new car.
3) He wants to do it.
4) I can do this work.
5) You must put your legs on the table.
6) You can come into my room.
7) She wants to buy a new dress.
8) We'd like to go home early.
9) You're supposed to finish this work.
10) Do you want me to call you up tonight?

translate:

1) You mustn't smoke here.
2) I'd like to swim in this lake.
3) Must I come tomorrow?
4) Do you want me to come on Saturday?
5) He'd like to help her, but he can't.
6) You're supposed to work on Saturday.
7) They have to make a lot of money in order to buy that car.
8) May I tell you his story?
9) I mustn't tell you.
10) · I'd like to come at Christmas.
11) If I must do it, I will.
12) Would you like to light my cigarette?
13) That must be wrong.
14) Can you understand him?
15) I'd like.to come with you.
16) May I open the window?
17) The children are allowed to go swimming.
18) I want you to listen to me now.
19) Nobody can always win.
20) They mustn't swim in this lake.
21) Don't be unhappy, I'm going to go with you! (3 translations)
22) Talk to him about the story! (3 translations)
23) Don't get off the bus yet! (3 translations)
24) Let's wait for her until five o'clock!
25) Let's go to the cinema!
26) Let's go out on New Year's Eve!
27) Don't forget this! (3 translations)

DATIVE OR ACCUSATIVE?

WO BIST DU?	Where are you?
Ich bin im Büro.	I'm at the office.
WOHIN GEHST DU?	Where are you going (to)?
Ich gehe ins Büro.	I'm going to the office.

note: — All prepositions (except zu and nach) take the accusative instead of the dative if they express a movement towards another place (going to, sitting down on, etc.).

— The following contractions are frequently used: in das = ins; an das = ans; auf das = auf.

STEHEN≠STELLEN–LIEGEN≠LEGEN–SITZEN≠SETZEN–HÄNGEN

WO STEHT DER TISCH?	Where's the table?
Er steht an der Wand.	It's against the wall.
WOHIN STELLST DU DEN TISCH?	Where are you putting the table?
Ich stelle den Tisch an die Wand.	I'm putting it against the wall.
WO LIEGT DAS BUCH?	Where's the book?
Es liegt auf dem Tisch.	It's on the table.
WOHIN LEGST DU DAS BUCH?	Where are you putting the book?
Ich lege es auf den Tisch.	I'm putting it on the table.
WO SITZT DIE KATZE?	Where's the cat?
Sie sitzt auf dem Stuhl.	It's on the chair.
WOHIN SETZT SIE DIE KATZE?	Where's she putting the cat?
Sie setzt sie auf den Stuhl.	She's putting it on the chair.
WO HÄNGT DAS BILD?	Where's the picture?
Es hängt an der Wand.	It's hanging on the wall.
WOHIN HÄNGST DU DAS BILD?	Where are you hanging the picture?
Ich hänge es an die Wand.	I'm hanging it on the wall.

note: — In German you always have to be very precise about the position of an object, if it's standing up, lying, sitting or hanging.

— There's a book on the table = Ein Buch liegt auf dem Tisch.
There's a car in the street = Ein Auto steht auf der Strasse.

— 'stehen, liegen, sitzen, hängen' are positions, whereas 'stellen, legen, setzen, hängen' are actions, where a movement's involved, therefore, the positions take the dative and the actions take the accusative.

insert the article, making contractions when possible, and then put the sentence into the interrogative using 'wo' or 'wohin':

1) Jeden Morgen arbeite ich in _____ Büro.
2) Jeden Morgen fahre ich mit _____ Bus zu _____ Büro.
3) Jetzt gehe ich in _____ Büro.
4) Der alte Mann steht den ganzen Tag an _____ Fenster.
5) Die alte Dame geht an _____ Fenster.
6) Einen Moment, bitte; Peter ist gerade an _____ Telefon.
7) Er geht an _____ Telefon.
8) Der Stuhl steht zwischen _____ Wand und _____ Tisch.
9) Sie stellt den Stuhl zwischen _____ Wand und _____ Tisch.
10) Der Whisky ist in _____ Esszimmer.
11) Er bringt den Whisky in _____ Esszimmer.
12) Mein Sohn ist jeden Morgen in _____ Schule.
13) Ihr Sohn geht auch in _____ Schule.
14) Ich fahre morgen in _____ Stadt.
15) Meine Freundin wohnt in _____ Stadt.
16) Auf _____ Tisch liegen vier Bücher.
17) Die Sekretärin legt die Bücher auf _____ Tisch.
18) Wir hängen das Bild sofort an _____ Wand.
19) In _____ Wohnzimmer hängt ein schönes Bild an _____ Wand.
20) Der kleine Hund sitzt auf _____ Stuhl.
21) Das Kind setzt seinen Hund auf _____ Stuhl.
22) Meine Freundin sitzt schon in _____ Bus.
23) Ich steige schnell in _____ Bus.
24) Alle meine Freunde studieren an _____ Universität.
25) Er geht zweimal pro Woche zu _____ Universität.
26) Die Studenten gehen in _____ Universität.
27) Auf _____ Strasse stehen viele Wagen.
28) Er stellt seinen Wagen auf _____ Strasse.

VOKABELN

	Übersetzung	Sinnverwandte Wörter	Gegenteil
1. das ist ein Kinderspiel	it's a cinch ≠ hard	leicht = easy	schwierig, anstrengend
2. /(die) Tasche /(die) Brieftasche	/pocket/wallet		
3. /(die) Bühne /(der) Regisseur	/stage/director		
4. (der) Komplex	hang-up		
5. nervös	nervous, uptight	aufgeregt, gereizt	
6. noch heute	this very day		
7. zustande bringen	to get on, to manage	Sie machen Fortschritte = you get on well	
8. falsch	false ≠ true, real	imitiert, unecht	wahr, echt
9. werfen	to throw		fangen = to catch
10. gewinnen	to win ≠ to lose		verlieren
11. na und?	so what?	so? = so?	
12. viel zu (viel)	far too (much)		genug = enough
13. Sieh mal an!	Well! well!	So! So!	
14. /(das) Steckenpferd /(der) Liebhaber	/hobby/fan	(das) Hobby, (der) Fan, (der) Zeitvertreib = pastime	
15. ernst	serious	schwer	
16. /Weihnachten /Ostern	/Christmas /Easter	Silvester = New Year's Eve	
17. wählen	to choose, to vote		
18. gerecht	fair ≠ unfair	gerade = straight	ungerecht
19. sich Sorgen machen	to be worried	besorgt, bange = worried, ich mache mir Sorgen = I'm worried	machen Sie sich keine Sorgen, keine Gedanken = don't worry

LEKTION 16

DER, DIE, DAS = WHICH, THAT, WHO

Der Mann, der spricht, . . . The man who's talking . . .
Die Frau, mit der er spricht, . . . The woman to whom he's talking . . .
Der Wagen, den ich fahre, . . . The car that I'm driving . . .

note: — This is very easy: in a relative sentence you simply repeat the article, but you must put it into the correct case.

insert the correct article and relative pronoun, and then put the sentence into the interrogative using welcher:

e.g. _____ Mann, _____ du kennst, ist mein Doktor.
  — Der Mann, den du kennst, ist mein Doktor.
  — Welcher Mann ist mein Doktor?

1) Ich kenne _____ Mann, mit _____ du sprichst.
2) Nehmen wir _____ Bus, _____ dort kommt?
3) Das ist _____ Frau, _____ mir im Büro hilft.
4) Alle Leute, _____ in diesem Büro arbeiten, sind Amerikaner.
5) Ich fahre mit _____ Wagen, _____ meinem Vater gehört.
6) _____ Student, mit _____ ich spreche, ist sehr helle.
7) Das ist _____ Zug, _____ ich jeden Morgen nehme.
8) Ich gehe in _____ Kino, _____ du sicher kennst.
9) Ist das _____ Buch, von _____ sie immer spricht?
10) _____ Person, _____ das Ding findet, kann es behalten.
11) Hilf doch _____ Frau, _____ dort an der Strasse steht.
12) Die Bullen können _____ Schuft, _____ sie folgen, nicht mehr finden.
13) _____ Mann, _____ wir entlassen, bekommt viel Geld.
14) _____ Lektion, _____ wir hier machen, ist nicht schwierig.
15) _____ Frau, _____ der grosse Wagen gehört, ist sehr reich.
16) Ich frage _____ Studenten, _____ alles weiss.
17) _____ U-Bahn, mit _____ wir fahren, ist sehr alt.
18) Sie schreibt _____ Mann, _____ sie seit gestern kennt.

94

```
┌─────────────────────────────────────────────────────────────────────┐
│ QUESTIONS WITH PREPOSITIONS                                           │
│                                                                       │
│ MIT WEM KOMMT ER?              With whom is he coming?                │
│                                                                       │
│ Er kommt mit seinem Freund.    He's coming with his friend.           │
│ Er kommt mit ihm.              He's coming with him.                  │
│                                                                       │
│ WOMIT KOMMT ER?                How's (with what) he coming?           │
│                                                                       │
│ Er kommt mit dem Bus.          He's coming by bus.                    │
│ Er kommt damit.                (He's coming by it.)                   │
└─────────────────────────────────────────────────────────────────────┘
```

note: — It's impossible to form a question with 'was' and a preposition;
         you have to use wo- and the preposition, or wor- plus preposition
         if it starts with a vowel.
       — For the answer you have to use da- or dar- (darin = in it); damit =
         with it; darauf = on it; daneben = beside it, etc.

answer the questions using a pronoun instead of the noun:
e.g. Kommt er mit dem Wagen?
     — Ja, er kommt damit.

1)   Wartest du auf deinen Freund?
2)   Warten Sie auf den Bus?
3)   Spricht er über seine Familie?
4)   Sprecht ihr über den neuen Film?
5)   Kommt sie mit ihrer Schwester?
6)   Kommen Sie mit dem Flugzeug?
7)   Sitzen Sie neben Klaus?
8)   Steht der Tisch neben dem Fenster?
9)   Ist das Ding für Ihr Auto?
10) Ist der Wagen für meine Familie?

translate:

1) That's the man, Mary's married to.
2) Who's the woman you've been waiting for since this morning?
3) The book which I'm reading now is very exciting.
4) The cat the children are playing with, is mine.
5) The actor you hate is in this film.
6) The sweater you're putting on is too dirty.
7) These are the friends who are going to travel with me.
8) The girl who looks very tired goes out every night.
9) The guy who she loves is a lawyer.
10) Things which happen every day aren't very interesting.
11) I'm helping the secretary who can't do the work alone.
12) She's writing to the man she's known for a week.

put into interrogative form, and then answer the question, substituting a pronoun for the underlined phrase:
e.g. Er kommt mit dem Bus.
    — Womit kommt er?
    — Er kommt damit.

1) Er spricht über das neue Buch von Günter Grass.
2) Wir sprechen über einen guten Schauspieler.
3) Sie warten auf ihren Lehrer.
4) Ich warte immer noch auf den Bus.
5) Dieser Preis ist für den Gewinner.
6) Das Geld ist für ein neues Auto.
7) Sie kommen mit dem Flugzeug.
8) Sie kommt immer mit ihrer Mutter zum Rendezvous.
9) Ich sitze zwischen zwei hübschen Mädchen.
10) Er steht zwischen dem Stuhl und dem Tisch.
11) Wir sind mit der Arbeit fertig.
12) Die junge Katze liegt auf dem Bett.
13) Der Lehrer ist gegen diese Idee.
14) Ich bin gegen diese Person.

```
┌─────────────────────────────────────────────────────────────────────┐
│  IN, NACH, ZU, AN, AUF        =   TO                                  │
│  WOHIN GEHST DU?                  Where are you going?                │
│                                                                       │
│  1) Ich gehe in das Kino.         I'm going to the cinema.            │
│  2) Ich fahre nach Paris.                   to Paris.                 │
│  3) Ich gehe zum Hofbräuhaus.               to the Hofbräuhaus.       │
│  4) Ich fahre an die See.                   to the seaside.           │
│  5) Ich gehe auf die Post.                  to the post-office.       │
└─────────────────────────────────────────────────────────────────────┘
```

note: — You have to translate 'to' by:
  1) in, if you enter somewhere;
  2) nach for cities and countries;
  3) zu for persons, places and sights;
  4) an, if you can't go inside (you don't drive into the sea);
  5) auf for public places and institutions (Bank, Post, Strasse, Markt, etc.).
  — Remember that zu and nach are always with the dative, while the other prepositions take the accusative here since they express a movement.

insert the correct preposition:

1) Geht ihr _____ die Schule?
2) Morgen fahren wir _____ Berlin.
3) Er geht _____ das Fenster.
4) Kommen Sie bitte _____ das Telefon.
5) Kleine Kinder sollen nicht allein _____ die Strasse gehen.
6) Alle Touristen gehen _____ dem Brandenburger Tor.
7) Gehen wir _____ das Zimmer nebenan.
8) Zuerst gehe ich _____ die Bank, dann _____ dem Bäcker.
9) Wenn du krank bist, musst du _____ das Krankenhaus oder _____ dem Doktor gehen.
10) Im Sommer fahren wir _____ die See oder _____ die Berge.

```
┌─────────────────────────────────────────────────────────────────────┐
│  WAS                          =   WHAT, THAT                          │
│                                                                       │
│  IST DAS ALLES, WAS ER            Is that all (that) he said?         │
│  GESAGT HAT?                                                          │
│                                                                       │
│  Ja, das ist alles, was er gesagt hat.   Yes, that's all (that) he said. │
│  Nein, das ist nicht alles, was er       No, that isn't all (that) he said. │
│      gesagt hat.                                                      │
└─────────────────────────────────────────────────────────────────────┘
```

translate, and then put into the interrogative form using **wo** or **wohin**:

1) Let's go to the market first.
2) Many children are playing in the street.
3) If you need bread you must go to the baker.
4) Let's have a big beer in the Hofbräuhaus.
5) This year I'd like to go to Heidelberg.
6) You can phone in the post-office.
7) I have a toothache, I must go to the dentist.
8) He must go to the station now.
9) They're at the seaside this month.
10) He's going to the bank this afternoon.

complete:

1) Auf _____ Strasse sind zu viel Autos.
2) Geht nicht auf_____ Strasse!
3) Ist sie immer noch auf _____ Post?
4) Ich gehe jeden Morgen auf_____ Markt.
5) Der Doktor geht in _____ Krankenhaus.
6) Soll ich an _____Telefon kommen.
7) Sie bleibt immer eine Stunde an _____Telefon.
8) Fahren Sie auch im Sommer an _____ See.
9) Sind Sie gern in _____ Bergen?
10) Ist das Frühstück schon auf_____Tisch.
11) Er stellt die Tassen auf _____Tisch.
12) Auf _____ Markt kann man alles kaufen.
13) Sie fährt ihren Sohn zu _____Schule.
14) Der kleine Junge geht in _____Schule.
15) Am Sonntag fahre ich zu mein _____Onkel.
16) Warum steht er die ganze Zeit an _____Fenster.
17) Ich muss heute nachmittag auf_____ Post und auf _____Bank gehen.
18) Arbeitet er auf_____ Bank?

```
ES = IT

es ist schön          = it's nice out        es regnet          → it rains

es ist kalt/warm/     = it's cold/warm/      es schneit         → it snows
heiss                   hot                  es scheint         → it seems
es ist sicher, dass   = it's certain that
                                             es kommt vor,      → it happens that
es ist wichtig,       = it's important       dass
dass                    that
                                             es ist möglich,    → it's possible
es ist selbstver-     = it's understood      dass                 that
standlich, dass         that
```

```
ES GIBT                              THERE IS, THERE ARE

GIBT ES VIELE LEUTE IN               Are there many people in Bonn?
BONN?

Ja, es gibt viele Leute in Bonn.     Yes, there are many people in Bonn.
Nein, es gibt nicht viele Leute      No, there aren't many people in
in Bonn.                             Bonn.
```

note: — This is, however, far less used than in English:
      — There are four of us = Wir sind vier.
      — There's a book on the table = Ein Buch liegt auf dem Tisch.

translate without using **es gibt**:
e.g. There are four books on the table.
      — Vier Bücher liegen auf dem Tisch.

1)   There are six of us.
2)   There are three chairs in this room.
3)   There are many children playing in the park.
4)   There are seven secretaries working in this office.
5)   There's one of us who can't come. (One of us can't come.)

translate:

1) Let's stay at home, it's too cold out.
2) It's quite hot here in the summer.
3) It's understood that you work when you're in the office.
4) It seems that he loves her very much.
5) It's important that you call me up tonight.
6) Is it possible that I'll finish the work tomorrow?
7) It happens that the planes to Frankfurt are a little late.
8) I like to be in the mountains when it snows.
9) It's certain that my boss won't be here.
10) It seems to me that you're wrong.
11) There are always many tourists in this city.
12) Is there a lot to do?
13) Are there any problems with this lesson?
14) There's a nice restaurant in this village.
15) There are several pills for (gegen!) toothache.
16) What's there to see?
17) There's nothing to do in this place.
18) Is there a lot of snow in winter.
19) Are you coming by tube (subway) or by bus?
20) I have to leave after breakfast.
21) It isn't certain that he's staying with his family.
22) It is impossible that I come after lunch.
23) It happens that there are fifty people here at lunchtime.
24) It never happens that I forget something.
25) It is understood that you come with your new friend.
26) Even in January it's quite warm here.
27) There are only four people in this restaurant.
28) There's a man I don't know on the phone.

VOKABELN

	Übersetzung	Sinnverwandte Wörter	Gegenteil
1. müde	tired ≠ to feel great	am Ende, kaputt, erschöpft = exhausted	in Form sein, sich besser fühlen = to feel better
2. krank	ill ≠ well		gesund, gut, sich gut fühlen = to feel well
3. sich erkälten	to catch a cold	(das) Fieber = fever	
4. niesen	to sneeze	Gesundheit! = God bless you!	
5. husten	to cough	die Halsschmerzen = sore throat	
6. (die) Medizin	medicine	(die) Tablette, (die) Pille = pill	
7. /(der) Zahnarzt /(die) Zahn- schmerzen	(dentist/toothache	(der) Zahn = tooth	
8. /Kopfschmerzen /Magenschmer- zen	/headache /stomach ache	(der) Magen = stomach	
9. das tut weh	it hurts	die Schmerzen = pain	
10. fertig?	ready?	ich bin fertig = I'm ready	
11. vorkommen	to happen, to occur	passieren, geschehen, stattfinden	
12. tragen	to carry (also: to wear)	bringen = to bring = mitbringen	
13. sich ausruhen	to rest	ruhig Blut = take it easy = nimm's leicht	
14. lachen	to laugh ≠ to cry	(das) Lächeln = smile	weinen, (die) Träne = tear
15. gut aussehen	to look well		schlecht aussehen = to look bad

LEKTION 17

THE COMPARATIVE FORM

JUNG	= young	**ALT**	= old
JÜNGER	= younger	**ÄLTER**	= older
DER JÜNGSTE **AM JÜNGSTEN**	= the youngest	**DER ÄLTESTE** **AM ÄLTESTEN**	= the oldest

note: — Most adjectives take the Umlaut in both comparative forms!
— Between 't' and 'st' and 'z' and 'st' add '-e'.
— The second form of the superlative is only used after the verb:
der jüngste Sohn = the youngest son; Peter ist am jüngsten =
Peter's the youngest.
— The comparative forms are declined as any other adjectives:
der jüngste Sohn → mein jüngster Sohn.
the youngest son   my youngest son.

Er ist jünger als ich. He's younger than me.
Er ist so jung wie ich. He's as young as me.
Er ist nicht so jung wie ich. He's not as young as me.
Er ist so jung, dass . . . . He's so young that . . . .

---

note: — Some adjectives have irregular comparative forms:
— gut, besser, am besten (good, better, best).
— hoch, höher, am höchsten (high, higher, highest).
— viel, mehr, am meisten (die meisten Leute = most people;
meistens = mostly)
— nahe, näher, am nächsten (near, nearer, nearest).

put the adjective into the comparative forms:

1)	schnell	7)	leicht
2)	gross	8)	hoch
3)	kalt	9)	warm
4)	sorgfältig	10)	schwierig
5)	interessant	11)	lang
6)	langsam	12)	kurz

translate:

1) He's younger than his sister.
2) This winter isn't as cold as the last one.
3) Your car's just as fast as mine.
4) He's so lazy that his teacher isn't very happy.
5) I hope to find a better doctor.
6) Who's older, your father or your mother?
7) My father's older than my mother.
8) She looks older than him.
9) I must find a dress which isn't longer than my coat.
10) Excuse me, but I can't come earlier.
11) Many people are kinder on vacation than at work.
12) I like cake better than bread. (use: schmecken)
13) In winter the nights are longer than in summer.
14) He's my best friend.
15) We have to find a cheaper restaurant.
16) *Love Story* is the saddest film I know.
17) I hope it's becoming more interesting.
18) He's so rich that he can spend as much money as he wants to.
19) Let's wait until its sunnier.
20) This lake isn't as deep as you think.

put the adjective into the superlative (second form):

1) Im Juni sind die Tage _____ (lang).
2) Im Dezember sind sie _____ (kurz).
3) Dieser Film dauert _____ (lang).
4) Findest du diesen Mantel _____ (schön)?
5) Gefällt Ihnen dieses Bild _____ (gut)?
6) Welchen Lehrer versteht ihr _____ (schlecht)?
7) _____ (interessant) ist New York, denke ich.
8) Dieser Weg zum Bahnhof ist _____ (schnell).

put the adjective into the superlative (fist form):

1) Sie ist _____ (gross) in der Familie.
2) Dieser Anruf ist _____ (wichtig) von allen.
3) Dieses Land ist das _____ (kalt) in Europa.
4) Mein _____ (alt) Sohn studiert in Deutschland.
5) Ihre _____ (jung) Tochter ist sehr hübsch.
6) Ich habe den _____ (modern) Wagen in dieser Stadt.
7) Sein _____ (gross) Fehler ist es, nie zuzuhören.
8) Der _____ (gut) Student bekommt einen Preis.
9) Die _____ (hoch) Häuser sind in New York, glaube ich.
10) Die _____ (viel) Leute machen im August Ferien.
11) Das ist der _____ (interessant) Film, den ich kenne.
12) Ist Peter Ihr _____ (alt) oder _____ (jung) Sohn?
13) Ist diese Lektion die _____ (schwierig) von allen?

put the adjective into the superlative (first form):

1) Er ist viel _____ (jung) _____ ich.
2) Dieser Berg ist _____ (hoch) _____ der.
3) Seine Arbeit ist _____ (sorgfältig) _____ deine.
4) Sie hat ein _____ (schön) Kleid _____ ihre Freundin.
5) Es macht nichts, wenn du _____ (spät) kommst.
6) Dein Zimmer ist heute noch _____ (unordentlich) _____ gestern.
7) In diesem Restaurant ist das Essen _____ (gut) _____ in dem.
8) Dieser Winter ist _____ (kalt) _____ der letzte.
9) Ich möchte gern einen _____ (warm) Mantel.
10) Dieses Buch kostet _____ (wenig) _____ das.
11) Mein Auto fährt _____ (schnell) als deins.
12) Ich brauche eine _____ (gut) Sekretärin.
13) Er ist _____ (arm) _____ sein Freund.
14) Je _____ (früh) je _____ (gut).

ADVERBS

GUT   = good, well

LEICHT   = easy, easily

SCHNELL   = quick, quickly, fast

note: — Adjectives can be used as adverbs
        without changing anything.
      — There are very few exceptions:
        glücklicherweise = luckily

NUMBERS

DER ERSTE	the first
DER ZWEITE	the second
DER DRITTE	the third
DER VIERTE	the fourth
DER ACHTZEHNTE	the eighteenth
DER NEUNZEHNTE	the nineteenth
DER ZWANZIGSTE	the twentieth
DER EINUNDZWANZIGSTE	the twenty-first

note: — You just add -te to the numbers, except for
     the first (der erste) and the third (der dritte).
       From twenty onwards you have to add -ste.
     — Ordinal numbers take adjective endings!

insert the correct endings as necessary, then put the sentence into the negative form:

1) Er ist ein gut ____ Schriftsteller.
2) Sie spielt sehr gut ____ .
3) Er arbeitet sehr sorgfältig ____ .
4) Das ist eine sehr sorgfältig ____ Arbeit.
5) Ich möchte gern ein schnell ____ schön ____ Auto kaufen.
6) Heute ist der zwei ____ Januar. '
7) Weihnachten ist am fünfundzwanzig ____ Dezember.
8) Claudia ist meine zweit ____ Frau.
9) Peter ist ihr erst ____ Freund.
10) Sie sieht sehr glücklich ____ aus.
11) Er ist ein sehr beschäftigt ____ Mann, aber sein Bruder ist auch sehr beschäftigt ____ .
12) Sie ist eine sehr fleissig ____ Sekretärin.
13) Sie kommt mit ihrem neuest ____ Freund.
14) Ich will meinen best ____ Freund anrufen.
15) Er zieht seinen zweit ____ Sohn vor.
16) Sie ist von ihrem erst ____ Mann geschieden.
17) Sein viert ____ Buch ist so gut wie die anderen.
18) Das ist die schwierigst ____ Übung.
19) Er ist der grösst ____ Mann, den ich kenne.
20) Das ist das höchst ____ Haus von Berlin.
21) Peter ist am jüngst ____
22) Ich will seinen neuest ____ Film sehen.
23) Ich kenne ein spannender ____ Buch.
24) Er möchte einen schneller ____ Wagen.
25) Ich muss einen wärmer ____ Pullover kaufen.
26) Januar ist der kältest ____ Monat.
27) Dieses Bild ist am schönst ____ .
28) Ich kenne einen schlechter ____ Kerl.

GERN, LIEBER, AM LIEBSTEN = TO LIKE, TO PREFER, TO LIKE BEST

Ich <u>trinke gern</u> Tee.	I <u>like (drinking)</u> tea.
Ich <u>trinke lieber</u> Kaffee.	I <u>prefer (drinking)</u> coffee.
Ich <u>trinke am liebsten</u> Whisky.	I <u>like best (drinking)</u> whisky.

IMMER + COMPARATIVE = MORE AND MORE

VERDIENST DU IMMER MEHR?	Do you earn more and more?
Ja, ich verdiene immer mehr.	Yes, I earn more and more.
Nein, ich verdiene immer weniger.	No, I earn less and less.

translate:

1) Do you like going to the cinema?
2) I prefer whisky to beer.
3) The exercises are becoming harder and harder.
4) I like reading novels best.
5) He works less and less.
6) As for me I prefer swimming in the sea.
7) On the whole I like working with him.
8) What do you like doing in your holidays?
9) I like walking in the mountains best.
10) She prefers skiing.
11) I like driving a very fast car best.
12) Do you prefer going to the cinema to going to the theatre?
13) She likes doing nothing.
14) He's driving faster and faster.

ADVERBEN UND SÄTZE 3

1. **je früher desto besser**	the sooner the better	14. **— vor kurzem** **— vor nicht langer Zeit**	— recently — not long ago
2. **am nächsten Tag**	the next day	15. **. . . genug**	enough . . .
3. **— am Tag /Abend** **— vorher**	— the day/night — before	16. **— nur** **— ich habe nur**	— only — I have only
4. **während, . . . lang**	while, during	17. **alle 14 Tage**	every other week
5. **wie oft?**	how often?	18. **— absichtlich** **— extra**	on purpose
6. **durchschnitt- lich**	on the average	19. **sobald wie**	as soon as
7. **vor allem**	above all	20. **was . . . betrifft**	as far as
8. **für den Fall, dass**	just in case	21. **mehrere**	several
9. **bald**	soon	22. **— ausserdem** **— darüber hinaus**	— besides — what's more
10. **noch einmal**	once more, again	23. **— im Grossen und Ganzen** **— im allge- meinen** **— die meisten**	— on the whole — in general — most of
11. **laut**	according to		
12. **von . . . an**	as of . . . from on		
13. **— vorausge- setzt, dass** **— da**	— given that — since	24. **was (mich) betrifft**	as for (me)
		25. **insofern als**	in so far as

VOKABELN

	Übersetzung	Sinnverwandte Wörter	Gegenteil
1. /telefonieren /(der) Anruf	/to call up/call	anrufen	
2. auflegen	to hang up ≠ to pick up	aufhängen	abnehmen
3. bleiben Sie am Apparat	hold on		
4. wer ist am Apparat	who's speaking?		
5. ich verbinde Sie mit . . .	I'll put you through to . . .		M . . . ist am Apparat = Mr . . . is on the line
6. /eine Prüfung machen/bestehen	/to take a test /to pass ≠ to fail		durchfallen
7. ich bin beschäftigt	I'm busy ≠ free		frei
8. wie Sie wünschen	as you like		
9. lustig	funny ≠ a drag	komisch	(sterbens) langweilig
10. (der) Freund	friend ≠ enemy	(der) Kumpel = pal	(der) Feind
11. 14 Tage	a fortnight		
12. wegen	on account of	das ist auf . . . zurückzuführen = it's due to . . .	warum? = why?
13. faul	lazy ≠ hard-working		fleissig
14. ich habe noch 2	I have two left ≠ I don't have any more		ich habe keine mehr
15. versuchen	to try		
16. (die) Verabredung	appointment	sich verabreden = to make an appointment	
17. hier ist (sind)	here is (are)		

LEKTION 18

GENITIVE = THE POSSESSIVE CASE

subject		genitive
(masc.)	**DER VATER** the father	**DER WAGEN DES VATERS** the car of the father, father's car
(fem.)	**DIE DAME** the lady	**DAS HAUS DER DAME** the house of the lady, the lady's house
(neut.)	**DAS KIND** the child	**DER VATER DES KINDES** the father of the child, the child's father
(plural)	**DIE KINDER** the children	**DAS ZIMMER DER KINDER** the room of the children, the children's room

note: — Masculine and neuter nouns add -s or -es in the singular.
  — Very often Germans form compound nouns:
    das Zimmer der Kinder = das Kinderzimmer;
    die Tür des Hauses = die Haustür.
  — With first names, the possessive case is as in English:
    Peters Frau = Peter's wife (but there's no apostrophe in German).

insert the correct endings:

1) Das Haus mein____ Vater____ ist nicht weit von hier.
2) Die Studenten dies____ Lehrerin sind sehr fleissig.
3) Das Zimmer mein____ Kinder ist immer unordentlich.
4) Ich komme während d____ Ferien mein____ Direktor____.
5) Das ist das Auto ein ____ reich ___ Mann ____ .
6) Der Vater d____ Mädchen____ lebt nicht mit seiner Mutter.
7) Das Kleid dies____ Frau ist sehr hübsch.
8) Das ist Peter____ Frau und nicht die sein____ Bruder ____ .
9) Er ist der neueste Freund mein____ jüngst____ Schwester.
10) Das ist der Roman ein____ interessant____ Schriftsteller____ .
11) Die Preise dies____ Restaurant____ sind sehr hoch.

110

```
PREPOSITIONS + GENITIVE

trotz des schlechten Wetters    =    in spite of the bad weather

während der Ferien              =    during the holidays

wegen eines Fehlers             =    because of a mistake

binnen einer Woche              =    within a week's time
```

note: — These four prepositions take the genitive!
— Adjectives take -en in the genitive.

insert the correct endings:

1) Wegen _____ Krankheit sein _____ Bruder_____ kann er nicht kommen.
2) Trotz sein ___ hoh ___ Alter_____ arbeitet er noch.
3) Während ____ Arbeit trinkt er sehr viel Kaffee.
4) Ich brauche das Resultat binnen ____ Monat _____ .
5) Er geht trotz _____ stark _____ Regen _____ spazieren.
6) Ich besuche dich während _____ nächst _____ Urlaub _____ .
7) Ich muss wegen _____ wichtig ___ Anruf ____ im Büro bleiben.
8) Trotz sein _____ Fieber_____ geht er aus.
9) Das ist der neue Wagen mein _____ Vater _____ .
10) Wegen sein _____ Sonnenbrand _____ geht er nicht schwimmen.
11) Das ist der Strand ein ___ sehr reich ___ Mann ____ .
12) Die Antwort dies ____ Schüler _____ ist richtig.
13) Er besteht seine Prüfung trotz ein ____ gross ___ Fehler _____ .
14) Wegen ihr_____ jüngst ____ Kind ___ arbeitet sieht nur halbtags.
15) Die Birne dies ____ Lampe ist kaputt.
16) Unglücklicherweise ist der Direktor dies ___ Abteilung nicht hier.

```
┌─────────────────────────────────────────────────────────────────┐
│  INTERROGATIVE PRONOUNS                                           │
│                        WER? =    WHO? (subject)                   │
│  WER SIEHT SIE?                  MEIN FREUND SIEHT MICH.          │
│  Who sees you?                   My friend sees me.               │
│                                                                   │
│                        WEN? =    WHO? WHOM? (direct object)       │
│  WEN SEHEN SIE?                  ICH SEHE MEINEN FREUND.          │
│  Who do you see?                 I see my friend.                 │
│                                                                   │
│                        WEM? =    (TO) WHOM? (indirect object)     │
│  WEM SCHREIBEN SIE?              ICH SCHREIBE MEINEM FREUND.      │
│  Who are you writing to?         I'm writing to my friend.        │
│                                                                   │
│                     WESSEN? =    WHOSE? (possessive case)         │
│  WESSEN WAGEN IST DAS?           DAS IST DER WAGEN MEINES         │
│  Whose car is it?                FREUNDES.                        │
│                                  It's my friend's car.            │
└─────────────────────────────────────────────────────────────────┘
```

put into the interrogative form and then answer the question, using possessives or pronouns:

e.g. Das ist der Wagen meines Vaters!
    — Wessen Wagen ist das?
    — Das ist sein Wagen.

1) Ich helfe meinem Vater gern.
2) Das ist das Zimmer meines jüngsten Sohnes.
3) Dieses Stück gefällt meinem Freund sehr.
4) Man nimmt den Jugendlichen fest.
5) Das ist die Frau meines Lehrers.
6) Ich sehe die Frau meines Freundes.
7) Die Frau seines Bruders kommt morgen.
8) Sie schreibt ihrem Freund einen Brief.
9) Das ist der Fleischer meiner Mutter.
10) Wir warten auf die Dame.

ETWAS – NICHTS	=	SOMETHING, ANYTHING
SEHEN SIE ETWAS?		Do you see anything?
Ja, ich sehe etwas.		Yes, I see something.
Nein, ich sehe nichts.		No, I don't see anything.

note: If 'anything' is positive it's translated by etwas.

ETWAS – KEIN	=	SOME – ANY
HABEN SIE ETWAS GELD?		Do you have some money?
Ja, ich habe etwas Geld.		Yes, I have some money.
Ja, ich habe etwas.		Yes, I have some.
Nein, ich habe kein Geld.		No. I don't have any money.
Nein, ich habe keins.		No, I don't have any.

note: — If kein is without a noun it takes an -s in the neuter.
— In the plural you have to use welche: Hat er Freunde?
Ja, er hat welche ≠ Nein, er hat keine.

answer in the affirmative, and then in the negative, without using nouns:

1) Haben Sie einen Wagen?
2) Verstehen sie etwas?
3) Hat er schon ein Buch?
4) Kann ich etwas für Sie tun?
5) Hat sie Probleme?
6) Lernen Sie etwas bei diesem Lehrer?
7) Haben Sie einen Photoapparat?
8) Gibt es etwas zu sehen?
9) Haben Sie etwas Kaffee?
10) Können Sie etwas verstehen?

translate:

1) Whose present are you carrying?
2) She's the same size as her sister.
3) Let's go into the ladies department first.
4) If the fur coats are in the sale, I'll buy one.
5) I'm exhausted, but it was worth it.
6) It wouldn't surprise me to see him there in spite of his fever.
7) He's so well off that he doesn't have to work.
8) The amount's higher than expected.
9) The men's department's on the third floor.
10) I'm twenty-one.
11) When? The sooner the better.
12) I'm coming during the weekend.
13) On the whole this supermarket's rather cheap.
14) Soon all these dresses will be on sale.
15) He doesn't see me on purpose.
16) I have to go to the doctor's every other week.
17) I'll call you as soon as I arrive.
18) The appointment is for the 5th of March.
19) I have to take a test in a fortnight.
20) Put me through to my father's secretary, please.
21) I have two minutes left.
22) I'm sorry, I don't have any more ideas.
23) I'm not ready yet.
24) Whose car's the fastest?
25) It's his broad who makes him so nervous.
26) You mustn't smoke in my director's room.

VOKABELN

	Übersetzung	Sinnverwandte Wörter	Gegenteil
1. (das) Geschenk	gift	schenken = to give	
2. wichtig	important ≠ it's beside the point		das hat nichts damit zu tun
3. welche Grösse haben Sie?	what size?		
4. (der) erste Stock	first floor	(das) Vorzimmer = lobby	
5. (die) Abteilung	department	(die) Damenabteilung = ladies department	
6. /(der) Lebensmittelladen/(der) Bäcker/(der) Fleischer	/grocery/baker /butcher	(der) Supermarkt = supermarket	
7. im Sonderangebot	on sale	im Ausvorkauf, spottbillig = dirt cheap	
8. ich habe es erwartet	I expected it	das würde mich nicht wundern = it wouldn't surprise me	unerwartet, unvorhergesehen = unexpected
9. reich	rich ≠ poor	wohlhabend = well off	arm, pleite = blank = broke
10. es war der Mühe wert	it was ≠ wasn't worth it		es war nicht der Mühe wert
11. (die) Summe	amount	(der) Betrag, (die) Quantität = quantity	
12. ach, du meine Güte!	goodness!	lieber Gott!	Gott sei dank! = thank goodness!
13. wie alt sind Sie?	how old are you?		
14. (die) Jugend	youth ≠ old age	(der) Jugendliche	(das) Alter
15. (der) Schmuck	jewellery	(der Ring = ring, (das) Armband = bracelet, (die) Halskette = necklace	

LEKTION 19

THE FUTURE TENSE

ich **werde** sprechen = I'll speak   **Ich werde nicht sprechen** = I won't
                                                                        speak

du **wirst** sprechen   du **wirst** nicht sprechen

er   er
sie **wird** sprechen   sie **wird** nicht sprechen
es   es

wir **werden** sprechen   wir **werden** nicht sprechen

ihr **werdet** sprechen   ihr **werdet** nicht sprechen

sie   sie
Sie **werden** sprechen   Sie **werden** nicht sprechen

note: — The future is *very rarely* used in German! (You use the present
        instead.)
      — *Werden* also means 'to become': Es wird sehr wichtig = It's
        becoming very important).

put the following sentences into the future:

1)   Er kommt nächstes Jahr.
2)   Sehr wahrscheinlich fällt er durch.
3)   Sie heiratet ihn.
4)   Er ist sehr erfolgreich.
5)   Die Polizisten nehmen ihn fest.
6)   Der Zug kommt morgen an.
7)   Du musst links abbiegen.
8)   Ich gehe ins Museum.
9)   An diesem Bahnhof steigen wir aus.
10) Ich höre bald auf.
11) Sie schreibt ihm einen Brief.
12) Er hilft seiner Mutter.
13) Ihr kommt zu spät.
14) Du weisst es nicht.

WIRST DU NÄCHSTEN MONAT KOMMEN?	Will you come next month?
Ja, ich <u>werde</u> nächsten Monat kommen.	Yes, I'<u>ll</u> <u>come</u> next month.
Nein, ich <u>werde</u> nicht nächsten Monat <u>kommen</u>.	No, I <u>won't come</u> next month.

note: As always the infinitive goes to the end.

translate, using first the present, then the future (in German either tense is correct):

1) There'll be many tourists here in the summer.
2) She'll be getting married in a fortnight.
3) I won't talk to him.
4) If I eat a lot, I'll gain weight.
5) We'll move out next month.
6) It's certain that they'll get a divorce.
7) Tomorrow we'll visit the most important monuments of this city.
8) If I get the diploma, I'll be very happy.
9) This piece will be a flop. (only future here)
10) I'll go to Munich if you like.
11) When will you listen to me?
12) We'll have to fix an appointment soon.
13) At Christmas I'll go skiing.
14) Tomorrow morning I'll get up earlier than you.
15) If I'm tired, I'll go to bed.
16) If the flat's (apartment's) big, I'll take it from the first of the month.
17) We won't come at Christmas, but at Easter.
18) They'll close the ladies' department next week.
19) You'll prefer this wine too.
20) He'll sell his old car and buy a new one.
21) I'll call you up on Monday.
22) He won't know.

Ich werde <u>nichts</u> tun.	I won't do <u>anything</u>.
Ich werde <u>nicht mehr</u> hier sein.	I won't be here <u>any more</u>.
Ich werde <u>kein</u> Geld <u>mehr</u> haben.	I won't have money <u>any longer</u>.
Es wird <u>niemand</u> hier sein.	There won't be <u>anybody</u> here.
Er wird <u>nie</u> zurückkommen.	He'll <u>never</u>/won't <u>ever</u> come back.
Er wird <u>noch nicht</u> dort sein.	He won't be there <u>yet</u>.
Er wird <u>noch kein</u> Haus haben.	He won't have <u>a</u> house <u>yet</u>.

put into the negative, and then into the future tense:
e.g. Sagt er etwas?
       — Nein, er sagt nichts.
       — Nein, er wird nichts sagen.

1) Ist er schon verheiratet?
2) Haben Sie noch Zeit?
3) Versteht ihr etwas?
4) Ist jemand im Büro?
5) Ist er schon auf der Bank?
6) Hat er schon einen neuen Job?
7) Müssen wir schon links abbiegen?
8) Kommt er je zurück?
9) Spricht er schon deutsch?
10) Lernt er noch englisch?
11) Kann man etwas für sie tun?
12) Will mir jemand helfen?

review: PUBLIC ENEMY NUMBER ONE — THE GERMAN PRESENT!!!

	= I'm reading (now) = **Ich lese jetzt.**
	= I read (often, every day) = **Ich lese oft, jeden Tag.**
ICH LESE	= I've been reading (for an hour) = **Ich lese seit einer Stunde.**
	= I'm going to read (tonight) = **Ich lese heute abend.**
	= I'll read (next weekend) = **Ich lese nächstes Wochenende.**

note: GERMANS LIVE IN THE PRESENT!!! You must get used to using it much more than we do in English. The possible translations are many.

SEIT + present = FOR/SINCE + present perfect

Wir sind seit fünf Jahren verheiratet.	=	We've been married for five years.
Er arbeitet seit Juni hier.	=	He has worked here since June.
Ich bin seit einer Woche hier.	=	I've been here for a week.
Seit wann sind Sie hier?	=	For how long have you been here?

translate:

1) I've been waiting for her since three o'clock.
2) How long have you been in this boring city?
3) He's been learning German for six months.
4) We've been driving for a day.
5) She's been visiting the museum since noon.
6) Have you been working since this morning?
7) I've been listening to music (hören) all afternoon.
8) Has she been here since Easter?
9) I'll write him tomorrow.
10) He has lived here since March.

GEGENTEIL 4

1. **lieben**
   to love
   ≠ **hassen**
   to hate

2. **aufstehen**
   to stand up
   ≠ **sich setzen**
   to sit down

3. **sich anziehen**
   to get dressed
   ≠ **sich ausziehen**
   to get undressed

4. **sich beeilen**
   to hurry up
   ≠ **sich Zeit nehmen**
   to take one's time

5. **zurückkommen**
   to come back
   ≠ **weggehen/ausgehen**
   to go away/out

6. **finden**
   to find
   ≠ **verlieren**
   to lose

7. **vergessen**
   to forget
   ≠ **sich erinnern**
   to remember

8. **gewinnen**
   to win
   ≠ **verlieren**
   to lose

9. **kaufen**
   to buy
   ≠ **verkaufen**
   to sell

10. **anziehen (Kleidung)**
    to put on (clothes)
    ≠ **ausziehen**
    to take off

11. **landen**
    to land
    ≠ **starten, abheben**
    to take off

12. **übereinstimmen mit**
    to agree with
    ≠ **uneins sein**
    to disagree

13. **anmachen, anschalten**
    to put on, to turn on
    ≠ **ausmachen, löschen**
    off

14. **einschlafen**
    to fall asleep
    ≠ **aufwachen**
    to wake up

15. **achtgeben auf**
    to pay attention to
    ≠ **nicht beachten**
    to ignore

16. **fragen**
    to ask
    ≠ **antworten**
    to answer

17. **schieben**
    to push
    ≠ **ziehen**
    to pull

18. **lachen**
    to laugh
    ≠ **weinen**
    to cry

19. **geben, schenken**
    to give, to give a gift
    ≠ **nehmen, annehmen**
    to take, to accept

20. **ausgehen**
    to go out
    ≠ **zu Hause bleiben**
    to stay at home

VOKABELN

	Übersetzung	Sinnverwandte Wörter	Gegenteil
1. wahrscheinlich	likely ≠ unlikely	sehr wahrscheinlich = most likely	unwahrscheinlich
2. /(die) Schule /(das) Gymnasium /(die) Klasse	/school/high school /class (grade room)	(die) Universität = university, (die) Note, (die) Zensur = mark	
3. nötig	necessary ≠ optional	es ist ein Muss = its a must	wahlfrei
4. (das) Diplom	diploma	graduiert = graduated	
5. durchfallen	to fail ≠ to succeed		bestehen, erfolgreich sein = to be successful
6. (der) Erfolg	hit ≠ failure, flop	(der) Treffer	(der) Misserfolg, (die) Niete, (der) Reinfall
7. erstaunlich	amazing, surprising	überraschend, unglaublich	
8. (der) Liebling	favourite	(der) Favorit, Lieblings-	
9. heiraten	to get married ≠ to get divorced	(die) Flitterwochen = honeymoon	sich scheiden lassen
10. (die) Hochzeit	wedding ≠ divorce		(die) Scheidung
11. besichtigen	to sightsee		
12. gehören	to belong to	besitzen = to own	
13. mein eigener	my own	meiner, e, es = mine	
14. (der) Tourist	tourist		
15. /(das) Museum /(die) Kirche	/museum/church	(die) Kunst = art, (das) Gebäude = monument	
16. geradeaus	straight ahead ≠ turn left		links abbiegen
17. rechts	to the right ≠ to the left		links
18. schweigen	to keep quiet	halt den Mund! = Schnauze! = shut up!	

LEKTION 20

PERFEKT = PAST

Gestern		yesterday.
Letzte Woche	**habe ich ein Buch gekauft** = I bought a book	last week.
Vor zwei Tagen		(have bought) two days
		ago.

---

ich habe gekauft = I bought   **ich habe nicht gekauft** = I didn't buy

du hast gekauft   **du hast nicht gekauft**

er
sie hat gekauft
es

er
sie hat nicht gekauft
es

wir haben gekauft   **wir haben nicht gekauft**

ihr habt gekauft   **ihr habt nicht gekauft**

sie
Sie haben gekauft

sie
Sie haben nicht gekauft

---

note: The Perfekt is formed with the present of haben and the past participle of the verb.

HAST DU DIE LEKTION GELERNT?   Did you learn the lesson?
(Have you learnt . . .)

Ja, ich habe die Lektion gelernt.   Yes, I (have) learned the lesson.
Nein, ich habe die Lektion nicht gelernt.   No, I didn't learn (haven't learned) the lesson.

122

INFINITIVE	PAST PARTICIPLE
machen	gemacht
sagen	gesagt
suchen	gesucht

note: — To form the past participle you have to drop the inifinitive ending
-en and add ge- at the beginning and -t at the end.
— But:
versagen → versagt; no ge- if the prefix isn't separable.
rasieren → rasiert; no ge- for verbs ending in -ieren.
anmachen→ angemacht; if the prefix is separable the ge- is
between the prefix and the verb.

review:

Ich habe es niemandem gesagt.	I didn't tell anybody.
Ich habe es nie gemacht.	I didn't ever do it.
Ich habe es noch nicht gesucht.	I haven't looked for it yet.
Er hat nichts verkauft.	He didn't sell anything.
Ich habe nicht mehr dort gewohnt.	I didn't live there any more.
Er hat keine Probleme mehr gehabt.	He didn't have problems any more.

put into the negative:

1) Er hat mich gesehen.
2) Er hat den Film schon gesehen.
3) Sie haben schon Ferien genommen.
4) Wir haben etwas gesucht.
5) Du hast noch hier gearbeitet.
6) Ich habe noch Geld gehabt.
7) Ihr habt jemanden eingeladen.
8) Er hat es immer gesagt.

put into the past tense, and then into the interrogative form:

1) Die Sonne scheint den ganzen Tag.
2) Er sitzt auf dem Platz dort.
3) Ich verstehe etwas.
4) Er liest ein gutes Buch.
5) Sie werfen das Papier weg?
6) Sie trägt ein hübsches Kleid.
7) Er macht nichts.
8) Ich rufe Sie an.
9) Sie weiss sicher, wo ihr Mann arbeitet.
10) Er empfiehlt ihr einen Rechtsanwalt.
11) Er schläft lange.
12) Wir nehmen den Bus.
13) Sie macht nie die Tür zu.
14) Er rasiert sich.
15) Der Fahrer wäscht den Wagen.
16) Du machst das Licht an.
17) Er zerbricht das Geschenk.
18) Man stiehlt ihren Diamanten.
19) Ich bekomme nicht viel Geld.
20) Er hilft der alten Frau.
21) Ich leihe ihm Geld, weil er keins hat.
22) Ich schneide das Fleisch mit dem grossen Messer.
23) Er trinkt gern Whisky.
24) Sie schwört ihm, bei ihm zu bleiben.
25) Der Film geginnt um 6 und hört um 8 auf.
26) Er spricht sehr schnell.
27) Er kann es.
28) Ich schreibe ihr einen Brief pro Woche.

```
HABEN (Perfekt)

ich habe gehabt = I had (have had)    ich habe nicht gehabt = I hadn't,
                                                              didn't have

du hast gehabt                         du hast nicht gehabt

er                                     er
sie  hat gehabt                        sie  hat nicht gehabt
es                                     es

wir haben gehabt                       wir haben nicht gehabt

ihr habt gehabt                        ihr habt nicht gehabt

sie                                    sie
Sie  haben gehabt                      Sie  haben nicht gehabt
```

```
JE(MALS) – NIE(MALS) = EVER – NEVER

HABEN SIE JE(MALS)              Did you ever smoke?
GERAUCHT?

Nein, ich habe nie(mals) geraucht.    No, I never smoked.
```

put into the negative:

1) Haben Sie diesen Film je gesehen?
2) Hast du je dieses Museum besucht?
3) Ist er je durchgefallen?
4) Hat sie ihn je gefragt?
5) Haben wir je einen Fehler gemacht?
6) Habe ich Sie je getroffen?
7) Haben Sie je jemanden geschlagen?
8) Haben wir Ihnen je geholfen?
9) Haben Sie je diesen Roman gelesen?
10) Haben sie je zu viel getrunken?

IRREGULAR VERBS (Perfekt)

1. **brechen** (to break)	**gebrochen**	35. **stehen** (to stand)	**gestanden**
2. **tun** (to do)	**getan**	36. **verstehen** (to understand)	**verstanden**
3. **essen** (to eat)	**gegessen**		
4. **geben** (to give)	**gegeben**	37. **finden** (to find)	**gefunden**
5. **wissen** (to know)	**gewusst**	38. **empfehlen** (to suggest)	**empfohlen**
6. **sehen** (to see)	**gesehen**		
7. **sprechen** (to speak)	**gesprochen**	39. **treffen (to meet)**	**getroffen**
8. **fangen** (to catch)	**gefangen**	40. **helfen** (to help)	**geholfen**
9. **nehmen** (to take)	**genommen**	41. **befehlen** (to order)	**befohlen**
10. **werfen** (to throw)	**geworfen**	42. **braten** (to roast)	**gebraten**
11. **behalten** (to keep)	**behalten**	43. **waschen** (to wash)	**gewaschen**
12. **tragen** (to wear, to carry)	**getragen**	44. **bitten** (to ask)	**gebeten**
		45. **giessen** (to pour)	**gegossen**
13. **können** (can, be able to)	**gekonnt**	46. **ziehen** (to draw)	**gezogen**
		47. **mogen** (to like)	**gemocht**
14. **müssen** (must, have to)	**gemusst**	48. **scheinen** (to seem, to shine)	**geschienen**
15. **lesen** (to read)	**gelesen**		
16. **fahren** (to drive)	**gefahren**	49. **rufen** (to call)	**gerufen**
17. **schlafen** (to sleep)	**geschlafen**	50. **streiten** (to argue)	**gestritten**
18. **lassen** (to let)	**gelassen**	51. **lügen** (to lie)	**gelogen**
19. **stehlen** (to steal)	**gestohlen**	52. **buchstabieren** (to spell)	**buchstabiert**
20. **schlagen** (to hit)	**geschlagen**		
21. **raten** (to guess)	**geraten**	53. **leiden** (to suffer)	**gelitten**
22. **bekommen** (to receive)	**bekommen**	54. **zurückweisen** (to refuse)	**zurückgewiesen**
23. **liegen** (to lie)	**gelegen**	55. **gewinnen** (to win)	**gewonnen**
24. **bringen** (to bring)	**gebracht**	56. **verbinden** (to connect)	**verbunden**
25. **schliessen** (to close)	**geschlossen**		
26. **leihen** (to lend)	**geliehen**	57. **schweigen** (to be silent)	**geschwiegen**
27. **schwören** (to swear)	**geschworen**		
28. **zerreissen** (to tear up)	**zerrissen**	58. **vergessen** (to forget)	**vergessen**
		59. **schieben** (to push)	**geschoben**
29. **schreiben** (to write)	**geschrieben**	60. **kennen** (to know)	**gekannt**
30. **beginnen** (to begin)	**begonnen**	61. **einladen** (to invite)	**eingeladen**
31. **trinken** (to drink)	**getrunken**	62. **schreien** (to shout)	**geschrien**
32. **denken** (to think)	**gedacht**	63. **schiessen** (to shoot)	**geschossen**
33. **schneiden** (to cut)	**geschnitten**	64. **übertreiben** (to exaggerate)	**übertrieben**
34. **sitzen** (to sit)	**gesessen**	65. **verbieten** (to forbid)	**verboten**

translate:

1) What did you do yesterday?
2) He ate a lot an hour ago.
3) He gave me a present last week.
4) It poured yesterday.
5) The rain stopped a while ago.
6) I hope that it didn't hurt.
7) What did he admit?
8) He never made a mistake.
9) How did you find her?
10) What did you suggest to your brother?
11) I had a nightmare last night.
12) He has already unpacked his baggage.
13) He brought me a newspaper this morning.
14) Why did you hit him?
15) She tore all his letters up two weeks ago.
16) Where did you meet him?
17) Do you like roast mutton?
18) I'm certain that I didn't receive your parcel.
19) I knew it. I was right!
20) I don't understand why you didn't help her.
21) They caught the bastard last week.
22) He put his raincoat on.
23) What did you think?
24) He was in a jam.
25) You were lucky.
26) I saw him only two days ago.
27) Why did you close the door?
28) Did he swear it?

VOKABELN

	Übersetzung	Sinnverwandte Wörter	Gegenteil
1. Sie haben Glück	you're lucky ≠ you're out of luck	ein glücklicher Zufall = a lucky break	Sie sind ein Pechvogel
2. gerade	a little while ago ≠ in a little while	vor einem Moment	in einem Augenblick
3. (die) Gesellschaft	company	Gesellschaft haben = Gäste haben = entertain	
4. /(das) Gepäck /packen	/baggage/to pack		auspacken = to unpack
5. (das) Ziel	aim, target	(die) Zielscheibe	
6. in der Klemme sitzen	in a jam, in a spot	in der Patsche sitzen	
7. stolz sein auf	to be proud of ≠ ashamed of		sich schämen
8. begeistert	enthusiastic ≠ I'm cool		es lässt ich kalt
9. (der) Traum	dream	(der) Alptraum = nightmare	
10. ich frage mich	I was wondering	ob = if	
11. (der) Fehler	mistake	(der) Irrtum = error	
12. (das) Paket	package		
13. (die) Firma	company, firm	(die) Gesellschaft	
14. erinnern Sie mich daran	remind me to		
15. erstklassig	first rate, second rate		zweitklassig, (die) Zeitverschwendung = waste of time
16. einsehen	recognize	erkennen, erblicken = to spot	
17. nur zu gut	only too well		

LEKTION 21

PERFEKT (Fortsetzung)

Gestern		yesterday.
Letzte Woche	**bin ich gegangen** = I went (have gone)	last week.
Vor zwei Tagen		two days ago.

note: Some verbs form their past with SEIN!

ich **bin** gegangen = I went	ich **bin** nicht gegangen = I didn't go
du **bist** gegangen	du **bist** nicht gegangen
er sie **ist** gegangen es	er sie **ist** nicht gegangen es
wir **sind** gegangen	wir **sind** nicht gegangen
ihr **seid** gegangen	ihr **seid** nicht gegangen
sie Sie **sind** gegangen	sie Sie **sind** nicht gegangen

IST SIE GEGANGEN?	Did she go? (has she gone?)
Ja, sie ist gegangen.	Yes, she went (has gone).
Nein, sie ist nicht gegangen.	No, she didn't go (hasn't gone).

IRREGULAR VERBS (Perfekt) — Fortsetzung

1. **sein** (to be)	**gewesen**
2. **fallen** (to fall)	**gefallen**
3. **sterben** (to die)	**gestorben**
4. **begegnen** (to meet)	**begegnet**
5. **gehen** (to go)	**gegangen**
6. **kommen** (to come)	**gekommen**
7. **rennen** (to run)	**gerannt**
8. **fahren** (to go)	**gefahren**
9. **fliegen** (to fly)	**geflogen**
10. **geschehen** (to occur)	**ist geschehen**
11. **werden** (to become)	**geworden**
12. **bleiben** (to stay)	**geblieben**
13. **gelingen** (to succeed)	**ist gelungen**
14. **schwimmen** (to swim)	**geschwommen**
15. **eintreten** (to enter)	**eingetreten**
16. **steigen** (to go up)	**gestiegen**
17. **aufstehen** (to get up)	**aufgestanden**
18. **folgen** (to follow)	**gefolgt**
19. **einziehen** (to move in)	**eingezogen**
20. **abbiegen** (to turn)	**abgebogen**
21. **aufwachen** (to wake up)	**aufgewacht**
22. **einschlafen** (to fall asleep)	**eingeschlafen**

note: All these verbs form their Perfekt with SEIN!

```
SEIN — (Perfekt)

ich bin gewesen = I was (have been)    ich bin nicht gewesen = I wasn't
                                                            (haven't been)

du bist gewesen                        du bist nicht gewesen

er                                     er
sie  ist gewesen                       sie  ist nicht gewesen
es                                     es

wir sind gewesen                       wir sind nicht gewesen

ihr seid gewesen                       ihr seid nicht gewesen

sie                                    sie
Sie  sind gewesen                      Sie  sind nicht gewesen
```

put into the past tense:

1) Ich bin in Berlin.
2) Das Buch fällt auf den Boden.
3) Ich bleibe eine Woche hier.
4) Er schwimmt sehr weit.
5) Tritt er ein?
6) Wo steigen Sie um?
7) Wann kommt der Zug an?
8) Er fliegt von New York nach Hamburg.
9) Er wird Ingenieur.
10) Ich fahre mit dem Bus.
11) Wo bist du?
12) Was passiert?
13) Es gelingt mir nicht.
14) Er bleibt hinter den anderen Studenten zurück.

131

insert the correct auxiliary verb:

1) Es ____ mir schlecht gegangen.
2) ____ er es wiederholt?
3) ____ sie dir wirklich geglaubt?
4) Wir ____ sehr früh aufgestanden.
5) Warum ____ es nicht gegangen?
6) Das Radio ____ nicht viel gekostet.
7) Ich ____ ihm gestern abend begegnet.
8) Was ____ er bekommen?
9) Es ____ auf ihn angekommen.
10) Sie ____ ihr Zimmer reserviert.
11) Ich ____ sehr braun geworden.
12) Weisst du, was geschehen ____ ?
13) Er ____ uns erblickt.
14) Die Sekretärin ____ wieder zu spät gekommen.
15) Was ____ aus ihr geworden?
16) Leider ____ ich nicht aufgewacht.
17) Er ____ seinen Pullover ausgezogen.
18) Wir ____ aus dem alten Haus ausgezogen.
19) Warum ____ du nicht geschwiegen?
20) Ich hoffe, dass die Polizisten Ihnen nicht gefolgt ____ .
21) Dann ____ wir rechts abgebogen.
22) Ich ____ ihn gut gekannt.
23) Sie ____ ihr Geschäft geschlossen.
24) Er ____ eingestiegen.
25) Wir ____ lange gewartet.
26) Sie ____ noch nie in Deutschland gewesen.
27) Der Zug ____ angekommen.
28) Er ____ Glück gehabt.

translate:

1) I was there for an hour.
2) I saw him a moment ago.
3) One out of six failed.
4) I was afraid in that park.
5) I hope that he caught up.
6) He trapped me.
7) He didn't do the dirty work.
8) We moved last week.
9) Why didn't she take off her coat?
10) I've been here for a month.
11) Where did she go afterwards?
12) He has already gone (US already went) in.
13) Did he cheat on you.
14) Who did you meet at the movies? (two translations)
15) They followed him into the cinema.
16) Did you succeed in doing it?
17) As usual he fell asleep.
18) I arrived an hour ago.
19) I had planned it.
20) Does she know what became of him?
21) I was very proud of him.
22) He died three years ago.
23) I called you right away.
24) I moved out in January.
25) Then I changed my clothes.
26) He came at eight as usual.
27) They elected the new director yesterday.
28) Did you succeed in becoming rich?

1. **ungefähr (eine Stunde)**	(an hour) or so	13. **— wirklich — tatsächlich**	— in fact — as a matter of fact
2. **seit wann?**	how long?		
3. **— in der Tat —wirklich**	indeed	14. **bis spätestens (Montag)**	by (Monday)
4. **— noch — immer noch — trotzdem**	— still	15. **von Anfang an**	from the first
		16. **— für immer — dauernd**	— for good — permanently
5. **eins von zehn**	one out of ten	17. **— den ganzen Tag — den ganzen Tag lang**	— all day long
6. **irrtümlich (erweise)**	by mistake		
7. **— ausser wenn — es sei denn, dass**	— unless	18. **— glücklicher- weise — zum Glück**	— fortunately — luckily
8. **ausserdem**	furthermore	19. **— überall — irgendwo**	— all over — anywhere
9. **gleichwohl**	all the same		
10. **— vor einem Moment — in einem Moment**	— a little while ago — in a little while	20. **— irgendwo — nirgendwo, nirgends**	— somewhere — nowhere
		21. **wie gewöhn- lich**	as usual
11. **eine Zeitlang**	for a while	22. **ausserdem, dazu**	in addition to
12. **bei weitem**	by far	23. **in diesem Fall**	if so
		24. **sozusagen**	so to speak

VOKABELN

	Übersetzung	Sinnverwandte Wörter	Gegenteil
1. (er ist mir) böse	angry ≠ content	wütend = furious, wütend werden = to lose one's temper	zufrieden
2. vorhaben	to plan to	die Absicht haben	
3. mutig	brave ≠ coward		(der) Feigling
4. sich fertig machen	to get ready	sich zurecht machen	ich bin fertig = ich bin so weit = I'm ready
5. gewöhnlich	usual ≠ unusual	typisch = typical	selten, ungewöhn- lich
6. sehr	very ≠ rather	ganz = quite	eher
7. sauber	clean ≠ dirty		schmutzig, dreckig
8. aufholen	to catch up ≠ to fall behind		zurückbleiben hinter
9. /noch etwas/wer noch? /was noch?	/something else /who else?/what else?	jemand anders = someone else, irgendwo anders = somewhere else	sonst nichts = nothing else
10. Angst haben	to be afraid	sich fürchten = to be frightened	
11. (die) Falle	trick	eine Falle stellen = to trap	
12. betrügen	to cheat (on)		
13. nach	according to	laut	
14. sich entschliessen	to make up one's mind		unentschlossen = undecided
15. (das) Ergebnis	result	(das) Resultat	
16. (der) Dummkopf	idiot	(der) Tor, (der) Esel note: (das) Tor = gate	

LEKTION 22

IMPERFEKT = WAS + -ING

ICH <u>SAH</u> FERN, **<u>WÄHREND</u> ER <u>LAS</u>.**
<u>ALS</u> ER <u>KAM</u>.

I was watching TV while he was reading.
when he came.

note: This tense is most often used for two actions taking place at the same time in the past.

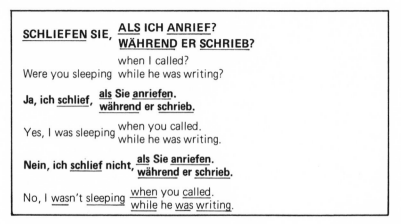

<u>SCHLIEFEN</u> SIE, **<u>ALS</u> ICH <u>ANRIEF</u>?**
<u>WÄHREND</u> ER <u>SCHRIEB</u>?

when I called?
Were you sleeping while he was writing?

Ja, ich <u>schlief</u>, **<u>als</u> Sie <u>anriefen</u>.**
<u>während</u> er <u>schrieb</u>.

Yes, I was sleeping when you called.
while he was writing.

Nein, ich <u>schlief</u> nicht, **<u>als</u> Sie <u>anriefen</u>.**
<u>während</u> er <u>schrieb</u>.

No, I <u>wasn't</u> <u>sleeping</u> <u>when</u> you <u>called</u>.
<u>while</u> he <u>was</u> <u>writing</u>.

note: Both verbs are normally in the Imperfekt.

136

```
IMPERFEKT OF A REGULAR VERB

ich sagte = I was saying . . .        ich sagte nicht = I wasn't saying . . .

du sagtest                            du sagtest nicht

er                                    er
sie  sagte                            sie  sagte nicht
es                                    es

wir sagten                            wir sagten nicht

ihr sagtet                            ihr sagtet nicht

sie                                   sie
Sie  sagten                           Sie  sagten nicht
```

note: — Watch out for the verbs ending in -ten:
      PRÄSENS: ich arbeite, du arbeitest, er arbeitet.
      IMPERFEKT: ich arbeitete, du arbeitetest, er arbeitetet.

```
IMPERFEKT OF AN IRREGULAR VERB

ich schrieb = I was writing           ich schrieb nicht = I wasn't writing

du schriebst                          du schriebst nicht

er                                    er
sie  schrieb                          sie  schrieb nicht
es                                    es

wir schrieben                         wir schrieben nicht

ihr schriebt                          ihr schriebt nicht

sie                                   sie  schrieben nicht
Sie  schrieben                        Sie
```

note: Irregular verbs don't have special Imperfekt endings; except for the
first and third person of the singular, which don't take any ending, you add
the endings of the Präsens.

IRREGULAR VERBS (Imperfekt)

1. **sein** (to be)	**war**		41. **sitzen** (to sit)	**sass**
2. **haben** (to have)	**hatte**		42. **fahren** (to go)	**fuhr**
3. **brechen** (to break)	**brach**		43. **stehen** (to stand)	**stand**
4. **tun** (to do)	**tat**		44. **verstehen** (to understand)	**verstand**
5. **essen** (to eat)	**ass**			
6. **fallen** (to fall)	**fiel**		45. **finden** (to find)	**fand**
7. **geben** (to give)	**gab**		46. **fliegen** (to fly)	**flog**
8. **wissen** (to know)	**wusste**		47. **empfehlen** (to suggest)	**empfahl**
9. **sehen** (to see)	**sah**			
10. **sprechen** (to speak)	**sprach**		48. **raten** (to advise)	**riet**
11. **fangen** (to catch)	**fing**		49. **treffen** (to meet)	**traf**
12. **nehmen** (to take)	**nahm**		50. **helfen** (to help)	**half**
13. **werfen** (to throw)	**warf**		51. **befehlen** (to order)	**befahl**
14. **behalten** (to keep)	**behielt**		52. **geschehen** (to happen)	**geschah**
15. **tragen** (to wear, carry)	**trug**			
			53. **werden** (to become)	**wurde**
16. **können** (can)	**konnte**		54. **entlassen** (to lay off)	**entliess**
17. **müssen** (must)	**musste**		55. **braten** (to roast)	**briet**
18. **lesen** (to read)	**las**		56. **waschen** (to wash)	**wusch**
19. **fahren** (to drive)	**fuhr**		57. **bleiben** (to stay)	**blieb**
20. **schlafen** (to sleep)	**schlief**		58. **bitten** (to ask for)	**bat**
21. **lassen** (to let)	**liess**		59. **giessen** (to pour)	**goss**
22. **stehlen** (to steal)	**stahl**		60. **mögen** (to like)	**mochte**
23. **sterben** (to die)	**starb**		61. **ziehen** (to draw)	**zog**
24. **schlagen** (to hit)	**schlug**		62. **gelingen** (to succeed)	**gelang**
25. **raten** (to guess)	**riet**		63. **erhalten** (to obtain)	**erhielt**
26. **bekommen** (to obtain)	**bekam**		64. **scheinen** (to seem, shine)	**schien**
27. **gehen** (to go)	**ging**		65. **schwimmen** (to swim)	**schwamm**
28. **liegen** (to lie down)	**lag**			
29. **bringen** (to bring)	**brachte**		66. **rufen** (to call)	**rief**
30. **kommen** (to come)	**kam**		67. **besitzen** (to possess, own)	**besass**
31. **schliessen** (to close)	**schloss**			
32. **leihen** (to lend)	**lieh**		68. **streiten** (to argue)	**stritt**
33. **schwören** (to swear)	**schwor**		69. **schiessen** (to shoot)	**schoss**
34. **zerreissen** (to tear up)	**zerriss**		70. **eintreten** (to enter)	**trat ein**
			71. **zurückweisen** (to refuse)	**wies zurück**
35. **schreiben** (to write)	**schrieb**			
36. **rennen** (to run)	**rannte**		72. **beschreiben** (to describe)	**beschrieb**
37. **beginnen** (to begin)	**begann**			
38. **trinken** (to drink)	**trank**		73. **reiten** (to ride)	**ritt**
39. **denken** (to think)	**dachte**		74. **steigen** (to go up)	**stieg**
40. **schneiden** (to cut)	**schnitt**			

insert the correct tense:

1) (gehen)   Ich _____ gestern ins Kino _____ .
                Ich _____ ins Kino, als er ankam.

2. (arbeiten)   Wir _____ gestern sechs Stunden _____ .
                Wir _____ , als sie eintraten.

3) (treffen)   Er _____ seine alte Freundin _____ .
                Er _____ sie, als er spazieren ging.

4) (trinken)   Sie _____ gestern Nacht vier Gin _____ .
                Sie _____ viel, während wir tanzten.

5) (helfen)   Meine Freundin _____ mir sehr _____ .
                Sie _____ mir, während du nichts tatest.

6) (sein)   Ich _____ sehr glücklich _____ .
                Ich _____ glücklich, weil sie zu mir zurückkam.

7) (umziehen)   Sie _____ sich gerade _____ .
                Sie _____ sich um, während wir warteten.

8) (verstehen) Ich _____ nichts _____ .
                Ich _____ nichts, als er seinen Dialekt sprachen.

9) (kommen)   Wir _____ gerade _____ .
                Wir _____ , als sie abfuhren.

10) (schlagen) Man _____ ihn _____ .
                Er _____ sie, als sie gehen wollte.

11) (beginnen) Du _____ dein erstes Buch _____ .
                Er _____ mit der Arbeit, als seine Kollegen aufhörten.

12) (sitzen)   Ich _____ den ganzen Abend allein zu Hause _____ .
                Ich _____ , während die anderen standen.

13) (schreiben) Sie _____ dir gestern nachmittag einen Brief _____ .
                Sie _____ , während er Radio hörte.

insert the correct forms of the verb:

1) Peter _____ (besuchen) uns, als wir zu Abend _____ (essen).
2) Der Vater _____ (verbieten) alles, während die Mutter alles _____ (erlauben).
3) Er _____ (lassen) mich im Stich, obwohl ich ihm _____ (trauen).
4) Wir _____ (treffen) ihn, als er auf dem Weg zu uns _____ (sein).
5) Diese Zeitung _____ (kritisieren) das Stück, während jene es _____ (loben).
6) Sie _____ (flüstern), obwohl er nichts verstehen _____ (können).
7) Er _____ (finden) sie reizend, solange sie nichts _____ (sagen).
8) Ich _____ (fahren) mit dem Wagen, obwohl ich die Stadt nicht _____ (kennen).
9) Er _____ (lesen), während sie das Essen _____ (vorbereiten).
10) Sie _____ (ausgehen), obwohl sie müde _____ (aussehen).
11) Der Regen _____ (fallen), obwohl die Sonne _____ (scheinen).
12) Er _____ (übertreiben), obwohl er _____ (wissen), das ihm keiner von uns _____ (glauben).
13) Ich _____ (mögen) ihn sehr, weil er jedem _____ (helfen).
14) Sie _____ (schlafen), während er wach neben ihr _____ (liegen).
15) Wir _____ (sprechen) Englisch, während der Lehrer nicht _____ (zuhören).
16) Er _____ (helfen) mir nicht, obwohl er _____ (sehen), dass ich grosse Probleme _____ (haben).
17) Der Boxer _____ (gewinnen) nicht, obwohl er sehr _____ (kämpfen).
18) Sie _____ (begegnen) ihrem Freund, als wir meinen Geburtstag _____ (feiern).
19) Die Ehefrau _____ (fliegen), während ihr Mann mit dem Auto _____ (fahren).
20) Ich _____ (schneiden) mir in den Finger, weil ich an etwas anderes _____ (denken).
21) Sie _____ (tragen) ein weisses Kleid, als sie _____ (heiraten).
22) Ich _____ (verdienen) meinen Lebensunterhalt allein, als ich _____ (studieren).

translate, using the correct tenses:

1) When he came in, I was watching TV and my husband was reading the newspaper.
2) What was your wife doing when you left this morning?
3) What were you talking about when I saw you?
4) What were you thinking about when he said that?
5) When the war started we were living in Europe.
6) When they were sitting in the café, the waiter came to their table and brought the menu.
7) I did that experiment when I was working for him.
8) While she was cutting the cake the guests took a seat.
9) When he left her she started to cry.
10) I did it because I had to.
11) It was snowing when we were on vacation.
12) As we were finishing the lesson, the teacher asked a difficult question.
13) He caught up with the others because he studied a lot.
14) I was crying while she was laughing.
15) I met him because we took the same tube (subway).
16) When I brought him his breakfast, he was still sleeping.
17) I woke up when I had that nightmare.
18) I was so hungry that I stole an apple.
19) Where were you driving when it happened?
20) We were entertaining when we had that terrible argument.
21) I noticed the mistake when I checked the bill.
22) I gave him a big tip, because he carried all my baggage.
23) He was washing his car while she was doing the housework.
24) The police caught him when he was on holiday.
25) I suggested it to her because she asked me.

ADVERBEN UND SÄTZE 5

1. **um zu**	so as to	14. **was auch immer sei**	regardless
2. **– gegenwärtig**	– at present	15. **kurz**	to make a long story short
– für den Moment	– for the time being		
3. **– übrigens**	– by the way	16. **wenn auch nur**	if only
– nebenbei	– incidentally	17. **unter den Umständen**	in the circumstances
4. **irgendwie**	somehow		
5. **– aber natürlich**	by all means	18. **bestimmt**	definitely
– auf alle Fälle		19. **für immer**	for good
6. **irgendwie**	in a way	20. **ganz und gar**	altogether
7. **überhaupt**	after all	21. **der Gipfel ist, dass**	on top of that
8. **– mehr und mehr**	more and more	22. **alles in allem**	all in all
– immer mehr		23. **was noch?**	what else?
9. **heute in 8 Tagen**	this time next week	24. **egal**	no matter
10. **am Abend darauf**	the following night	25. **später**	later on
11. **– in einer Woche**	– a week from today	26. **solange wie**	as long as
– in acht Tagen		27. **wer, was . . . auch immer**	whatever
12. **kurz vorher**	shortly before	28. **bis jetzt**	up to now
13. **ausser**	apart from		

VOKABELN (a)

	Übersetzung	Sinnverwandte Wörter	Gegenteil
1. ich ginge lieber	I'd prefer going	ich möchte lieber = I'd rather	
2. (der) Besucher	visitor	(der) Gast = guest	(der) Gastgeber = host
3. /enttäuschen /(die) Enttäuschung	/to disappoint /disappointment	er hat mich im Stich gelassen = he let me down	
4. verdienen	to earn	seinen Lebensunterhalt verdienen = to earn a living	
5. viel Spass!	enjoy yourself!	wir haben uns gut amüsiert = we had a good time	
6. übertreiben	to exaggerate	zu weit gehen = to go too far	
7. es trifft sich, dass	it happens that		
8. (die) Erfahrung	experience		
9. ich finde dass	I feel that	ich denke dass = I think that	
10. feiern	to celebrate	(die) Party, (das) Fest = party	
11. frech	naughty ≠ good	(das) Balg = brat	brav, artig
12. Gäste haben	to entertain	(der) Empfang = party	
13. erlauben	to permit ≠ to forbid		verbieten, untersagen
14. lieber als	rather than		
15. herzlich willkommen!	welcome!	machen Sie es sich gemütlich = make yourself at home	
16. kämpfen	to fight, to struggle		

VOKABELN (b)

	Übersetzung	Sinnverwandte Wörter	Gegenteil
1. jemand	someone ≠ no-one	irgendjemand = anyone, jeder = everybody	niemand, jeder = anyone
2. überall	everywhere		nirgends = nowhere
3. (der) Artikel	item	etwas = something	
4. /(die) Geschichte /(der) Roman	/story/novel	(die) Belletristik = fiction	
5. ich bezweifle es	I doubt it ≠ I don't doubt it	ich habe es vermutet = I thought as much	ich bezweifle es nicht
6. das gleiche wie	the same as ≠ different from	ähnlich = similar to, egal = the same thing	verschieden von
7. kritisieren	to criticize	abschiessen = to down	loben = to praise
8. Fortschritte machen	to make progress	verbessern = to improve	
9. gerade	straight		krumm = crooked
10. schützen	to protect		
11. sehen Sie nach!	make sure!		
12. brüllen	to yell ≠ to whisper	schreien = to shout	flüstern
13. was für ein Getue!	what a fuss!	viel Aufhebens machen = to make a fuss	
14. (der) Streit	argument	(der) Zank = quarrel	
15. Haupt-	main	führend = leading	Neben- = minor
16. ich bin es leid!	I've had it	ich habe die Nase voll! = I'm fed up!	
17. wach	awake ≠ asleep		eingeschlafen
18. bemerken	to notice		
19. /(der) Zoo/(das) Tier/(das) Haustier	/zoo/animal/pet	(der) Tiger = tiger, (der) Löwe = lion, (der) Elefant = elephant, (der) Vogel = bird, (der) Affe = monkey, (der) Bär = bear, (die) Ente = duck	

LEKTION 23

WENN = IF (CONDITIONAL II)

WENN ICH GELD <u>HÄTTE</u>, <u>KAUFTE</u> ICH EINEN WAGEN.
                     <u>WÜRDE</u> ICH EINEN WAGEN <u>KAUFEN</u>.

   conditional   conditional

<u>If</u> I <u>had</u> the money,   I'd <u>buy</u> a car.

WENN SIE GELD <u>HÄTTEN</u>, <u>KAUFTEN</u> SIE EINEN WAGEN?
                      <u>WÜRDEN</u> SIE EINEN WAGEN <u>KAUFEN</u>?

If you had the money,   would you buy a car?

Ja, <u>wenn</u> ich Geld <u>hätte</u>, **<u>kaufte</u> ich einen Wagen.**
                           <u>würde</u> ich einen Wagen <u>kaufen</u>.

Nein, <u>wenn</u> ich Geld <u>hätte</u>, **<u>kaufte</u> ich keinen Wagen.**
                             <u>würde</u> ich keinen Wagen <u>kaufen</u>.

note: — Both sentences are in the second conditional form!
      — würde = would
      — There are two ways of expressing it:
         a) regular verbs take their Imperfekt form; irregular verbs add the
            Umlaut and <u>-e</u>: ich fuhr = I was driving; ich führe = I'd drive.
         b) würde + infinitive

IRREGULAR CONDITIONAL FORMS

ich hätte	I'd have	**ich sähe**	I'd see
du hättest	you'd have	**du sähest**	you'd see
er	he	**er**	he
sie hätte	she 'd have	**sie sähe**	she 'd see
es	it	**es**	it
wir hätten	we'd have	**wir sähen**	we'd see
ihr hättet	you'd have	**ihr sähet**	you'd see
sie **hätten**	they 'd have	**sie** **sähen**	they 'd see
Sie	you	**Sie**	you

note: — This is fairly easy; just add an Umlaut to the Imperfekt form and -e
to the singular forms and the second person of the plural.
— You can use würde + infinitive only in one of the two sentences.

put the verbs into both of the second conditional forms:
e.g. Ich kam
— Ich käme, ich würde kommen.

1)	er geht	9)	er nimmt
2)	du nimmst	10)	sie isst
3)	ich komme	11)	wir essen
4)	sie fahren	12)	du vergisst
5)	ihr zeigt	13)	wir helfen
6)	sie findet	14)	er trifft
7)	es scheint	15)	sie geben
8)	du gibst	16)	er liess

put into the second form of the conditional:

1) Wenn ich müde bin, gehe ich schlafen.
2) Wenn das Wetter schlecht ist, bleibe ich zu Hause.
3) Wenn der Doktor Zeit hat, kommt er.
4) Wenn die Wohnung gross genug ist, nehme ich sie.
5) Wenn er übertreibt, sage ich es ihm.
6) Wenn ich allein bin, bin ich traurig.
7) Wenn er mich mit ihr sieht, wird er wütend.
8) Wenn sie dich liebt, tut sie das nicht.
9) Wenn du kommst, freue ich mich.
10) Wenn es schneit, fahren wir ski.
11) Wenn du mir den Wagen empfiehlst, nehme ich ihn.
12) Wenn ich Zahnschmerzen habe, gehe ich zum Zahnarzt.
13) Wenn ich zu spät komme, bleibe ich länger.
14) Wenn es schneit, fahre ich in die Berge.

complete without using **würde**:

1) Wenn ich Zeit _____ (haben), _____ (fahren) ich in die Berge.
2) Wenn er _____ (kommen), _____ (sein) ich glücklich.
3) Wenn du mich _____ (belügen), _____ (sprechen) ich nie mehr mit dir.
4) Wenn er ihr _____ (trauen), _____ (schweigen) er nicht.
5) Wenn sie ihn _____ (langweilen), _____ (ausgehen) er nicht mit ihr.
6) Wenn ihr bald _____ (kommen), _____ (können) ihr uns helfen.
7) Wenn ihr Mann so viel _____ (verdienen), _____ (brauchen) sie nicht arbeiten zu gehen.
8) Wenn das mein Kind _____ (machen), _____ (verbieten) ich es ihm.
9) Wenn er ein Buch _____ (schrieben), _____ (kaufen) ich es sofort.
10) Wenn diese Übungen einfach _____ (sein), _____ (lernen) Sie nichts.
11) Wenn er mir Geld _____ (leihen), _____ (helfen) er mir sehr.
12) Wenn du _____ (wollen), _____ (können) du.
13) Wenn der Kellner nicht höflich _____ (sein), _____ (geben) ich ihm kein Trinkgeld.
14) Wenn ich ihn _____ (sehen), _____ (sagen) ich es ihm sofort.

translate and then give the first form of the conditional:

1) If I had more time, I'd visit you.
2) If you spoke German, would you go to Germany?
3) If you could, would you help me?
4) If the movie was a flop, we wouldn't see it.
5) If you walked straight ahead, you'd find the monument.
6) If they studied hard, they'd get their diplomas.
7) If she couldn't come, she'd ring (call) you up.
8) If we didn't have to work tonight, we'd go dancing.
9) If that book belonged to you, would you lend it to me?
10) If you were late every day, would your boss fire you?
11) If you went to Berlin, would you see the Wall?
12) If he weren't so shy, he'd kiss his broad.
13) If that fur coat were on sale, she'd buy it.
14) If you were able to do it, would you?
15) If he told you everything, you wouldn't believe him.
16) If I met the woman of my life today, I'd marry her tomorrow.
17) If I had to, I'd borrow the money from him.
18) If you liked Africa, would you move there?
19) If he beat you, would you leave him?
20) If you were looking for a job, would you buy the morning papers?
21) If you went there by car, you'd have to drive carefully.
22) If he didn't love her, he wouldn't live with her.
23) Even if you told me the truth, I wouldn't believe you any more.
24) If you went to the dentist, would you take a pill before?
25) If you were fed up, would you quit?
26) If it were sunny outside, would we go for a walk?

VOKABELN

	Übersetzung	Sinnverwandte Wörter	Gegenteil
1. schlagen	to hit, to beat	prügeln = to spank	
2. lügen	to lie ≠ to tell the truth	(die) Lüge = lie	(die) Wahrheit sagen
3. ausehen	to look	Sie sehen müde aus = you look tired	
4. als ob	as though		
5. (der) Norden	North	(der) Süden, (der) Westen, (der) Osten	
6. das hört sich gut an	it sounds good	ich bin dabei = I'm game	
7. so ein Durcheinander!	what a mess!		
8. /meine Familie fehlt mir/ich fehle meiner Familie	/I miss my family /my family misses me		
9. Gehen wir	let's go	komm doch = come on	
10. schüchtern	shy ≠ brazen		unverschämt
11. /Frankreich/die Vereinigten Staaten/Italien /China	/France/USA /Italy/China	französisch, amerikanisch, italienisch,chinesisch	
13. vorherig	previous ≠ the latter		der letztere
14. /Deutschland /Spanien/England /Afrika	/Germany/Spain /England/Africa	deutsch, spanisch, englisch, afrikanisch	
16. raten	to guess (note: also to advise)	über den Daumen gepeilt = guesswork	
17. und ob!	you bet!		
18. schwanger	pregnant		(die) Abtreibung = abortion

LEKTION 24

INFINITIVES

OHNE ZU bezahlen	without paying
UM ZU helfen	in order to help
ANSTATT ZU essen	instead of eating

note: — These three prepositions are followed by the infinitive.
— Don't forget to put the verb at the end.
— If the verb's separable the zu is in the middle: um anzukommen = in order to arrive.

ES GEWOHNT SEIN ZU = TO BE USED TO

BIST DU ES GEWOHNT, FRÜH AUFZUSTEHEN?
Are you used to getting up early?

Ja, ich bin es gewohnt.	Yes, I'm used to it.
Ja, ich bin es gewohnt, früh aufzustehen.	Yes, I'm used to getting up early.

note: Infinitive after es gewohnt sein.

FRÜHER + past = USED TO

HAST DU FRÜHER GERAUCHT? Did you use to smoke?

Ja, ich habe früher geraucht.	Yes, I used to smoke.
Nein, ich habe nie geraucht.	No, I didn't use to smoke.

note: In the negative Germans use nie = never.

insert the correct form of the verb:

1) Er ging aus ohne (essen).
2) Er kam um (uns helfen).
3) Er nahm ein Taxi um (rechtzeitig ankommen).
4) Anstatt (fernsehen) gingen wir spazieren.
5) Ich bin es gewohnt (lange schlafen).
6) Ich habe früher (öfter schreiben).
7) Sie hat früher (besser aussehen).
8) Er ist es gewohnt (alle hereinlegen).
9) Wir sind früher (jedes Wochenende kommen).
10) Er ist es nicht gewohnt (allein sein).

```
┌─────────────────────────────────────────────────────────────┐
│  DESSEN, DEREN          =  WHOSE/OF WHICH                     │
│  masculine/neuter                                             │
│                                                               │
│  Der Mann,                  The man                           │
│      dessen Bruder ich kenne, . . .    whose brother I know . . . │
│  Das Haus, dessen Besitzer tot  The house, whose owner's dead . . . │
│      ist, . . .                                               │
│                                                               │
│  feminine/plural                                              │
│                                                               │
│  Die Frau,                  The woman,                        │
│      deren Sohn hier arbeitet, . . .   whose son's working here . . . │
│  Die Kinder,                The children,                     │
│      deren Vater ich nicht sein    whose father I wouldn't like │
│      möchte, . . .               to be . . .                  │
└─────────────────────────────────────────────────────────────┘
```

note: The verb has to be at the end of the relative sentence.

```
┌─────────────────────────────────────────────────────────────┐
│  DENEN = (TO) WHOM (plural)                                   │
│                                                               │
│  Das sind die Kinder,                                         │
│          denen ich die Bücher geschenkt habe.                 │
│                                                               │
│  These are the children,                                      │
│          (to) whom I gave the books as a present.             │
└─────────────────────────────────────────────────────────────┘
```

note: This form's only valid for the plural. In the singular you just repeat the article: Das ist das Kind, dem ich das Buch geschenkt habe.

complete:

1) Die Studentin, a) ____ Sie mir vorgestellt haben, . . .
   b) ____ ich gestern begegnet bin, . . .
   c) ____ ich gestern getroffen habe, . . .
   d) ____ Vater gestorben ist, . . .
   e) ____ Mutter mein Englischlehrerin war, . . .
   f) von ____ ich gerade komme, . . .
2) Der Student, a) mit ____ wir gesprochen haben, . . .
   b) ____ Mutter mir geschrieben hat, . . .
   c) ____ du nach der Zeit gefragt hast, . . .
   d) ____ neben mir sitzt, . . .
   e) über ____ wir lachen, . . .
   f) ____ Familie sehr arm ist, . . .
3) Die Studenten, a) ____ das Examen bestanden haben, . . .
   b) ____ Eltern wir eingeladen haben, . . .
   c) ____ mit uns gefahren sind, . . .
   d) mit ____ wir an die See gefahren sind, . . .
   e) von ____ wir viel gehört haben, . . .
   f) für ____ ich die Bücher bestellt habe, . . .
4) Das Haus, a) in ____ wir wohnen, . . .
   b) ____ Wohnungen sehr klein sind, . . .
   c) ____ wir vor zehn Jahren gekauft haben, . . .
   d) ____ Fenster sehr gross sind, . . .
   e) für ____ er sein ganzes Geld spart, . . .
   f) ____ mir so gut gefällt, . . .
5) Die Freunde a) ____ Geburtstag ich nie vergesse, . . .
   b) ____ bei mir wohnen, . . .
   c) ____ ich traue, . . .
   d) mit ____ wir heute abend ausgehen, . . .
   e) auf ____ ich warte, . . .
   f) ____ Examen sehr schwer war, . . .

```
┌─────────────────────────────────────────────────────────────────┐
│  PRESENT PARTICIPLE                                               │
│                                                                   │
│  das weinende Kind              =    the crying child             │
│                                                                   │
│  die ermüdende Arbeit           =    the tiring work              │
└─────────────────────────────────────────────────────────────────┘
```

note: — Simple: just add -d to the infinitive.
　　　 — Present participles are mainly used as adjectives in German, so they
　　　　　take the adjective endings.
　　　 — BUT: English present participles are very often translated by a
　　　　　subordinate clause:
　　　　　while talking = während er spricht, sprach;
　　　　　before going = bevor ich gehe.

translate:

1)　He looked out of the window while talking.
2)　a crying baby
3)　a flourishing business
4)　the shining sun
5)　The boss doesn't like employees sleeping in the office.
6)　an exciting film
7)　Many people complain about the rising prices.
8)　the falling leaves
9)　He watches the children swimming in the sea.
10)　the girls dancing in the corner
11)　a burning house
12)　an aching tooth
13)　I hate this tiring job.
14)　I don't like people shouting all the time.
15)　a well-off man
16)　Before going he kissed her.
17)　You mustn't talk too much while driving.
18)　After reading this book I'll write to my friends about it.

OB	=	WHETHER
WAS FRAGEN SIE MICH?		What are you asking me?
Ich frage Sie, **ob Sie heute abend kommen.**		I'm asking you <u>whether</u> you'll come tonight.

note: No future and verb at the end!

FRAGEN, BITTEN	TO ASK
WAS FRAGE ICH SIE?	What am I asking you?
Ich frage Sie, <u>ob</u> Sie **Zeit haben.**	I'm asking you whether you have time.
WONACH FRAGE ICH SIE?	What am I asking you?
Ich frage sie <u>nach</u> dem Weg.	I'm asking you the way.
WORUM BITTE ICH SIE?	What am I asking you for?
Ich <u>bitte</u> Sie <u>um</u> ein Bier.	I'm asking you for a beer.
WORUM BITTE ICH SIE?	What am I asking you for?
Ich <u>bitte</u> Sie, mir ein Bier <u>zu</u> geben.	I'm asking you to give me a beer.

note: — fragen = to ask a question.
        — fragen nach = to ask for an information.
        — bitten um = to ask for something.
        — bitten . . . zu = to ask someone to do something.

insert the correct verb and, if necessary, a preposition:

1) Er ____ mich, pünktlich zu kommen.
2) Sie ____ ihn ____ der Zeit.
3) Ich ____ Sie ____ eine Zigarette.
4) Sie ____ mich, ob ich noch allein bin.
5) Meine Mutter ____ mich ____ dem Resultat meiner Prüfung.
6) Er ____ sie, ihn morgen anzurufen.
7) Ich ____ Sie ____ Entschuldigung.
8) Er ____ ihn, ob er ihm helfen kann.
9) Wor ____ ____ er sie?
10) Wo ____ ____ sie ihn?

154

change the direct into the indirect question:
e.g. Ich frage Sie: 'Kommen Sie morgen abend?'
    — Ich frage Sie, ob Sie morgen abend kommen.

1) Er fragt sie: 'Bist du verheiratet?'
2) Die Mutter fragt die Kinder: 'Habt ihr schon gegessen?'
3) Der Vater fragt seine Tochter: 'Willst du schon wieder ausgehen?'
4) Meine Freundin fragt mich: 'Wo bist du gestern abend gewesen?'
5) Sie fragt ihn: 'Gehört dir der schöne Sportwagen?'
6) Ich weiss nicht: 'Habe ich dir das Geld zurückgegeben?'
7) Sie möchte wissen: 'Peter, kann ich dir helfen?'
8) Der Boss fragt sie: 'Wer von euch ist heute zu spät gekommen?'
9) Die Kinder fragen: 'Dürfen wir ins Kino gehen?'
10) Sie fragen ihn: 'Gefällt dir diese Musik?'
11) Ich frage dich: 'Willst du es mir erzählen?'
12) Er fragt seine Freundin: 'Willst du mich heiraten?'

translate:

1) He asked me whether I saw you last night.
2) I didn't know the city, so I asked the first man I saw for the station.
3) You always ask your friends for cigarettes.
4) I only asked him to lend me five marks.
5) What did you ask him for? (two translations)
6) She asked her boss for a better job.
7) He asked me for the time.
8) I'm asking her for a rendezvous.
9) I asked him for a light.
10) May I ask you for a cigarette?
11) May I ask you to close the window?
12) The tourist asked the woman for the post-office.
13) She asked for my father.
14) Can you ask Judy, whose work is careless, to come to my office.
15) Although he asked her several times already, he's asking her again for a date.
16) She asked me why I was so proud of my daughter.

VOKABELN

	Übersetzung	Sinnverwandte Wörter	Gegenteil
1. halbtags	part time ≠ full time		full time
2. (die) Gewerk-schaft	union	streiken = to go on strike	
3. bekannt	famous ≠ unknown	berühmt	unbekannt
4. sich beklagen	to complain	meckern = to kick	zufrieden sein = to be content
5. (der) Grund	reason	(die) Erklärung = explanation, (die) Einzelheit = detail	(die) Tatsache = fact
6. (die) Idee	idea	(der) Gedanke = thought	
7. einsehen	to realize	klar erkennen	ich war mir dessen nicht bewusst = I didn't realise
8. (der) Unfall	accident	(das) Unglück, (die) Katastrophe	
9. ärgern	to annoy	belästigen	
10. er fällt mir auf den Wecker	he's a pain in the neck	(der) Arsch = pain in the ass	
11. Mumm haben	to have guts	dreist sein	
12. sich streiten	to argue ≠ to get on	sich zanken = to quarrel	sich verstehen
13. klar	clear ≠ vague	deutlich, offen-sichtlich = obvious	undeutlich, verschwommen
14. überreden	to persuade	überzeugen = to convince	
15. ich kann nicht ...	I don't know how to ...		
16. für den Fall, dass	in case		

LEKTION 25

ZEITENFOLGE = SEQUENCE OF TIME

ICH DENKE, ER KOMMT.   I think he'll come.
present   +   present

ICH HABE GEDACHT, ER KÄME. I thought he'd come.
    past   +   conditional

note: — Once again Germans use the present when we use the future!
      — You will often find the Imperfekt used instead of the Perfekt
        without the meaning really changing,
        e.g. Ich habe gedacht, er käme = Ich dachte, er käme.

ICH DENKE,   ICH KANN ES MACHEN.
I think   I'll be able to do it.

ICH DACHTE,   ICH KÖNNTE ES MACHEN.
I thought   I could do it.

WENN ER ZEIT HAT, KOMMT ER.
If he has time, he'll come.

WENN ER ZEIT HÄTTE, KÄME ER.
If he had time, he'd come.

157

put the following sentences into the past, using the Imperfekt for the first part:

1) Ich denke, ich fahre morgen ab.
2) Er denkt, er muss es bald machen.
3) Sie denkt, er will sie heiraten.
4) Wenn ich genug Geld habe, kaufe ich dieses Haus.
5) Ich denke, dass er es machen muss.
6) Wir denken, dass es regnen wird.
7) Wir hoffen, dass sie auch kommt.
8) Du denkst, sie glaubt dir alles.
9) Wenn du willst, kannst du das Examen bestehen.
10) Sie denken, dass ich sie nicht sehe.
11) Ich glaube, dass er es allein machen kann.
12) Wenn er nicht kommt, bin ich ihm böse.
13) Er denkt, dass er durchfällt.

translate and then put into the present tense:

1) I thought she'd ask me again.
2) She hoped he'd marry her.
3) She thought he loved her more.
4) If I were alone I'd try to get to know interesting people.
5) If he played a dirty trick on me, I'd hustle him too.
6) She thought he was trying to con her.
7) I thought the murderer was in prison.
8) If somebody shot your friend, would you gun him down?
9) I thought the murderer escaped from prison.
10) All of us thought the prices would go down.
11) The candidate thought they'd vote for him.
12) If you smoked pot, I'd try it.
13) He said that he'd be on time.
14) The director thought that I'd forget it.
15) If she knew that, she wouldn't go out with him.
16) He said that we'd hear from him.

SOLLEN	=	SOMEONE WANTS ME TO . . .
Ich soll heute kommen.		(He) <u>wants</u> me to come today.
Ich sollte heute kommen.		(He) <u>wanted</u> me to come today.

note: Can be he, she, they, etc.

SOLLTE	=	SHOULD, OUGHT TO
SOLLTE ICH SIE ANRUFEN?		Should I call her?
Ja, Sie sollten sie anrufen.		Yes, you should call her.
Nein, Sie sollten sie nicht anrufen.		No, you shouldn't call her.

note: Remember: You don't have to call her = Sie brauchen sie nicht anzurufen.

ALS OB	=	AS THOUGH, AS IF
KÖNNEN SIE ES MACHEN?		Can you do it?
Als ob ich es nicht könnte!		As though/if I couldn't do it!

note: — After 'als ob' you have to put the Conditional II.
      — 'Tun, als ob' = to pretend.

translate:

1) Do you want me to give him a ring (call him up)?
2) She wanted me to go dancing with her.
3) You should prevent this nonsense.
4) He pretends to be very rich.
5) They wanted him to speak slower.
6) As though he didn't know it!
7) They wanted her to come with her pretty sister.
8) He came back, as if nothing could worry him.
9) He shouldn't say that.
10) I was supposed to go there, too.

answer the question in the affirmative and then in the negative:
e.g. Sollte ich sie besuchen?
     — Ja, Sie sollten sie besuchen.
     — Nein, Sie sollten sie nicht besuchen.

1) Sollten wir ihr einen Vorschlag machen?
2) Sollte er seinen Eltern die Wahrheit sagen?
3) Sollte ich versuchen, ihn zu überreden?
4) Sollte sie zum Doktor gehen?
5) Sollten wir diesen Kandidaten wählen?
6) Sollten sie den Schuft laufen lassen?
7) Sollten wir ihm sagen, was wir von ihm halten.
8) Sollten Sie sie heute anrufen?
9) Sollte ich es ihr sagen?
10) Sollte sie auch kommen.
11) Sollten wir es noch einmal versuchen?
12) Sollte er es übersetzen?
13) Sollte sie daran denken?
14) Sollten sie es wissen?
15) Solltest du ein Zimmer reservieren?
16) Sollte man es tun?

```
EINANDER                    =   EACH OTHER

Sie lieben einander.            They love each other.

Sie sprechen miteinander.       They're talking to each other.

Sie gehen nacheinander weg.     They're leaving one after the other.
```

note: — einander is mainly used together with a preposition:
- miteinander = with each other;
- füreinander = for each other;
- gegeneinander = against each other.

translate:

1) They never talk to each other.
2) They hate each other.
3) They live close to each other.
4) The little boy and the little girl always play with each other.
5) They think about each other all the time.
6) We don't live far from each other.
7) They came in one after the other.
8) They were fighting each other.

```
SCHON — NOCH NICHT          =   ALREADY — NOT YET

IST ER SCHON GEKOMMEN?          Has he already come?

Ja, er ist schon gekommen.      Yes, he has already come.
Nein, er ist noch nicht gekommen.  No, he hasn't come yet.
Nein, noch nicht.               No, not yet.
```

put into the negative:

1) Er hat schon angerufen.
2) Er hat schon eine neue Freundin gefunden.
3) Sie ist noch in Berlin.
4) Der Direktor hat noch einen Mercedes.
5) Wir haben schon ein Examen gemacht.
6) Sie haben gesagt, dass sie mitkommen.

VOKABELN

	Übersetzung	Sinnverwandte Wörter	Gegenteil
1. (das) Feuer	fire	(der) Feuerwehrmann = fireman	
2. /(der) Gangster /(der) Schurke	/gangster/crook	(der) Bandit, (der) Dieb = thief, (der) Räuber = robber	
3. stehlen	to steal, to swipe	stibitzen	
4. festnehmen	to arrest ≠ to release, let go	schnappen = to nab	freilassen, laufen lassen
5. (das) Gefängnis	prison, jail	hinter schwedischen Gardinen = in the clink	
6. (der) Einbruch	burglary	(der) Überfall = hold-up	
7. /töten/(der) Mörder/(der) Mord	/to kill/murderer /murder	(der) Totschläger = killer	(das) Opfer = victim
8. /schiessen/um die Ecke bringen	/to shoot/to gun down	(der) Revolver = gun, (die) Pistole, (die) Kugel = bullet	
9. ehrlich	honest ≠ crooked	anständig = straight	unehrlich
10. einen Streich spielen	to play a dirty trick	(der) Tiefschlag = low deal	
11. (das) Schmiergeld	bribe	der goldene Hand-schlag = kickback	
12. (der) Journalist	journalist	(der) Reporter	
13. (der) Kandidat	candidate	wählen = to vote	
14. (die) Droge	drug	(das) Haschisch = pot	
15. fliehen	to escape	sich davonmachen	
16. hereinlegen	to hustle	betrügen = to con	
17. (die) Unterwelt	underworld		
18. seine Politik ist es ...	his policy is ...		
19. (der) Umstand	circumstances		

LEKTION 26

MÜSSEN (Perfekt)

1) **Ich musste gestern gehen.**   **Ich brauchte gestern nicht zu gehen.**
                                        (Ich musste gestern nicht gehen.)
   I had to go yesterday.   I didn't have to go yesterday.

                                        Ich durfte gestern nicht gehen.
                                        i wasn't allowed to go yesterday.

2) **Ich hätte gestern gehen müssen.**   **Ich hätte gestern nicht gehen müssen.**
   Ich hätte gestern gehen sollen.   **Ich hätte gestern nicht gehen sollen.**
   I should   I shouldn't
   I ought to have gone yesterday.   I oughtn't to have gone yesterday.

note: — 'ich musste nicht' is rarely used.
      — The second construction's very easy: You use the form of 'hätte'
        and you put the infinitive of 'sollen' or 'müssen' to the end of the
        sentence. Even the main verb stays in the infinitive! Here, too,
        müssen is rather rarely used.
      — Er ist nicht gekommen, er <u>muss</u> krank <u>gewesen</u> <u>sein</u> = he didn't
        come, he <u>must have been</u> sick. Notice the two infinitives here!
      — Er ist nicht gekommen, er <u>soll</u> krank <u>sein</u> = he didn't come he <u>is said</u>
        <u>to be</u> ill.

answer in the negative:

1) Musstest du am Wochenende arbeiten?
2) Hätte ich dich anrufen sollen?
3) Sollte ich ihn auch einladen?
4) Musstet ihr zweimal pro Woche auf die Bank gehen?
5) Mussten wir viel Kies für das Auto bezahlen?
6) Hätten sie mehr arbeiten müssen?
7) Musstest du dich über sie beklagen?
8) Hätte sie netter zu ihm sein sollen?
9) Musstet ihr gegeneinander kämpfen?
10) Hättest du deiner Frau ein Geburtstaggeschenk geben sollen?

put the following sentences into the past, and then into the future tense:
e.g. Ich muss auf die Bank gehen.
    – Ich musste auf die Bank gehen.
    – Ich werde auf die Bank gehen müssen.

1) Ich muss früh schlafen gehen.
2) Du musst es gleich machen.
3) Sie müssen mich zuerst fragen.
4) Sie muss ihn heute abend anrufen.
5) Du musst mir von deiner Reise erzählen.
6) Ich muss auf ihn warten.
7) Ihr müsst dem Lehrer zuhören.
8) Er muss eine bessere Arbeit finden.
9) Wir müssen versuchen, bessere Noten zu bekommen.
10) Sie müssen gegen die Gewerkschaft kämpfen.

translate:

1) He said he had to leave her.
2) The children weren't allowed to stay up late.
3) He should have listened to you.
4) You should have worked quicker.
5) The cops had to arrest him.
6) The journalist had to write an article about the new candidate.
7) We should have waited for the bus.
8) Why didn't he come? He mustn't be in Munich.
9) I haven't seen him for a long time, he must be in prison again.
10) She said she had to lose weight.
11) I had to finish this work first.
12) He should have given me an example.
13) You shouldn't be afraid in the dark.
14) He should wear a coat.
15) I should have bought that painting.
16) Before the reception I had to go to the hairdresser.
17) The streets were wet. It must have rained.
18) They shouldn't have given him a bribe.
19) He shouldn't ask for a kickback.
20) He's so funny, he must have smoked pot.
21) I didn't have to go yesterday.
22) Did you have to tell him that?
23) Her baby should have been born yesterday.
24) What on earth should we have done?
25) He's not at home. He must be in his office.
26) He wasn't allowed to go with us to the seaside.
27) We didn't have to take the test yesterday.
28) I had to tell him that I was fed up.

GERADE + present	=	IN THE MIDST OF
WAS MACHEN SIE GERADE?		What are you doing now?
Ich esse gerade.		I'm eating now.
		(I'm in the midst of eating.)

GERADE + past	=	HAVE JUST
HAST DU GERADE GEGESSEN?		Have you just eaten?
Ja, ich habe gerade gegessen.		Yes, I've just eaten.
Nein, ich habe nicht gerade gegessen.		No, I haven't just eaten.

translate:

1) Thank you, I've just had a drink.
2) I was (in the midst of) eating when he called me up.
3) I'm reading your letter right now.
4) We've just come from there.
5) Has he just left?
6) He's just escaped from prison.
7) I'm in the midst of watching the film which you recommended.
8) I've just lost five pounds.
9) He's there now.
10) I was just thinking of you, when I got your letter.
11) He's just arrived.
12) We were (in the midst of) watching television when my mother came in.
13) We've just passed our exam.
14) Don't disturb me; I'm in the midst of doing my homework.
15) Has he just heard about it?
16) The cops have just caught him.
17) I was (in the midst of) sleeping when the house caught fire.

166

answer in the affirmative and then in the negative:

1) Er hat es dir gesagt, nicht wahr?
2) Hast du Zeit?
3) Wenn du es bekämest, wärest du froh, nicht wahr?
4) Sind wir schon einmal hier gewesen?
5) Verstehen Sie mich gut?
6) Ist das alles, was du von ihm bekommen hast?
7) · Weisst du, wohin er gefahren ist?
8) Hast du meinen Kugelschreiber genommen?
9) Hast du eine Wohnung gefunden?
10) Ich hätte kommen sollen, nicht wahr?
11) Du solltest es sofort tun, nicht wahr?
12) Er hat jemanden hereingelegt, nicht wahr?

translate:

1) I had to do it, didn't I?
2) Did you know what he wanted to do?
3) We'll love each other, won't we?
4) He didn't marry her, I hope. Yes, he did marry her.
5) You should help her, shouldn't you?
6) What did he want?
7) I wonder what he'll do.
8) Now I know what I should have done.
9) She looks well, doesn't she?
10) She has a nice figure, hasn't she?
11) If you knew, what I know, you wouldn't trust her.
12) Of course, I said what I had to say.
13) He left her alone, didn't he?
14) You don't drive, do you? Yes, I do.
15) He isn't your friend, is he? Yes, he is.
16) You didn't con her, did you? Yes, I did.

TO GET: How to translate.

BEKOMMEN, ERHALTEN

Ich habe es gestern bekommen.
I got it yesterday.

Wann bekomme ich es?
When will I get it?

WERDEN

Er wird alt.
He's getting old.

Es wird interessant.
It's getting interesting.

ANKOMMEN

Wir sind spät angekommen.
We got there late.

Sein Fett abbekommen!
Du wirst dein Fett abbekommen.
You're going to get it.

KAPIEREN, VERSTEHEN

Kapiert?
Get it?

Ich verstehe Sie nicht.
I don't get you.

BESCHAFFEN

Kannst du mir das Buch beschaffen.
Can you get me that book?

Er hat es sich auf dem Markt beschafft.
He got it in the market.

VERBUNDEN WERDEN

Bist du mit ihm verbunden worden?
Did you get him?

Ich habe keine Verbindung mit ihr bekommen.
I didn't get her.

VERDIENEN

Ich verdiene zehn Mark pro Stunde.
I get ten marks an hour.

translate:

1) Soon it'll get dark earlier.
2) Could you repeat please? I didn't get it.
3) I hope, I'll get more money next month.
4) If you don't shut up, you're going to get it.
5) Did you get there yesterday or this morning?
6) When you go to Germany, can you get me some German wine?
7) I must have tried twenty times, but I couldn't get her.
8) Where did he get this beautiful jacket?
9) I think, you should try to get your diploma this year.
10) Could you explain it to me; I don't get it.

VOKABELN

	Übersetzung	Sinnverwandte Wörter	Gegenteil
1. beenden	to complete ≠ to start	fertigmachen	anfangen, beginnen
2. /(die) Bedingung /(der) Zustand	/condition/state	(die) Lage = position	
3. nicht klappen	to go wrong	schlechter werden = sich verschlechtern = to get worse	besser werden = sich verbessern = to get better
4. (das) Beispiel	example	(der) Fall = case	
5. (das) Licht	light ≠ dark		(die) Dunkelheit
6. /(die) Frucht /(der) Pfirsich /(der) Apfel /(die) Orange	/fruit/peach /apple/orange	das Obst = fruits, (die) Pampelmuse = grapefruit	
7. soso	so-so	nichts Weltbewegendes = no great shakes	prima, toll = out of this world
8. (der) Bart	beard	sich rasieren = to shave	
9. /(das) Gemälde /(der) Künstler	/painting/artist	(das) Bild, malen = to paint	
10. (der) Schriftsteller	writer	(der) Roman = novel	
11. /(die) Figur /(die) Diät	/figure/diet	(das) Gesicht = face	
12. (der) Körper	body	(der) Hals = neck, (die) Schulter = shoulder	
13. mager	underweight ≠ overweight	schlank = slim	zu dick, fett
14. abnehmen	to lose weight ≠ to gain weight	schlanker werden	zunehmen
15. /(der) Friseursalon/Waschen und Legen	/beauty parlour /shampoo and set	(der) Friseur = hairdresser, barber	
16. hätten Sie etwas dagegen?	would you mind? ≠ no I don't mind		ich habe nichts dagegen = das stört mich nicht

LEKTION 27

PLUSQUAMPERFEKT = past perfect or pluperfect

ALS ICH EINTRAT, **HATTEN SIE SCHON GEGESSEN.**
WAREN SIE SCHON AUSGEGANGEN.

When I came in   they had already eaten.
                      they had already gone out.

note: — This is the same structure as in English (an action 'paster' than past).
      — The past action is generally in the Imperfekt.
      — The verbs conjugated with SEIN in the past are also conjugated with SEIN in this tense (see page 131).

WAR ER SCHON AUSGEGANGEN, ALS ICH ANRIEF?
Had he already gone out, when I called?

Ja, er war schon ausgegangen, als Sie anriefen.
Nein, er war noch nicht ausgegangen, als Sie anriefen.

translate:

1) By the time she came, it had already got(ten) dark.
2) When she refused this job, she had already accepted another one.
3) She didn't believe him, because he hadn't always told her the truth.
4) I didn't dance, because my leg hurt.
5) The thief ran, because he had spotted the cops.
6) She didn't answer because she had fallen asleep.
7) He was afraid, because someone had followed him.
8) When we had had a swim, we went for some food.
9) After having lit his cigarette, he gave it to her.
10) I thought he had already told you.

insert the imperfekt form, and then the plusquamperfekt:

e.g. Als ich ____ (kommen), ____(essen) sie schon ____ .
     Als ich kam, hatten sie schon gegessen.

1) Er ____ (ankommen) schon ____ , als ich in den Bahnhof ____
    (gehen).
2) Er ____ (lesen) das Buch, das mir gut ____ ____ (gefallen).
3) Ich ____ (spielen) oft die Musik, die wir an jenem Abend ____ ____
    (hören).
4) Ich ____ (wissen) nicht, dass du ihn vorher ____ ____ (kennen).
5) Ich ____ (helfen) dir, weil du mich darum ____ ____ (bitten).
6) Als du mich ____ (anrufen), ____ ich schon ____ ____ (schlafen
    gehen).
7) Als ich den Hörer abnehmen ____ (wollen), ____ sie schon ____ (auf-
    hängen).
8) Ich ____ (rufen) ihn, da er mich nicht ____ ____ (sehen).
9) Ich ____ (glauben) ihm nie mehr, weil er mich einmal ____ ____
    (belügen).
10) Er ____ (sein) sehr böse, weil ich ____ ____ (vergessen) ihn einzu-
    laden.
11) Als sie mir ____ (gratulieren), ____ ich das Examen noch nicht ____
    (bestehen).
12) Als sie mit ihm ____ (tanzen), ____ er schon zu viel ____ (trinken).
13) Als er mir seinen Doktor ____ (empfehlen), ____ ich schon einen
    anderen ____ (finden).
14) Ich ____ schon lange ____ (aufstehen), als sie mich ____ (wecken).
15) Als er mich ____ (bitten), rechts abzubiegen, ____ ich schon links
    ____ (abbiegen).
16) Als er ____ (eintreten), ____ sie schon ____ (einschlafen).
17) Als ich seinen ersten Roman ____ ____ (lesen), ____ (müssen) ich
    alle lesen.
18) Sie ____ (vorstellen) mich ihrem Vater, der gerade nach Hause ____
    ____ (kommen).
19) Als ich ____ ____ (verstehen), was er wirklich ____(wollen), ____
    (sagen) ich nein.
20) Sie ____ (tragen) das Kleid, das sie gestern ____ ____(kaufen).

```
WANN, WENN, ALS          =  WHEN

WANN KOMMT ER?              When's he coming?

Ich weiss nicht, wann er kommt.   I don't know when he's coming.
Wenn er kommt, spielen wir Schach. When he comes, we'll play chess.
Als er kam, spielten wir Schach.   When he came, we played chess.
```

note: — wann = when (which day, month, what time, etc.).
       — wenn is only used in the present, als in the past.

translate:

1) When will he be here?
2) I don't know when he arrived.
3) When I see him, I'll tell him.
4) When I saw him, I told him.
5) Can you tell me when the film starts?
6) I'd like to know when he'll take his exams.
7) When he was sixty, he retired.
8) She doesn't know when she'll get this job.
9) When will you retire?
10) When I see the sea I'm happy.
11) When he threatened me, I got mad.
12) When I got the letter, I read it right away.
13) When will this job be vacant (free)?
14) Every time I see him, we talk about music.
15) She had already gone out when I called.
16) Did he tell you what had happened?
17) I don't know when I'll be able to do it.
18) By the time I came home, he had fallen asleep.
19) Each time I see him he looks very tired.
20) When did you meet him?

VOKABELN

	Übersetzung	Sinnverwandte Wörter	Gegenteil
1. Sie sollten lieber	you'd better		
2. /(die) Post/(die) Briefmarke	/post office/stamp	mit Luftpost = by airmail	
3. ich warne Sie	I warn you	drohen = to threaten	
4. hartnäckig	stubborn ≠ accommodating	eigensinnig, dickköpfig	zuvorkommend
5. umziehen	to move	einziehen = to move in = ausziehen	
6. (die) Erde	earth, land	(das) Eigentum = property	
7. /(der) Berg /(der) See	/mountain/lake	(der) Fluss = river	note: (die) See = sea
8. /(der) Umschlag /(die) Postkarte	/envelope/postcard	(der) Brief = letter	
9. annehmen	to accept ≠ to refuse	zulassen = to admit	zurückweisen, verweigern = deny
10. abgemacht	settled ≠ in the air	festgesetzt = set	im Ungewissen
11. (die) Stellung	situation	(die) Tätigkeit = function	
12. (der) Lastwagen	truck	(der) Lkw	
13. (der) Teil	part ≠ whole		(das) Ganze
14. in den Ruhestand treten	to retire	zurücktreten = to resign	
14. es sieht so aus	it looks like	es scheint, dass = it seems that	
16. bummsen	to screw, to fuck	ficken	
17. beschreiben	to describe	schildern = to portray	
18. dieses Scheissbuch	this fucking book	dieses verdammte Buch	
19. (der) Unsinn	nonsense	dumm, doof = silly	

173

LEKTION 28

CONDITIONAL III

1) **Wenn ich Geld habe, kaufe ich einen Wagen.**
   If I have the money, I'll buy a car.

2) **Wenn ich Geld hätte, kaufte ich einen Wagen.**
   If I had the money, I'd buy a car.

3) **WENN ICH GELD GEHABT HÄTTE, HÄTTE ICH EINEN WAGEN GEKAUFT.**
   If I had had the money, I would have bought a car.

note: This third form is formed by the conditional of haben or sein and the past participle. Pay attention to the position of the words!!!

WENN SIE DAS GEWUSST HÄTTEN, HÄTTEN SIE IHN EINGELADEN?
If you had known that, would you have invited him?

Ja, wenn ich das gewusst hätte, hätte ich ihn eingeladen.
Nein, wenn ich das gewusst hätte, hätte ich ihn nicht eingeladen.

put into the conditional forms II and III:

1) Wenn ich Zeit habe, komme ich.
2) Wenn der Direktor nicht im Büro ist, arbeite ich nicht.
3) Wenn ich kein Geld habe, bleibe ich zu Hause.
4) Wenn das Wetter schön ist, gehe ich spazieren.
5) Wenn ich mit der U-Bahn fahre, komme ich pünktlich.
6) Wenn ich Ferien habe, lese ich viel.
7) Wenn mein Hemd schmutzig ist, wasche ich es.
8) Wenn ich müde bin, gehe ich schlafen.
9) Wenn ich einen schweren Kopf habe, nehme ich ein Aspirin.
10) Wenn es mir gleich ist, sage ich nichts.

put into the conditional forms I, II and III:
e.g. Wenn ich Zeit _____ (haben), _____ (kommen) ich.
 — Wenn ich Zeit habe, komme ich.
 — Wenn ich Zeit hätte, käme ich.
 — Wenn ich Zeit gehabt hätte, wäre ich gekommen.

1) Wenn er mich mit ihr _____ (sehen), _____ (werden) er wütend.
2) Wenn du mir den Wagen _____ (empfehlen), _____ (nehmen) ich ihn.
3) Wenn du _____ (wollen), _____ (können) du.
4) Wenn es _____ (schneien), _____ (fahren) wir Ski.
5) Wenn sie dich _____ (lieben), _____ (tun) sie das nicht.
6) Wenn er mir das Geld _____ (leihen), _____ (helfen) er mir sehr.
7) Wenn er ein Buch _____ (schreiben), _____ (kaufen) ich es sofort.
8) Wenn das mein Kind _____ (machen), _____ (verbieten) ich es ihm.
9) Wenn diese Übungen einfach _____ (sein), _____ (lernen) sie nichts.
10) Wenn sie ihn (langweilen), _____ (ausgehen) er nicht mit ihr.
11) Wenn sie ihm _____ (trauen), _____ (schweigen) er nicht.
12) Wenn du mich _____ (belügen), _____ (sprachen) ich nie mehr mit dir.
13) Wenn er _____ (kommen), _____ (sein) ich glücklich.
14) Wenn er Zeit _____ (haben), _____ (fahren) wir in die Berge.
15) Wenn sie noch einmal zu spät _____ (kommen), _____ (feuern) ich sie.
16) Wenn es nicht _____ (regnen), _____ (spazierengehen) wir.
17) Wenn das Stück ein Reinfall _____ (werden), _____ (verlieren) er sein ganzes Geld.
18) Wenn du weniger _____ (rauchen), _____ (sein) du gesünder.
19) Wenn ich _____ (durchfallen), _____ (machen) ich die Prüfung noch einmal.
20) Wenn du mir _____ (schreiben), _____ (antworten) ich dir sofort.
21) Wenn er mich darum _____ (bitten), _____ (geben) ich es ihm.
22) Wenn sie in dieser Stadt _____ (wohnen), _____ (besuchen) ich sie öfter.
23) Wenn du richtig _____ (suchen), _____ (finden) du es.
24) Wenn er mich _____ (einladen), _____ (einladen) ich ihn auch.
25) Wenn ich _____ (müssen), _____ (tun) ich es.
26) Wenn ich es _____ (wissen), _____ (sagen) ich es dir.

CAREFUL!

WENN ICH <u>HÄTTE</u> GEHEN MÜSSEN, <u>WÄRE</u> ICH <u>GEGANGEN</u>.

If I <u>had had to go</u>, I <u>would have</u>.

note: — If there are three verbs in a sentence you have to leave the second auxiliary and the main verb in the infinitive!
— Also the position changes: the form of 'hätte' comes first, then the main verb and then the second auxiliary.
— In German you can't drop the verb in the second sentence.
— LASSEN in the sense of 'to have something done' is considered an auxiliary.

translate:

1) If you had had to work on Sunday, would you have?
2) If you could have done it, would you have?
3) If you could do it, would you?
4) If she had had to leave him, she would have.
5) If I could have prevented him, I would have.
6) If I had wanted to win the game, I would have.
7) If she had had to let him go, she would have.
8) If he had wanted to marry her, he could have.
9) If I had been allowed to go with you, I would have.
10) If we had wanted to pass the exams, we would have.
11) If he had had to do it, he would have.
12) If the doctor could have done something, he would have.
13) If I had had a new dress made, I would have gone to the party.
14) If the children had been allowed to go to the beach, they would have.
15) If they could have phoned, they would have.
16) If you had wanted to talk to me, you could have.

SEIN

Wenn ich krank bin, gehe ich zum Arzt.
If I'm sick, I'll go to the doctor.

Wenn ich krank wäre, ginge ich zum Arzt.
If I were sick, I'd go to the doctor.

Wenn ich krank gewesen wäre, wäre ich zum Arzt gegangen.
If I had been sick, I would have gone to the doctor.

KÖNNEN

Wenn ich kann, komme ich.
If I can, I'll come.

Wenn ich könnte, käme ich.
If I could, I'd come.

Wenn ich gekonnt hätte, wäre ich gekommen.
If I could have, I would have come.

MÜSSEN

Wenn ich es machen muss, mache ich es.
If I have to do it, I will.

Wenn ich es machen müsste, machte ich es.
If I had to do it, I would.

Wenn ich es hätte machen müssen, hätte ich es gemacht.
If I had had to do it, I would have.

note: — Auxiliary + past participle = two infinitives!
— If there are three verbs in one sentence, the two infinitives are at
the end (first the infinitive of the verb, then of the auxiliary.

translate, and then give the second and first forms of the conditional:

1) If I had found a solution, I would have been happier.
2) If I had won, I would have got a prize.
3) If I had bought this apartment, you could have lived with me.
4) If you had felt better, would you have come with us?
5) If we had taken the bus sooner, we would have arrived on time.
6) If he had driven slower, he wouldn't have had an accident.
7) If the police had followed the murderer by car, they would have caught him.
8) If it hadn't been so ridiculous, I would have believed it.
9) If I had been fed up, I would have quit.
10) If it had been sunny outside, we would have gone for a walk.
11) If I had liked her better, I would have moved into her apartment.
12) If I had had to, I would have borrowed the money from him.
13) If you had been looking for a job, would you have bought the morning papers?
14) Even if you had told me the truth, I wouldn't have believed you.
15) If he hadn't been so shy, he would have kissed her.
16) If he had studied hard, he would have got his diplomas?
17) If the movie had been a flop, he would have lost all his dough.
18) If the fur coat had been in the sale, I would have bought it.
19) If she hadn't been able to come, she would have let you know.
20) If we hadn't had to work tonight, we would have gone dancing.
21) If you had walked straight ahead, you would have found the church
22) If you had spoken German, would you have gone to Germany?
23) If I had looked for it, I would have found it.
24) If he had been shrewd enough, he would have persuaded him.
25) If you had seen him first, would you have spoken to him?
26) If it hadn't been raining, we wouldn't have been at home.
27) If you hadn't lost your umbrella, we wouldn't have got wet now.

VOKABELN

	Übersetzung	Sinnverwandte Wörter	Gegenteil
1. /mieten /vermieten	/to rent/to let	untermieten = to sublet	(der) Mieter = tenant
2. (der) Hauswirt	owner	(der) Hausbesitzer	
3. (die) Methode	method	(das) System = system, (die) Art = way, (der) Stil = style	
4. gewöhnlich	ordinary ≠ exceptional	alltäglich = commonplace	aussergewöhnlich, klasse = far-out
5. modisch	in ≠ old-fashioned	in (Mode)	altmodisch
6. (das) Wort	word	(der) Satz = sentence	
7. (das) Gas	gas	(das) (Erd)öl = oil	
8. /(das) Geräusch	noise ≠ silence	(der) Lärm, (das) Getöse = racket	(die) Stille
9. vergebens	in vain	vergeblich, nutzlos = useless, zu nichts nütze = to no avail	
10. ich kann ihn nicht riechen	I can't bear him		ich bin wild auf = I'm wild about
11. klug	clever	gescheit, listig = shrewd	
12. verursachen	to cause, to bring on	bewirken, hervor-rufen	
13. (der) Einfaltspinsel	sucker		
14. /(die) Welt/im Ausland	/world/abroad		im Inland = at home
15. widersinnig, absurd	absurd ≠ logical	lächerlich = ridiculous	logisch, praktisch = practical
16. das schlägt alles!	that beats all! that's the limit!	das ist die Höhe! das ist der Gipfel!	
17. ich habe eine Stunde gebraucht	it took me an hour		
18. erreichen	to reach, get to		

LEKTION 29

REFLEXIVE VERBS – SICH WASCHEN

ich wasche mich	ich wasche mich nicht
du wäschst dich	du wäschst dich nicht
er	er
sie wäscht sich	sie wäscht sich nicht
es	es
man	man
wir waschen uns	wir waschen uns nicht
ihr wascht euch	ihr wascht euch nicht
sie waschen sich	sie waschen sich nicht
Sie	Sie

note: Reflexive verbs are extremely frequent in German. Mistakes are not very important, but you should try to get used to the structure: ich wasche mich = I wash (myself).

WASCHEN SIE SICH JEDEN TAG?
Do you wash everyday?

Ja, ich wasche mich jeden Tag.
Nein, ich wasche mich nicht jeden Tag.

ICH WASCHE MICH.	I wash.
ICH WASCHE MIR DIE HÄNDE.	I wash my hands.
DU WÄSCHST DICH.	You wash.
DU WÄSCHST DIR DIE HÄNDE.	You wash your hands.

note: — No possessive pronouns for the parts of your body.
— If a reflexive verb has a direct object, mich becomes mir and dich becomes dir.

REFLEXIVE VERBS

1. **sich anziehen** (to get dressed)
2. **sich ausziehen** (to get undressed)
3. **sich umziehen** (to change one's clothes)
4. **sich entscheiden** (to make up one's mind)
5. **sich irren** (to be wrong)
6. **sich beeilen** (to hurry)
7. **sich ausruhen** (to rest)
8. **sich fühlen** (to feel well, etc.)
9. **sich verstehen mit** (to get on with)
10. **sich interessieren für** (to be interested in)
11. **sich wünschen** (to wish)
12. **sich ausschlafen** (to sleep in)
13. **sich verschlafen** (to oversleep)
14. **sich verspäten** (to be late)
15. **sich schämen** (to be ashamed)
16. **sich entschuldigen bei** (to excuse oneself)
17. **sich vorstellen** (to imagine)
18. **sich . . . brechen** (to break one's . . .)
19. **sich bedienen** (to help oneself)
20. **sich ansehen** (to watch)
21. **sich aussuchen** (to choose)
22. **sich aufregen** (to get mad/excited)
23. **sich fertigmachen** (to get ready)
24. **sich rasieren** (to shave)
25. **sich scheiden lassen** (to get a divorce)
26. **sich Zeit nehmen** (to take one's time)
27. **sich Sorgen machen um** (to worry about)
28. **sich drehen** (to turn)
29. **sich aufhalten** (to stay)
30. **sich setzen** (to sit down)
31. **sich legen** (to lie down)
32. **sich ärgern** (to get angry)
33. **sich wundern** (to be astonished)
34. **sich fragen** (to wonder)
35. **sich streiten** (to have an argument)
36. **sich die Zähne putzen** (to brush one's teeth)
37. **sich freuen über** (to be glad about)
38. **sich freuen auf** (to be looking forward to)
39. **sich verlaufen** (to lose one's way)
40. **sich kämmen** (to comb)
41. **sich erkälten** (to catch a cold)
42. **sich amüsieren** (to have a good time)
43. **sich verabreden** (to make a date)
44. **sich erinnern an** (to remember)
45. **sich fürchten** (to be frightened)
46. **sich beklagen** (to complain)
47. **sich zanken** (to quarrel)
48. **sich davonmachen** (to escape)
49. **sich erfüllen** (to come true)
50. **sich gewöhnen an** (to get used to)
51. **sich vermehren** (to increase)
52. **sich vermindern** (to decrease)
53. **sich verbessern** (to improve)
54. **sich verschlechtern** (to get worse)
55. **sich verloben** (to get engaged)

insert the reflexive pronoun, then put the sentence into the interrogative:
e.g. Ich wasche ____.

  — Ich wasche mich.
  — Wer wascht sich?

1) Er fühlt ____ gut.
2) Sie muss ____ beeilen, weil es spät ist.
3) Sie waschen ____ im Badezimmer.
4) Du wäschst ____ das Gesicht.
5) Ich putze ____ die Zähne.
6) Am Sonntag können wir ____ ausschlafen.
7) Wir streiten ____ um den Wagen.
8) Sie hat ____ nie verspätet.
9) Er schämt ____ nicht.
10) Ich freue ____ auf die Ferien.
11) Er würde ____ nicht wundern.
12) Du kämmst ____ das Haar.
13) Sie freut ____ über das schöne Wetter.
14) Alle Träume erfüllen ____ nicht.
15) Sein Deutsch hat ____ verbessert.
16) Sie verloben ____ nächste Woche.
17) Er hat ____ geirrt.
18) Wir sehen ____ einen spannenden Film an.
19) Er regt ____ über seine Schwester auf.
20) Ich verstehe ____ mit ihr.
21) Ich ziehe ____ aus, weil ich schlafen gehen möchte.
22) Sie macht ____ für die Party fertig.
23) Ihr interessiert ____ für Musik.
24) Wir entschuldigen ____ bei unserem Lehrer.
25) Sie lassen ____ bald scheiden.
26) Ich mache ____ um meine Mutter Sorgen.
27) Ich setze ____ auf einen Stuhl.
28) Ihr erinnert ____ an die Ferien.

translate:

1) Let's hurry!
2) I'm getting dressed right now.
3) What are you interested in?
4) I shaved while she changed.
5) If he made up his mind we wouldn't have to worry any longer.
6) We could leave if she got ready now.
7) If we married now we'd get a divorce tomorrow.
8) Don't get mad! (3 translations)
9) What would you choose?
10) All dreams don't come true.
11) The situation will improve.
12) I'm looking forward to your birthday party.
13) Every time they have an argument, he gets mad.
14) Take your time!
15) On Sundays I sleep in, and on Mondays I oversleep.
16) What's he complaining about?
17) You'll get used to his behaviour.
18) Tonight I want to have a good time.
19) He caught a cold when we were in the mountains.
20) First they quarrelled, and then he escaped.
21) Do you remember him?
22) I broke my leg when we had the accident.
23) Excuse yourself! (3 translations)
24) Let's make a date for Monday.
25) I lost my way when I was coming back from the station.
26) I must lie down on my bed for a few minutes.
27) He's getting on well with his wife.
28) I wonder whether my translation's correct.

VOKABELN

	Übersetzung	Sinnverwandte Wörter	Gegenteil
1. er hat es geschafft	he managed	es ist ihm gelungen = he succeeded	
2. riesig	huge ≠ tiny	enorm	winzig
3. /(der) Ausländer /(der) Fremde	/foreigner /stranger		
4. /offen/offen gesagt	/frank/frankly ≠ to beat about the bush	ehrlich = honestly	wie die Katze um den heissen Brei schleichen
5. (die) Gewohnheit	habit	sich gewöhnen an = to get used to	
6. fahren	to drive	lenken, reiten = to ride	
7. sich vorstellen	to imagine	so tun als ob = to pretend, einreden = to make believe	
8. steigen	to increase ≠ to decrease	sich vermehren, heraufgehen = to go up	fallen, sich vermindern, heruntergehen
9. /es passt mir/es steht mir	/it fits/it suits me		zu grooss = loose, zu eng = tight
10. (der) Fahrgast	passenger ≠ driver		(der) Fahrer
11. freundlich	friendly ≠ unfriendly		unfreundlich, kalt = cold
12. (die) Unterbrechung	break	(die) Pause = pause	
13. seither	ever since		
14. der springende Punkt ist	the point is ≠ that's not the point		darum geht es nicht, das hat nichts damit zu tun
15. ruhig	calm ≠ excited		aufgeregt
16. verhindern	to prevent	ich muss lachen = I can't help laughing	
17. (die) Stärke	strength ≠ weakness	die starke Seite = strong point	(die) Schwäche, (die) schwache Seite = weak point

LEKTION 30

HAST DU DICH ENTSCHIEDEN?   Did you make up your mind?

Ja, ich habe mich entschieden.   Yes, I made up my mind.
Nein, ich habe mich nicht   No, I didn't make up my mind.
entschieden.

note: All reflexive verbs form their Perfekt and Plusquamperfekt with the forms of haben.

put into the past tense, and then into the interrogative:
e.g. Sie wäscht sich im Badezimmer.
      — Sie hat sich im Badezimmer gewaschen.
      — Wo hat sie sich gewaschen?

1) Sie kämmt sich mit ihrem neuen Kamm.
2) Ich putze mir am Morgen und am Abend die Zähne.
3) Er streitet sich immer mit seiner Frau.
4) Sie verspätet sich wieder, weil sie sich verschlafen hat.
5) Wir fühlen uns schlecht.
6) Der Junge rasiert sich schon.
7) Er beklagt sich beim Direktor über seine Sekretärin.
8) Er nimmt sich Zeit.
9) Wir amüsieren uns in einer Diskothek.
10) Ich interessiere mich für Blues.
11) Sie verabreden sich für nächste Woche.
12) Sie zanken sich um einen Sitzplatz.
13) Wir verstehen uns gut mit unseren Kollegen.
14) Die alte Dame setzt sich in den grossen Sessel.
15) Wenn er sich ärgert, streiten sie sich.
16) Du erkältest dich immer im Januar.
17) Sie sehen sich das Stück an.
18) Wir können uns Zeit nehmen.

translate:

1) Can you imagine that she fainted?
2) I'm sorry, I was wrong.
3) The situation temporarily got worse.
4) If you had improved, your mother would have been very glad.
5) Harry lost his way again.
6) Do you brush your teeth with a hard toothbrush?
7) Practically all were interested in the conversation.
8) You should be ashamed to take that gossip seriously.
9) If I took my time, we'd never get there.
10) If she beats about the bush again, I'll get mad.
11) Let's lie down in the grass to have a rest.
12) If the beer's stale, you'll have to complain about it.
13) If this plan had come true, I would have fainted.
14) I can't get used to the new car.
15) Are you looking forward to your next vacation?
16) Look! The restaurant in that skyscraper is revolving.
17) You should have excused yourself.
18) I cut myself when I want to shave quickly.
19) If you took your time, your work would be better.
20) Did you make an appointment with her?
21) Aren't you ashamed?
22) If I had hurried, I wouldn't have been late.
23) Imagine what you could do if you had good contacts.
24) Stop worrying about him!
25) If they caught him, he'd try to escape.
26) Let's get engaged!
27) Are you frightened in the dark?
28) Do you like watching the moon?

SELBST = MYSELF, YOURSELF, HIMSELF, etc.

MACHST DU ES SELBST?	Are you doing it yourself?
Ja, ich mache es <u>selbst</u>.	Yes, I'm doing it myself.
Nein, ich mache es nicht <u>selbst</u>.	No, I'm not doing it myself.

note: selbst doesn't change.

FÜR WEN KAUFT ER DIE ZEITUNG?	For whom does he buy the newspaper?
Er kauft die Zeitung für <u>ihn</u>.	He buys the newspaper for <u>him</u>.
Er kauft die Zeitung für <u>sich</u>.	He buys the newspaper for <u>himself</u>.

note: Very often the <u>selbst</u> is left out.

translate:

1) He did it himself.
2) Did you buy the book for yourself or your friend?
3) If I could have done it myself, I would have.
4) I'm amazed that she's doing it herself.
5) Did you see the accident yourself?
6) We've made the present ourselves.
7) Tell him yourself!
8) The old lady talks to herself.
9) He only likes himself.
10) They're going to ask him themselves.
11) I cooked the steak myself.
12) We could have done it ourselves.
13) I didn't write the letter myself.
14) You should have invited him yourself.

VOKABELN

	Übersetzung	Sinnverwandte Wörter	Gegenteil
1. /**(die) Seife**/**(das) Handtuch**/**(die) Zahnbürste**	/soap/towel/tooth-brush	(die) Zahnpaste = toothpaste	
2. /**(die) Decke** /**(das) Kopfkissen**	/blanket/pillow	(das) Laken = sheet	
3. /**so gut wie alle** /**so sehr(viel)**	/practically all /so very much	fast alle(s) = nearly all	
4. /**wann auch immer, immer wenn/wo auch immer, irgendwo**	/whenever/wherever	was auch immer = whatever	
5. (**die) Unterhaltung**	conversation	plaudern = to chat	
6. **sich erfüllen**	to come true	Wirklichkeit werden	
7. **Kontakte**	contacts	Beziehungen, Bindungen = ties	
8. **dauernd**	permanent ≠ temporary	ständig	zeitweilig
9. (**der) Wolkenkratzer**	skyscraper	(die) Sicht = sight	
10. **weiter**	further ≠ nearer		näher
11. /**(der) Klatsch**/**klatschen**	/gossip/to gossip		
12. **frisch**	fresh ≠ stale		abgestanden, verdorben, ranzig
13. **draussen**	outside, outdoor ≠ inside, indoor		innen, drinnen
14. **ohnmächtig werden**	to faint	in Ohnmacht fallen	
15. /**(der) Himmel** /**(der) Stern**	/sky, heaven/star	(der) Mond = moon	(die) Hölle = hell
16. /**(der) Baum**/**(die) Blume**/**(der) Garten**/**(der) Hof**	/tree/flower/garden /yard	(der) Park = park, (der) Wald = forest, (das) Gras = grass	
17. **ich wäre fast gefallen**	I almost fell		
18. **sachte! sachte!**	come, come!	erzähl mir nichts! = I don't buy it!	
19. (**das) Leben** /**lebendig**	/life/alive		(der) Tod = death, tot = dead
20. **sterben**	to die ≠ to be born		geboren werden

LEKTION 31

REVISION OF THE DECLENSIONS

NOMINATIVE

DER GROSSE MANN, EIN GROSSER MANN —
The tall woman,   the tall man

DIE GROSSE FRAU, EINE GROSSE FRAU —   GEHT SPAZIEREN.
the tall woman   , a tall woman   is going for a walk.

DAS GROSSE MÄDCHEN, EIN GROSSES MÄDCHEN —
the tall girl,   a tall girl

DIE GROSSEN KINDER, GROSSE KINDER —   GEHEN SPAZIEREN.
The tall children,   tall children   are going for a walk..

---

note: — The nominative is used tor the subject of the sentence!
　　　— The adjectives take -e in the singular and -en in the plural, -er after
　　　　ein masculine and -es after ein neuter.
　　　— Without an article the adjectives take -e in the plural.

ACCUSATIVE

ICH SEHE   DEN GROSSEN MANN, EINEN GROSSEN MANN.
I see   the tall man,   a tall man.

---

note: — The accusative's used for the direct object!
　　　— Only the masculine changes; the articles and adjectives take -en.

189

insert the correct endings:

1) Der Vater fragt sein ＿＿ ältest ＿＿ Sohn.
2) Ich habe ein ＿＿ neu ＿＿ Wagen, und mein ＿＿ Frau hat auch
   ein ＿＿ neu ＿＿ Auto.
3) D＿＿ jung ＿＿ Tochter besucht oft ihr ＿＿ alt ＿＿ Vater und
   ihr ＿＿ alt ＿＿ Mutter.
4) Steigen wir auf d ＿＿ hoh ＿＿ Wolkenkratzer!
5) Er bekommt ein ＿＿ sehr gut ＿＿ Gehalt.
6) Dies ＿＿ neu ＿＿ Grosshandel hat schon viele wichtig ＿＿ Kunden.
7) Wir brauchen ein ＿＿ neu ＿＿ Computer.
8) Dies ＿＿ Gesellschaft baut d ＿＿ höchst ＿＿ Wolkenkratzer.
9) Wenn wir in ein ＿＿ billiger ＿＿ Geschäft gingen, könntest du
   ein ＿＿ neu ＿＿ Pelzmantel bekommen.
10) Dort spielen unser ＿＿ klein ＿＿ Kinder, aber es sind auch
    gross ＿＿ Kinder dort.
11) ＿＿ Lehrer fragt d ＿＿ best ＿＿ Schüler und d ＿＿
    best ＿＿ Schülerin.

translate:

1) We bought a beautiful blue car.
2) Our new apartment should have at least three big rooms.
3) My youngest daughter and my youngest son are watching an
   interesting film.
4) Last year we had a very long and cold winter.
5) I'd like to drink a (cup of) sweet hot tea.
6) We saw a huge tree, beautiful flowers, a small garden, and a clean yard.
7) We walked through a big park, a dark forest and high grass.
8) I am giving you a new piece of soap, a clean towel and a new
   toothbrush.
9) You need a warm blanket, a soft pillow, and a white sheet.
10) She bought a yellow shirt, a brown suit, a black tie, a green dress, a
    blue coat and black shoes.
11) At Christmas she gave me an interesting book, a red scarf, and a
    beautiful pipe.

DATIVE

DEM GROSSEN MANN, EINEM GROSSEN MANN.
to the tall man,   to a tall man.

DER GROSSEN FRAU, EINER GROSSEN FRAU.

ICH GEBE ES   to the tall woman,   to a tall woman.

I give it   **DEM GROSSEN MÄDCHEN, EINEM GROSSEN MÄDCHEN.**
to the tall girl,   to a tall girl.

DEN GROSSEN KINDERN, GROSSEN KINDERN.
to the tall children,   to tall children.

note: — The dative is used for the indirect object (in English very often translated by 'to').
— der and das become dem; die feminine changes to der.
— die plural changes to den, also the noun takes -n in the plural.
— All adjectives take -en.

insert the correct endings:

1) D____ schön ____ Haus gehört d____ jung ____ Mann, d____ mit sein ____ hübsch ____ Frau und ihr____ beid ____ Kinder ____ in d____ erst____ Stock wohnt.
2) In d____ neu ____ Supermarkt gibt man d____ erst ____ Kunden ein ____ klein ____ Flasche Whisky.
3) Wir helfen d____ jung ____ Engländer, d____ nett ____ Amerikanerin, d____ braun ____ Italiener, d____ charmant ____ Franzosen und d____ reizend ____ Japanerinnen deutsch zu lernen.
4) Der gut ____ Lehrer antwortet d____ gut ____ Schüler ____ sowie d____ schlecht ____ .
5) Ich gebe d____ freundlich ____ Arzt und d____ nett ____ Krankenschwester ein klein ____ Geschenk.

DES GROSSEN MANNES, EINES GROSSEN MANNES.

of the tall man,   of a tall man.

DER GROSSEN FRAU, EINER GROSSEN FRAU.

DAS IST DER WAGEN of the tall woman,   of a tall woman.
It's the car

DES GROSSEN MÄDCHENS, EINES GROSSEN MÄDCHENS.

of the tall girl,   of a tall girl.

DER GROSSEN KINDER.

of the tall children.

note: — The genitive is the possessive case (in English 'of')!
      — The masculine and neuter articles take -es, the nouns -s or -es.
      — The feminine and the plural take -er.
      — All adjectives take -en.

insert the correct endings:

1) Er ist d___ jüngst ___ Bruder sein ___ zweit ___ Frau.
2) Ist das d___ Wagen dein ___ Vater ___ , dein ___ Onkel ___ ,
   dein ___ Tante oder d___ Herr ___ von nebenan.
3) Das ist Peter___ Frau.
4) Trotz d___ schlecht ___ und kalt ___ Wetter ___ fuhren wir zu
   d___ Gartenparty unser ___ neu ___ Freunde.
5) Wegen ein ___ sehr schlecht ___ Note hat er d___ schwer ___
   Examen nicht bestanden.
6) Ist das d___ Büro d___ neu ___ Ingenieur ___ , d___ erst ___
   Direktor ___ oder d___ alt ___ Sekretärin.
7) Während mein___ nächst ___ Sommerferien fahre ich mit d___
   gross ___ Wagen mein___ älter ___ Bruder ___ durch Europa.

translate:

1) When I was a kid, I always wanted to become a big gangster.
2) There are my pal's big children.
3) If I could have helped my sister, I would have.
4) When I met him, he was wearing a white suit, a white shirt and a black tie.
5) I gave some sweets to the little children.
6) He's sitting between a heavy chair and the old-fashioned desk.
7) I don't fight with little boys.
8) I need the letter within half an hour.
9) In spite of the hot sun we were playing a tiring game.
10) During the boring discussion many people fell asleep.
11) My best friend's against your good idea.
12) I wouldn't mind a glass of cold German beer.
13) I don't trust this crooked bastard.
14) I had a big accident with my brother's car.
15) He's trying to set up a small business in this old house.
16) He fired his young, hard-working and careful worker.
17) The unsuccessful writer lives in a small cheap room.
18) I don't understand any of this painter's paintings.
19) The bulb of the big lamp in our cosy living-room's broken.
20) The police arrested the young man, who stole the rich lady's real diamond.
21) When good friends move to another country I try to visit them every summer.
22) Young people often don't care for old people.
23) He lost his new watch and his expensive pen.
24) I get mad when I read a boring book or see a bad film.
25) Is it this man's or that man's car?
26) He gets a lot of money for beautiful little things, which he makes in his little room on the seventh floor.

VOKABELN

	Übersetzung	Sinnverwandte Wörter	Gegenteil
1. herstellen	to manufacture	machen = to make	
2. (die) Versammlung	meeting		
3. (die) Fabrik	factory		
4. (der) Markt	market		
5. organisieren	to organize	veranstalten, gründen = to set up	
6. (der) Einzelhandel	retail ≠ wholesale		(der) Grosshandel
7. (das) Personal	staff	(die) Mitarbeiter	
8. einstellen	to hire ≠ to fire	anstellen = to take on	feuern, kündigen
9. /(der) Ingenieur /(die) Brücke	/engineer/bridge		
10. /abgemacht/(das) Riesengeschäft /(die) Grossindustrie	/it's a deal/it's a big deal/big business	ein Geschäft(auf-) machen = to put a deal together	
11. bauen	to build	konstruieren	
12. (die) Maschine	machine	(der) Computer = computer	
13. (die) Anzeige	ad	werben = to advertise	
14. (der) Werbefilm	commercial		
15. (der) Kunde	client ≠ salesman		(der) Verkäufer
16. /(das) Einkommen/(die) Steuern	/income/taxes		
17. (das) Gehalt	salary	(der) Lohn = pay,	
18. /(das) Risiko /gewagt	/risk/risky	(das) Wagnis/heikel, es darauf ankommen lassen = to take a chance	
19. ausserdem, dazu	in addition to that	sowohl als auch = as well as	

LEKTION 32

VERBS REVIEW

PRÄSENS — THE PROBLEM!!!

ICH ARBEITE JEDEN TAG.   I work every day.

ICH ARBEITE JETZT.   I'm working now.

ICH ARBEITE SEIT EINER   I've been working for an hour.
STUNDE.

ICH ARBEITE NÄCHSTE WOCHE.   I'm going to work next week.

note: The German Präsens is so extensively used that its meaning can be tricky to grasp.

FUTURE

ICH WERDE **MORGEN**   **ARBEITEN.**   I'll work   tomorrow.
                 IN ZWEI TAGEN   in two days.

note: The future isn't used a lot! The infinitive goes to the end.

PERFEKT

            LETZTE WOCHE   last week.
ICH HABE **GESTERN**   **GEARBEITET.** I worked   yesterday.
            VOR ZWEI TAGEN   two days ago.
                                (I have worked.)

IMPERFEKT — THE OTHER PROBLEM

ICH <u>**ARBEITETE**</u> **ALS IHR** <u>**KAMT**</u>.
WÄHREND SIE <u>SPRACHEN</u>.

I <u>was</u> work<u>ing</u> when you <u>came</u>.
while you <u>were</u> talk<u>ing</u>.

note: Distinguish between:
 I worked yesterday = Ich habe gestern gearbeitet.
 I was working when you came = Ich arbeitete, als Sie kamen.

PLUSQUAMPERFEKT

ALS ICH <u>KAM</u>, <u>**HATTEN**</u> **SIE SCHON** <u>GEGESSEN</u>.
<u>**WAREN**</u> **SIE SCHON** <u>AUSGEGANGEN</u>.

When I <u>came</u> they <u>had</u> already <u>eaten</u>.
they <u>had</u> already <u>left</u>.

WENN = IF

WENN ICH GELD <u>**HABE**</u>, <u>**KAUFE**</u> **ICH EINEN WAGEN.**
If I have money, I'll buy a car.

WENN ICH GELD <u>**HÄTTE**</u>, <u>**KAUFTE**</u> **ICH EINEN WAGEN.**
If I had money, I'd buy a car.

WENN ICH GELD <u>**GEHABT HÄTTE**</u>, <u>**HÄTTE**</u> **ICH EINEN WAGEN**
<u>**GEKAUFT**</u>.

translate:

1) When I had that nightmare, I was afraid.
2) I always get up early.
3) Are you eating now? Do you always eat so early?
4) I listened to the radio when I couldn't sleep.
5) We met him last week in the mountains.
6) Did you meet her when you were at the seaside?
7) This piece will be a flop because of its director.
8) Was she here this morning?
9) What were you doing when I called?
10) I got angry instead of forgiving her.
11) When the little girl was playing with her doll, she broke it.
12) Have you ever been to Munich? Yes, I went last week.
13) Will they fire him because he's in the union?
14) They went on strike in order to earn more money.
15) I'm going to be there at ten.
16) Every summer we go to the south.
17) Did you hear their stupid conversation?
18) I've known her for two years.
19) She went to the country yesterday.
20) I'll get up before you.
21) I got angry when he tore the book apart.
22) Will you go with us tonight?
23) Why didn't you help him?
24) She has been waiting for him since lunchtime.
25) What am I going to do?
26) I used to go abroad once a year.
27) I'm not used to eating German food.
28) Will she ever forgive me?

put the sentences into the conditional, using first form II and then form III:

1) Wenn ich Zeit habe, fahre ich in die Berge.
2) Wenn ich eine Lösung finde, bin ich glücklich.
3) Wenn ich das Geld bekomme, leihe ich dir etwas.
4) Wenn ich ihn treffe, entschuldige ich mich bei ihm.
5) Wenn ich kann, mache ich es.
6) Wenn du es willst, kannst du es machen.
7) Wenn ich den Ring verliere, werde ich sehr traurig sein.
8) Wenn ich sie besser kenne, frage ich sie.
9) Wenn du nicht allein gehen willst, gehe ich mit.
10) Wenn er mit ihr spricht, wird er rot.
11) Wenn die Sonne nicht scheint, bleibe ich zu Hause.
12) Wenn er nicht sorgfältiger arbeitet, feuere ich ihn.
13) Wenn du mir versprichst zu schweigen, sage ich es dir.
14) Wenn Sie es ihm erzählen, traue ich Ihnen nicht mehr.

translate:

1) If he came too late, I wouldn't wait.
2) If she can't come, she'll call you.
3) If I had been alone, I would have gone to bed.
4) If I had had to do it, I would have.
5) If I don't have to work, I'll play with the children.
6) If you can't manage, I'll help you.
7) If he had told me about it, I would have known a solution.
8) If the gangster had had to kill the cop, he would have.
9) If they put up the prices, they'll lose a lot of money.
10) If you had seen the film, you would have cried too.
11) If he lost this fight, he'd give up this sport.

translate:

1) Do we have to go now? Yes, we must.
2) You should have told her.
3) You didn't have to tell me.
4) Do you really think I should have told her?
5) Though I'm delighted to see you, I must go now.
6) I absolutely want you to do it.
7) He can't help laughing while that teacher's speaking.
8) I almost bought that old clock yesterday.
9) She doesn't think that I can do it.
10) He should have told you the truth.
11) I've been working here for one year.
12) How could you drink that much?
13) You have to do it now. I had to do it yesterday.
14) We didn't have to work last week.
15) He wasn't allowed to come with us.
16) May I ask you a question?
17) He didn't come, he must have been sick.
18) I can't find my umbrella, I must have lost it.
19) She can't have finished yet.
20) They shouldn't have got married.
21) You mustn't wash this sweater.
22) I was disappointed since he couldn't travel with us.
23) How should I have done it?
24) He didn't have to leave so early.
25) He thinks he can't be wrong.
26) You've been talking for an hour.
27) Thank God! I won't have to do it alone.
28) Were you working while we were eating?

VOKABELN

	Übersetzung	Sinnverwandte Wörter	Gegenteil
1. /(das) Versprechen/(das) Geheimnis	/promise/secret	ein Versprechen halten = to keep a promise	
2. /(der) Tip/(der) Anhaltspunkt	/tip/clue	anspielen auf = to hint	
3. (die) Erleichterung	relief	erleichtern = to relieve	
4. reparieren	to repair ≠ to break		zerbrechen, kaputt machen
5. (die) Belohnung	reward	(der) Preis = prize	
6. /(die) Strasse /(die) Autobahn	/road/highway		
7. was wollen Sie damit sagen?	what do you mean?	was verstehen Sie darunter?	
8. liefern	to supply	versorgen mit	
9. leise	in a whisper	im Flüsterton	laut = aloud
10. beschädigen	to damage	verletzen, schaden = to harm	
11. (der) Friede(n)	peace ≠ war	(die) Armee = army	(der) Krieg
12. kochen	to cook, to boil	braten = to roast	
13. /nähen/(die) Nadel	/to sew/needle	(der) Faden = thread, (das) Bügeleisen = iron, waschen = to wash	
14. üben	to practise	(die) Übung = exercise	
15. (die) Bibliothek	library	(die) Bücherei	
16. (der) Liebling	darling	(der) Liebhaber = lover	
17. gern	I'm willing	einverstanden	
18. (der) Mist	bullshit	du bist ein Arsch = you're an ass	
19. wirklich	like crazy	echt	
20. was in aller Welt!	what on earth!	mein Gott! = my God!	
21. /vorschlagen /(der) Vorschlag	/to suggest /suggestion	raten = to advise, (der) Rat = piece of advice	
22. ich bin schuld	it's my fault		

VERBEN UND PRÄPOSITIONEN (VERBS AND PREPOSITIONS) 1

a) fill in the blanks in the second column as far as you can;
b) fold the page back to check your answer;
c) read the translation of the sentence for further clarification.

1. come in

Er ist ____ das Zimmer getreten.

2. a. to talk to
   b. to talk about

a. Ich habe ____ meinem Vater gesprochen.
b. Wir sprachen ____ Sie.
   Wir sprachen ____ Ihnen.

3. to depend on

Das kommt ____ Sie an.
Das hängt ____ Ihnen ab.

4. to agree with

Ich stimme ____ Ihnen überein.

5. to be interested in

Sie interessiert sich ____ ihre Arbeit.

6. to take care of

Er kümmert sich ____ deine Probleme.

7. to live in

Sie wohnt ____ Berlin.

8. married to

Sie ist ____ einem Amerikaner verheiratet.

9. amazed at/surprised at

Ich wundere mich ____ sein Benehmen.

10. to go to

Ich gehe ____ Paris./ ____ das Büro./ _____
_____ Hause./ ____ Friseur./ _____ Fenster./
_____ Markt.

11. to be afraid of

Sie hat Angst ____ ihm.

12. to be mad at

Ich bin wütend ____ ihn.

13. to be worried about

Er macht sich Sorgen ____ seinen Sohn.

14. to be proud of

Er ist stolz ____ seine Frau.

15. to feel like

Ich habe Lust ____ einen Kaffee. Wor ____
haben Sie Lust?

16. to look like

Er sieht ____ sein Vater aus.

17. a. to get used to

   b. to be used to

a. Ich werde mich nie ____ seine Art zu
   sprechen gewöhnen.
b. Ich bin nicht ____ sein Benehmen gewöhnt.

18. to get in ≠ to get out

Steig ____ das Auto ≠ Steig ____ dem Auto.

19. to stop

Er hat ____ dem Rauchen aufgehört.

20. a. to think about (think
       something over)
    b. think about (someone)
    c. to think about (opinion)

a. Denken Sie ____ das, was er gesagt hat./
   Denken Sie ____ seinen Rat nach.
b. Ich denke ____ dich.
c. Was halten Sie ____ seinem Rat.

1. **(ein) treten in**	He came into the room.
2. a. **sprechen mit**	a. I talked to my father.
b. **sprechen uber** + acc **sprechen von**	b. We were talking about you.
3. **ankommen auf** + acc /**abhängen von**	It depends on you.
4. **übereinstimmen mit**	I agree with you.
5. **sich interessieren für**	She's interested in her work.
6. **sich kümmern um**	He takes care of your problems.
7. **wohnen in**	She lives in Berlin.
8. **verheiratet mit**	She's married to an American.
9. **sich wundern über** + acc	I'm amazed/surprised at his behaviour.
10. **gehen in/nach/zu/an /auf**	I'm going to Paris./to the office./home./ /to the hairdresser./to the window./to the market.
11. **Angst haben vor** + dat	She's afraid of him.
12. **wütend sein auf** + acc	I'm mad at him.
13. **sich Sorgen machen um**	He's worried about his son.
14. **stolz sein auf**	He's proud of his wife.
15. **Lust haben auf** + acc	I feel like coffee. What do you feel like?
16. **aussehen wie**	He looks like his father.
17. a. **sich gewöhnen an** + acc	I'll never get used to his way of speaking.
b. **gewöhnt sein an**	I'm not used to his manners.
18. **steigen in ≠ aus**	Get in the car. ≠ Get out of the car.
19. **aufhören mit**	He stopped smoking.
20. a. **denken an/ nachdenken über** + acc	a. Think about what he said. Think his advice over.
b. **denken an**	b. I think about you.
c. **halten von**	c. What do you think about his advice.

VERBEN UND PRÄPOSITIONEN 2

1. to laugh at/make fun of — **Machen Sie sich nicht ____ mich lustig.**

2. to have a part in the (business) — **Sind Sie ____ dem Geschäft beteiligt?**

3. on behalf of — **Ich rufe Sie im Namen ____ Herrn X an.**

4. near ≠ far from — **Er wohnt in der Nähe ____ mir (or: in meiner Nähe) ≠ weit ____ mir.**

5. to be about — **Wor ____ handelt es sich?**

6. to apologize — **Ich entschuldige mich ____ die Störung.**

7. to look like — **Ich stand ____ ein Idiot da.**

8. to be good at — **Er ist gut ____ Geschichte.**

9. to regret — **Ich bedaure, ihn nicht gesehen ____ haben.**

10. to be aware of — **Hatten Sie ____ seiner Scheidung Kenntnis?**

11. so as to/in order to — **____ gut ____ sprechen, mache ich einen Kurs.**

12. to be pleased /delighted — **Es freut mich, Sie ____ sehen/Ich bin glücklich, Sie ____ sehen.**

13. to be lacking in — **Es fehlt mir ____ Zeit.**

14. to forget to — **Ich habe vergessen, es Ihnen ____ sagen.**

15. to expect to — **Ich habe nicht erwartet, Sie hier ____ sehen.**

16. to try to — **Versuchen Sie ____ kommen.**

17. to wait for — **Sie wartet seit heute morgen ____ ihren Mann.**

18. to complain about — **Beklagen Sie sich nicht ____ mich!**

19. to remember — **Ich erinnere mich ____ ihn.**

20. crazy about — **Ich bin verrückt ____ ihr.**

VERBEN UND PRÄPOSITIONEN 2

1. **sich lustig machen über** + acc	Don't laugh/make fun of me.
2. **an dem Geschäft beteiligt sein**	Have you a part in the business?
3. **im Namen von**	I'm calling you on behalf of Mr. Q.
4. **in der Nähe von** ≠ **weit von**	He lives near me ≠ far from me.
5. **sich handeln um**	What is it about?
6. **sich entschuldigen für**	I apologize for having disturbed you.
7. **dastehen wie**	I looked like an idiot.
8. **gut sein in**	He's good at history.
9. **bedauern zu**	I regret not having seen him.
10. **Kenntnis haben von**	Were you aware of his divorce?
11. **um zu**	In order to speak well I take lessons.
12. **es freut(mich) zu /glücklich sein zu**	I'm pleased to see you.
13. **fehlen an**	I'm lacking in time.
14. **vergessen zu**	I forgot to tell you.
15. **erwarten zu**	I didn't expect to see you here.
16. **versuchen zu**	Try to come.
17. **warten auf** + acc	She's been waiting for her husband since this morning.
18. **sich beklagen über +** acc	Don't complain about me.
19. **sich erinnern an +** acc	I remember him.
20. **verrückt nach**	I'm crazy about her.

VERBEN UND PRÄPOSITIONEN 3

1. it's okay for — Es geht _____ sechs Uhr.

2. to come back from — Er ist _____ New York zurückgekommen.

3. a. to ask for — Er bittet mich _____ eine Zigarette.
   b. to ask for (information) — Sie fragt ihn _____ dem Weg.
   c. to ask to — Ich bitte Sie, mir _____ helfen.

4. to answer — Ich muss noch _____ seinen Brief antworten.

5. to help with — Ich helfe ihm _____ der Arbeit.

6. to tell about — Er erzählte mir _____ seiner Reise.

7. to plan to — Ich habe vor, diese Woche _____ gehen.

8. you're right ≠ wrong — Sie haben recht ≠ unrecht, sofort _____ gehen.

9. I'd be happy to — Es wäre mir ein Vergnügen, Sie wieder _____ sehen.

10. it's . . . — Es ist wichtig, es _____ tun.
    nötig, es _____ tun.
    leicht, es _____ tun.
    normal, es _____ tun.

11. to look forward to — Ich freue mich _____ die Ferien.

12. to be glad about — Ich freue mich _____ dieses Geschenk.

13. to get on with — Er versteht sich gut _____ ihr.

14. to invite to — Er hat mich _____ seiner Party eingeladen.

15. begin — Er hat _____ der Arbeit begonnen.

16. to suffer from — Er leidet _____ Zahnschmerzen.

17. to argue/have an argument about — Sie streiten sich _____ den Wagen.

18. to get excited about — Er regt sich _____ seine Arbeit auf.

19. I succeed in — Es gelingt mir nicht, die Tür _____ öffnen.

VERBEN UND PRÄPOSITIONEN 3

1. **es geht um**	It's okay for six o'clock.
2. **zurückkommen aus**	He came back from New York.
3. a. **bitten um**	He asks me for a cigarette.
b. **fragen nach**	She's asking him for the way.
c. **bitten zu**	I'm asking you to help me.
4. **antworten auf** + acc	I still have to answer his letter.
5. **helfen bei**	I'm helping him with his work.
6. **erzählen von**	He was telling me about his trip.
7. **vorhaben zu**	I plan to go this week.
8. **recht ≠ unrecht haben**	You're right ≠ wrong to go at once.
9. **es wäre mir ein Vergnügen zu**	I'd be happy to see you again.
10. **es ist**	It's important to do it.
	necessary to do it.
	easy to do it.
	normal to do it.
11. **sich freuen auf** + acc	I'm looking forward to my holidays.
12. **sich freuen über** + acc	I'm glad about this present.
13. **sich gut verstehen mit**	He's getting on with her.
14. **einladen zu**	He invited me to his party.
15. **beginnen mit**	He began his work.
16. **leiden an** + dat	He suffers from toothache.
17. **sich streiten um**	They're having an argument about the car.
18. **sich aufregen über**	He's getting excited about his work.
19. **es gelingt mir zu**	I don't succeed in opening the door.

REDENSARTEN (IDIOMS) 1

1. to go for a walk   **Wir werden _____ .**

2. all the same   **_____ vielen Dank!**

3. I don't care/it's all   **Es ___ ___ ___ .**
   the same to me   **Es ___ ___ ___ .**

4. I'd like you to meet   **Ich mochte Ihnen Peter _____ .**
   . . . /pleased to   **_____ .**
   meet you

5. it doesn't matter   **Das ___ ___ .**

6. that's the limit/that   **Das ist ____ ____ !/Das ist ____ ____ !**
   takes the cake

7. to be on the line/   **Herr Müller ist ___ ___ ./Bleiben ___ ___ ___ .**
   to hang on

8. How are you?/Fine   **Wie geht es ___ ?/Danke, ___ , ___ ___ ?**
   thank you and you?

9. to make a mistake   **Ich habe ___ ___ ___ .**
       Ich habe ___ ___ .

10. straight or on the   **Pur ___ ___ ___ .**
    rocks.

11. do you have a light?   **Haben Sie ___ ?**

12. to have a drink   **Wollen wir heute abend ___ ___ ?**

13. too bad ≠ all the   **Zu ____ . ≠ Um ____ ____ .**
    better

14. on the other hand   **Er ist nicht sehr helle, aber ___ ___ ___ ___**
        ist er sehr charmant.

15. to be sick of/fed up   **Ich habe ___ ___ ___ .**

16. it isn't worth it   **Es ist nicht ___ ___ ___ .**

17. How goes it?/No   **Wie ___ ?/Es ___ ___ .**
    good.

18. I feel that   **Ich ___ , dass sie unrecht hat.**

19. I'm starving ≠ full   **Ich sterbe ___ ___ . ≠ ich bin ___ .**

20. some more . . .   **___ ___ Brot, bitte.**

21. to change one's mind   **Er hat es sich ___ ___ .**

22. to dial   **Ich habe ___ ___ ___ .**

REDENSARTEN 1

1. **spazierengehen**	We'll go for a walk.
2. **trotzdem**	Many thanks all the same.
3. **es ist mir gleich/es ist mir einerlei**	I don't care. It's all the same to me.
4. **ich möchte Ihnen . . . vorstellen/angenehm**	I'd like you to meet Peter./Pleased to meet you.
5. **das macht nichts**	It doesn't matter.
6. **das ist der Gipfel/ das ist das Beste**	That's the limit./That takes the cake.
7. **am Apparat sein/am Apparat bleiben**	Mr. Müller's on the line./Hang on!
8. **Wie geht es Ihnen? Danke, gut, und Ihnen?**	How are you? Fine thanks and you?
9. **einen Fehler machen /sich irren**	I made a mistake.
10. **pur oder mit Eis**	Straight or on the rocks?
11. **Haben Sie Feuer?**	Do you have a light?
12. **einen trinken**	Shall we have a drink tonight?
13. **zu dumm ≠ um so besser**	too bad ≠ all the better
14. **auf der anderen Seite**	He isn't very bright, but on the other hand he's very charming.
15. **die Nase voll haben**	I'm fed up.
16. **nicht der Mühe wert sein**	It isn't worth it.
17. **Wie gehts?/Es geht nicht.**	How goes it?/No good.
18. **Ich fühle, dass**	I feel that she's wrong.
19. **vor Hunger sterben ≠ satt sein**	I'm starving ≠ I'm full.
20. **noch etwas . . .**	Some more bread please.
21. **es sich anders überlegen**	He changed his mind.
22. **die Nummer wählen**	I dialled.

REDENSARTEN 2

1. to make a fortune | **Er ist in Amerika** ____ ___.
2. to do someone a favour | **Könnten Sie mir** ____ ____ ___?
3. to stand in line | **Vor dem Kino muss man** ____ ___.
4. to make an appointment | **Der Rechtsanwalt hat** ____ ___.
5. to earn a living | **Verdient er gut** ____ ___?
6. to get on someone's nerves | **Sie geht mir** ____ ____ ___.
7. to be late ≠ early | **Er kommt oft** ____ ___ ./ ≠ ____ ___.
8. I don't buy it | **Nicht** ____ ___.
9. to make an effort | **Man muss** ____ ___.
10. to go shopping | **Gehen wir** ____!
11. to feel under the weather/out of sorts ≠ to feel great | **Ich fühle** ____ ____ ./Es geht ____ ___ . ≠ **Es geht mir** ___ . **Ich bin** ____ ___ .
12. to do the dishes | **Heute muss ich** ____ .
13. to take turns | **Wir machen es** ____ .
14. you gotta be kidding | **Das kann nicht** ____ ____ ___!
15. what a pain in the neck | **So ein** ___ !/**So ein** ____!
16. to mean | **Was wollen Sie** ____ ____ ?
17. to tell the truth | **Um** ____ ____ ____ ___, **ich mag ihn nicht.**
18. that goes without saying | **Das versteht** ___ ____ ___ .
19. that's all the more reason | **Das ist** ____ ___ ___ ___ ___, **sie zu verlassen.**
20. help yourself! | **Bedienen** ____ ___!
21. it's not my cup of tea | **Das** ___ ___ ___ ___ ./**Das macht mich** ____ ___ .
22. to make a fuss | **Machen Sie** ___ ___ !
 Machen Sie sich ____ ___ !

209

REDENSARTEN 2

1. **reich werden**	He made a fortune in America.
2. **jemandem einen Gefallen tun**	Could you do me a favour?
3. **Schlange stehen**	You have to queue (stand in line) for the cinema.
4. **sich verabreden**	The lawyer made an appointment.
5. **seinen Lebensunterhalt verdienen**	Does he earn a good living?
6. **jemandem auf die Nerven gehen**	She gets on my nerves.
7. **zu spät ≠ zu früh kommen**	He's often late ≠ early.
8. **nicht mir mir**	I don't buy it!
9. **sich anstrengen**	You have to make an effort.
10. **einkaufen gehen**	Let's go shopping!
11. **sich schlecht fühlen /es geht (mir) schlecht ≠ es geht (mir) blendend/in Form sein**	I feel under the weather. ≠ I feel great.
12. **abwaschen**	I have to do the dishes today.
13. **es abwechselnd machen**	We'll take turns.
14. **das kann nicht dein Ernst sein!**	You gotta be kidding!
15. **so ein Mist(thing)/ So ein Arsch(person)**	What a pain in the neck!
16. **damit sagen wollen**	What do you mean?
17. **um die Wahrheit zu sagen**	To tell the truth, I don't like him.
18. **das versteht sich von selbst**	That goes without saying.
19. **das ist ein um so triftigerer Grund**	That's all the more reason to leave her.
20. **Bedienen Sie sich!**	Help yourself!
21. **das ist nicht mein Fall /das macht mich nicht an**	It's not my cup of tea.
22. **Geschichten/Umstände machen**	Don't make a fuss.

REDENSARTEN 3

1. to be successful

Das Stück hat ___ ___ .

2. to take a nap

Ich bin müde und werde ___ ___ ___ .

3. on the face of it

___ ___ ___ ___ würde ich sagen, dass Sie recht haben.

4. to hurt

Tut es ___ ___ ?

5. I don't give a damn

Das ist mir ___ ___ ./Ich scher mich ___ ___ ___ .

6. time's up

Die Zeit ___ ___ .

7. to fall behind ≠ to catch up

Ich bin hinter den anderen ___ , ich muss ___ .

8. what's up?

Was ___ ___?

9. to give up

Ich gebe ___ .

10. I don't want to put you out/you're not putting me out

Ich will ___ ___ ___ ./Sie ___ ___ ___ .

11. to get over

Ich komme nicht ___ ___ .

12. I didn't realize

Es ___ ___ ___ ___ .

13. to worry

Sie macht ___ ___ ___ ihren Sohn.

14. to cut off (phone)

Man hat uns ___ .

15. to have a good time

Wir haben uns ___ ___ .

16. to be lucky ≠ unlucky

Ich habe ___ . ≠ ___ .

17. do you mind if . . . ? I don't mind

Haben Sie ___ ___ , ___ ich rauche.
Ich habe ___ ___ .

18. Did you enjoy it? /I enjoyed it.

Hat es ___ ___ ?
Es ___ ___ ___ .

19. Get lost!

Hau ___ ?

20. Fuck off!/Screw off!

Leck mich ___ ___ !

21. Kiss me!

Küss mich!

22. You're an ass!

Du bist ___ ___ .

211

REDENSARTEN 3

1. **grossen Erfolg haben.**	The play's successful.
2. **ein Nickerchen machen**	I'm tired and I'm going to take a nap.
3. **auf den ersten Blick**	On the face of it, I'd say you're right.
4. **wehtun**	Does it hurt you?
5. **das ist mir ganz egal /ich scher mich den Teufel darum**	I don't give a damn.
6. **die Zeit ist um**	Time's up.
7. **zurückbleiben hinter ≠ aufholen**	I've fallen behind, I must catch up.
8. **was ist los?**	What's up?
9. **aufgeben**	I give up.
10. **ich will sie nicht stören /Sie stören mich nicht**	I don't want to put you out./ You're not putting me out.
11. **darüber hinwegkommen**	I can't get over it.
12. **es war mir nicht klar**	I didn't realize.
13. **sich Sorgen machen um**	She worries about her son.
14. **unterbrechen**	We were cut off.
15. **sich gut amüsieren**	We had a good time.
16. **Glück ≠ Pech haben**	I'm lucky ≠ unlucky.
17. **Haben Sie etwas dagegen, wenn . . . ? /Ich habe nichts dagegen**	Do you mind if I smoke? I don't mind.
18. **Hat es dir gefallen? /Es hat mir gefallen.**	Did you enjoy it? I enjoyed it.
19. **Hau ab!**	Get lost!
20. **Leck mich am Arsch!**	Fuck off!
21. **Küss mich!**	Kiss me!
22. **Du bist ein Arschloch.**	You're an ass!

CONGRATULATIONS!!

You are no longer a beginner.
You can now go on to *Gimmick I—
gesprochenes Deutsch,* the first uncen-
sored, realistic vocabulary learning book.

Key/Übersetzung

Lektion 1, page 1
1) Die Maus ist weiss. 2) Ist der Stuhl gross? 3) Bis bald! 4) Das Buch ist rot. 5) Ist der Kugelschreiber schwarz oder weiss? 6) Das ist ein rosa Telefon. 7) Die Armbanduhr ist klein, aber die Uhr ist gross. 8) Ist das eine weisse Wand? 9) Ist das eine Katze oder ein Hund? 10) Mist! 11) Ist das ein blauer Wecker? 12) Auf Wiedersehen!

Lektion 1, page 2
1) dicke 2) schwarzer 3) grosse 4) rotes 5) weisses 6) blaue 7) grosser 8) blaues 9) kleine 10) schwarzer 11) rote 12) grosses.

Lektion 1, page 3
1) die. Ist die Tür weiss? 2) der. Ist der Tisch gross? 3) das. Ist das Haus klein? 4) der. Ist der Kugelschreiber blau? 5) die. Ist die Maus weiss? 6) das. Ist das Buch marineblau? 7) das. Ist das Telefon rosa? 8) der. Ist der Wecker schwarz? 9) die. Ist die Frau blau. 10) die. Ist die Katze klein? 11) die. Ist die Buchhandlung klein? 12) die. Ist die Armbanduhr blau? 13) der. Ist der Kuli rot? 14) die. Ist die Katze dick? 15) der. Ist der Bleistift gross?

Lektion 1, page 4
1) Ja, das ist ein schwarzer Stuhl. 2) Ja, das ist ein rotes Telefon. 3) Ja, das ist ein Kugelschreiber. 4) Ja, das ist ein grosser Tisch. 5) Ja, der Wecker ist rosa. 6) Ja, das ist ein grosses Haus. 7) Ja, die Frau ist dick. 8) Ja, das ist ein Hund. 9) Ja, die Maus ist schwarz. 10) Ja, die Buchhandlung ist klein. 11) Ja, das ist eine weisse Maus. 12) Ja, die Armbanduhr ist marineblau.

Lektion 1, page 4
1) Das ist ein grosser Wagen. Ist das . . . ? 2) Der Wagen ist gross und weiss. Ist der Wagen . . . ? 3) Die Frau ist blau. Ist die Frau . . . ? 4) Die Tür ist rot und blau. Ist die Tür . . . ? 5) Der Tisch ist klein. Ist der Tisch . . . ? 6) Das ist ein grosses Haus. Ist das ein . . . ? 7) Die Buchhandlung ist gross. Ist die Buchhandlung . . . ? 8) Das ist ein grosser Stuhl. Ist das . . . ? 9) Die Maus ist schwarz. Ist die Maus . . . ? 10) Das ist ein grosser Wecker. Ist das . . . ? 11) Das ist ein schwarzer Kuli. Ist das ein   . ? 12) Der Mann ist dick. Ist der Mann . . . ? 13) Die Mauer ist weiss. Ist die Mauer . . . ? 14) Das ist eine grosse Buchhandlung. Ist das . . . ?

Lektion 2, page 6

1) Können Sie wiederholen, bitte? 2) Das Mädchen ist nicht alt und ich auch nicht. 3) Wie geht es Ihnen? Danke, gut, und Ihnen? 4) Peter ist stark und ich auch. 5) Ist das ein Junge oder ein Mädchen? 6) Der alte Mann ist dick. 7) Peter ist reich, aber John ist arm. 8) Das ist keine leichte Lektion. 9) Aber die Hausaufgabe ist nicht schwer. 10) Das ist falsch.

Lektion 2, page 7

1) Das ist kein Aschenbecher. Ist das . . . ? 2) Es ist nicht so spät. Ist es . . . ? 3) Das ist kein brauner Regenmantel. Ist das . . . ? 4) Die Musik ist nicht laut. Ist die Musik . . . ? 5) Das ist kein alter Wagen. Ist das . . . ? 6) Das ist keine lange Pfeife. Ist das . . . ? 7) Das ist kein schwarzer Schuh. Ist das ein . . . ? 8) Das Kind ist nicht jung. Ist das Kind . . . ? 9) Die Tür ist nicht weiss. Ist die Tür . . . ? 10) Das ist keine schwere Hausaufgabe. Ist das eine . . . ? 11) Der reiche Mann ist nicht gut. Ist der reiche Mann . . . ? 12) Das ist keine breite Strasse. Ist das . . . ? 13) Die Musik ist nicht gut. Ist die Musik . . . ? 14) Das ist kein kleiner Schlüssel. Ist das ein . . . ? 15) Die Lektion ist nicht leicht. Ist die Lektion . . . ? 16) Das ist nicht Lektion 3. Ist das . . . ? 17) Das ist kein grosses Zimmer. Ist das ein . . . ? 18) Das dicke Papier ist nicht weiss. Ist das dicke Papier . . . ? 19) Das ist nicht richtig. Ist das . . . ? 20) Das kleine Kind ist kein Mädchen. Ist das kleine Kind . . . ? 21) Der alte Mann ist nicht reich. Ist der alte Mann . . . ? 22) Der braune Aschenbecher ist nicht schwer. Ist der braune Aschenbecher . . . ? 23) Die dicke Frau ist nicht alt. Ist die dicke Frau . . . ? 24) Das keine blaue Schachtel. Ist das . . . ? 25) Das ist kein guter Mann. Ist das . . . ? 26) Das ist keine schöne Pfeife. Ist das . . . ? 27) Die junge Frau ist nicht schön. Ist die junge Frau . . . ? 28) Das ist keine enge Strasse. Ist das . . . ?

Lektion 2, page 8

1) lange. Das ist keine lange Strasse. Ist das . . . ? 2) brauner. Das ist kein brauner Hut. Ist das . . . ? 3) grosser, neuer. Das ist kein grosser, neuer Wagen. Ist das . . . ? 4) kleines. Das ist kein kleines Kind. Ist das . . . ? 5) dicker. Das ist kein dicker Mann. Ist das . . . ? 6) schöne. Das ist keine schöne Pfeife. Ist das . . . ? 7) brauner. Das ist kein brauner Schuh. Ist das . . . ? 8) langer, schwarzer. Das ist kein langer schwarzer Regenmantel. Ist das . . . ? 9) starker. Das ist kein starker Mann. Ist das . . . ? 10) stark. Peter ist nicht stark. Ist Peter . . . ? 11) kleines. Maria ist kein kleines Mädchen. Ist Maria . . . ? 12) grosse. Das ist keine grosse Uhr. Ist das . . . ? 13) schwerer. Das ist kein schwerer Tisch. Ist das . . . ? 14) weisse. Das ist keine weisse Mauer. Ist das . . . ? 15) jung. Frau Schmidt ist nicht jung. Ist Frau Schmidt . . . ? 16) schwere. Das ist keine schwere Lektion. Ist das . . . ? 17) leichte. Das ist keine leichte Hausaufgabe. Ist das . . . ? 18) rot. Das Buch ist nicht rot. Ist das Buch . . . ? 19) grosse. Das ist keine grosse Buchhandlung. Ist das . . . ?

20) klein. Der Tisch ist nicht klein. Ist der Tisch . . . ? 21) lauter. Das ist
kein lauter Wecker. Ist das . . . ? 22) weisse. Das ist keine weisse Maus. Ist
das . . . ? 23) armer. Das ist kein armer Mann. Ist das . . . ? 24) neues. Das
ist kein neues Feuerzeug. Ist das . . . ? 25) alte. Das ist keine alte Schachtel.
Ist das . . . ? 26) junges. Brigitte ist kein junges Mädchen. Ist Brigitte . . . ?
27) starker, dicker. Das ist kein starker, dicker Mann. Ist das . . . ? 28)
kleiner. Peter ist kein kleiner Junge. Ist Peter . . . ?

Lektion 3, page 12

1) Die Autos sind nicht neu. Ist das Auto neu? 2) Das sind keine langen
Strassen. Ist das eine lange Strasse? 3) Das sind keine starken Männer. Ist
das ein starker Mann? 4) Das sind keine kleinen Kinder. Ist das ein kleines
Kind? 5) Das sind keine schwarzen Schuhe. Ist das ein schwarzer Schuh?
6) Das sind keine blauen Taschentücher. Ist das ein blaues Taschentuch?
7) Das sind keine modernen Kleider. Ist das ein modernes Kleid? 8) Das sind
keine weissen Hüte. Ist das ein weisser Hut? 9) Das sind keine leichten
Hausaufgaben. Ist das eine leichte Hausaufgabe? 10) Das sind keine kurzen
Hosen. Ist das eine kurze Hose? 11) Das sind keine grünen Handschuhe. Ist
das ein grüner Handschuh? 12) Das sind keine grossen Zimmer. Ist das ein
grosses Zimmer? 13) Das sind keine langen Röcke. Ist das ein langer Rock?
14) Das sind keine schwarzen Anzüge; Ist das ein schwarzer Anzug? 15) Das
sind keine breiten Schlipse. Ist das ein breiter Schlips? 16) Das sind keine
braunen Jacken. Ist das eine braune Jacke? 17) Das sind keine langen
Zigaretten. Ist das eine lange Zigarette? 18) Die Lektionen sind nicht
schwer. Ist die Lektion schwer? 19) Das sind keine guten Lehrerinnen. Ist
das eine gute Lehrerin? 20) Die Strassen sind nicht breit. Ist die Strasse
breit? 21) Das sind keine weissen Wände. Ist das weisse Wand? 22) Das sind
keine grossen Häuser. Ist das ein grosses Haus? 23) Das sind keine alten
Uhren. Ist das eine alte Uhr? 24) Die Parks sind nicht grün. Ist der Park
grün? 25) Das sind keine schönen Bilder. Ist das ein schönes Bild? 26) Die
Abende sind nicht lang. Ist der Abend lang? 27) Das sind keine jungen
Töchter. Ist das eine junge Tochter? 28) Das sind keine schlechten
Menschen. Ist das ein schlechter Mensch?

Lektion 3, page 13

1) kleines 2) kleine 3) schwachen 4) braunen 5) neuen 6) alter 7) kurze
8) schöner 9) schweren 10) reiche 11) armer 12) rotes 13) grüne
14) grosser 15) gute 16) schlechter.

Lektion 3, page 14

1) die neuen Hüte 2) die alten Frauen 3) die grossen Bäume 4) die kleinen
Kinder 5) die neuen Autos 6) die jungen Mütter 7) die kleinen Schwestern
8) die reichen Männer 9) die blauen Seen 10) die roten Taxis 11) die

grünen Parks 12) die roten Äpfel 13) lange Abende 14) die jungen Väter
15) grüne Äpfel 16) die kleinen Brüder 17) die blauen Meere 18) die guten
Menschen 19) die kleinen Schwestern 20) blaue Augen 21) schwarze Taxis
22) die neuen Kinos 23) die schönen Töchter 24) schlechte Bilder 25)
weisse Hemden 26) breite Schlipse 27) die schwarzen Anzüge 28) die
kurzen Tage 29) die weissen Hosen 30) die grossen Zoos.

Lektion 3, page 15
1) Wie geht es Ihnen? 2) Es ist so spät. 3) Das ist neue Kleidung. 4) Seine
jungen Schwestern sind klein. 5) Der alte Mann ist dick. 6) Das sind grüne
Bäume. 7) Die roten Bücher sind gross. 8) Die neuen Handschuhe sind
weiss. 9) Was ist los? 10) Nichts Besonderes. 11) Ist das alles? 12) Das
sind breite Strassen. 13) Bitte. 14) Die Hausaufgaben sind lang, aber leicht.

Lektion 3, page 15
1) Grosse Wagen sind laut. Sind grosse Wagen . . . ? 2) Das sind weisse
Hemden. Sind das . . . ? 3) Das sind grosse Bäume. Sind das . . . ? 4) Grosse
Männer sind stark. Sind grosse Männer . . . ? 5) Das sind schwarze Strümpfe.
Sind das . . . ? 6) Das Buch und das Bild sind blau. Sind das Buch . . . ?
7) Das sind schwarze Taxis. Sind das . . . ? 8) Die Lektionen sind leicht. Sind
die Lektionen . . . ? 9) Die Hausaufgabe ist schwer. Ist die Hausaufgabe . . . ?
10) Das weisse Papier ist dünn. Ist das . . . ? 11) Der neue Pullover ist blau.
Ist der neue Pullover . . . ? 12) Das sind enge Strassen. Sind das . . . ?

Lektion 4, page 19
1) Ihre Hausaufgabe ist nicht schwer. 2) Deine Augen sind nicht blau.
3) Seine Ohren sind nicht gross und rot. 4) Das Buch ist nicht dein (Ihr,
euer) Buch. Es ist nicht deins (Ihres, eures). 5) Paris ist nicht in der Nähe
von London. 6) Seine blaue Hose ist nicht kurz. 7) Ihr Kind ist nicht in
Paris. 8) Das ist nicht unser Wagen. 9) Das ist nicht ihr Kleid. Das ist nicht
ihres. 10) Die Buchhandlung ist nicht weit von hier. 11) Seine Biene ist
nicht reich. 12) Dein (Ihr, euer) Wagen ist nicht dort. 13) Ihr Kerl ist nicht
schwach. 14) Mein neues Haus ist nicht in der Nähe von Hamburg. 15) Mein
alter Freund ist nicht hier. 16) Mein Mantel ist nicht rot und deiner auch
nicht. 17) Seine Frau ist nicht dick. 18) Unsre Lektion ist nicht schwer.
19) Der kleine See ist nicht dort drüben. 20) Ihre Nägel sind nicht rot.
21) Mein brauner Regenschirm ist nicht neu. 22) Seine Nase ist nicht gross.

Lektion 4, page 20
1) deine 2) meins 3) unsres 4) seine 5) ihre 6) ihrer 7) ihre 8) ihre
9) mein(e)s 10) seiner 11) unsre 12) eurer 13) ihrer 14) ihre 15) eure
16) seine 17) unsre 18) deine 19) meiner 20) ihre 21) meiner 22) unsre
23) seiner 24) mein(e)s 25) deiner.

Lektion 4, page 21

1) neuer 2) braunen 3) neues 4) neues 5) neue 6) breite 7) rotes
8) grünen 9) grossen 10) kleinen 11) alte 12) neue.

Lektion 4, page 22

1) eine weisse Katze 2) die schwarze Maus 3) grosse Hunde 4) ein schwerer
Tisch 5) die schwarzen Stühle 6) eine weisse Wand 7) mein neues Telefon
8) ihr blauer Kugelschreiber 9) dein kurzer Bleistift 10) ihr alter Wecker
11) meine neue Armbanduhr 12) grosse Uhren 13) eine kleine Tür 14) das
kleine rote Buch 15) unsre neue Buchhandlung 16) meine schwere Hausaufgabe 17) schöne Frauen 18) leise Musik 19) die breiten Strassen 20) ein
starker Mann 21) das dicke Papier 22) ein dünnes Mädchen 23) eine leichte
Lektion 24) ihr alter Wagen (altes Auto) 25) die reichen Männer 26) arme
Kerle 27) seine neue Biene 28) ein reicher Typ 29) kleine Kinder 30) das
dicke Mädchen 31) eine braune Schachtel 32) der grosse Schlüssel 33) ihre
schwarzen Schuhe 34) weisse Socken 35) die grünen Hausschuhe 36) ein
schwerer Aschenbecher 37) neue Feuerzeuge 38) die lange Pfeife 39) ein
grüner Hut 40) ein weisser Regenmantel 41) lange Mäntel 42) ein enges
Hemd 43) der blaue Schlips 44) seine neuen Jacken 45) ihre schwarzen
Strümpfe 46) breite Hosen 47) die neuen Stiefel 48) ein langer Schal 49)
weisse Taschentücher 50) die alte Tafel 51) weisse Kreide 52) ein kurzer
Nagel 53) der alte Vater 54) rote Bilder 55) der grüne Park 56) die grossen
Fenster 57) ihre grünen Augen 58) seine roten Ohren 59) ein roter Mund
60) ihre langen Beine.

Lektion 5, page 24

1) Es ist zehn vor vier. 2) Es ist viertel vor drei. 3) Es ist sechs Uhr in New
York und Mittag in Bonn. 4) Halb fünf? Einverstanden! 5) Samstag um
Mitternacht? Auf keinen Fall! 6) Es ist nicht viertel vor eins, es ist viertel
nach eins. 7) Ist die Lektion um halb zwei? 8) Fünf vor sechs oder fünf
nach sechs, es ist mir einerlei. 9) Ist es halb acht oder halb neun? 10) Vier
Uhr am Morgen oder am Nachmittag?

Lektion 5, page 25

1) Sind jene Häuser weit von Berlin? 2) Sind jene Flugzeuge deine? 3) Sind
diese Zimmer gross? 4) Sind jene Hemden eng? 5) Sind diese Uhren meine
und jene ihre? 6) Sind jene Kleider sexy.

Lektion 5, page 26

1) dieser, jener 2) dieses, jenes 3) dieser, jener 4) diese, jene 5) dieses,
jenes 6) diese, jene 7) dieser, jener 8) dieser, jener 9) dieses, jenes 10)
diese, jene 11) dieser, jener 12) dieses, jenes 13) diese, jene 14) dieser,
jener 15) dieser, jener 16) diese, jene 17) dieses, jenes 18) dieses, jenes

19) diese, jene 20) dieses, jenes 21) dieser, jener 22) dieser, jener 23)
dieses, jenes 24) dieses, jenes

Lektion 5, page 27

1) welcher 2) welcher 3) welches 4) welcher 5) welche 6) welche
7) welche 8) welcher 9) welche 10) welcher 11) welches 12) welches
13) welches 14) welcher 15) welches 16) welcher 17) welches 18) welche
19) welche 20) welcher 21) welche 22) welche(s) 23) welche 24) welches
25) welche 26) welche 27) welches 28) welcher 29) welcher 30) welche
31) welcher 32) welcher 33) welche 34) welche 35) welcher 36) welcher
37) welche 38) welche 39) welcher 40) welche

Lektion 5, page 28

1) Welches Buch ist meins? Dieses oder jenes? 2) Januar ist natürlich ein
kalter Monat. 3) Welche Jahreszeit ist heiss: Winter oder Sommer? 4) Wie
spät ist es? Es ist Mitternacht. 5) Dieser Wagen ist weiss, aber jener ist
schwarz. 6) Ist morgen Dienstag? 7) Ist das dein Taxi oder meins?
8) Diese U-Bahn ist voll, aber jene ist leer. 9) Dieser Bahnhof ist nicht weit
von hier. 10) Viertel vor zehn? Das geht klar!

Lektion 5, page 28

1) Diese Frau ist (nicht) dünn, aber jene ist (nicht) dick. Sind diese Frauen
. . . ? 2) Ein weisser Wagen ist (nicht) schön. Sind weisse Wagen . . . ?
3) Das kleine Kind ist (nicht) hier. Sind die . . . ? 4) Jenes Hemd ist (nicht)
weiss, aber dieses ist (nicht) schwarz. Sind jene . . . ? 5) Diese Buch ist
(nicht) neu, aber jenes ist (nicht) alt. Sind diese . . . ? 6) Ein grüner Park ist
(nicht) in der Nähe. Sind grüne . . . ? 7) Dieses neue Buch ist (nicht)
interessant. Sind diese . . . ? 8) Mein brauner Pullover ist (nicht) schmutzig.
Sind meine . . . ? 9) Jener Rock ist (nicht) eng, aber dieser ist (nicht) weit.
Sind jene . . . ? 10) Dieser Tag ist (nicht) kurz. Sind diese . . . ? 11) Mein
alter Freund ist (nicht) hier. Sind meine . . . ? 12) Dieser warme Monat ist
(nicht) schön. Sind diese . . . ? 13) Dieser Kerl ist (nicht) interessant. Sind
diese . . . ? 14) Diese U-Bahn ist (nicht) voll. Sind diese . . . ? 15) Diese
Lektion ist (nicht) langweilig. Sind diese . . . ? 16) Diese Strasse ist (nicht)
gefährlich, aber jene ist (nicht) sicher. Sind diese . . . ? 17) Jene Flasche ist
(nicht) leer. Sind jene . . . ? 18) Dieser Lehrer ist (nicht) gut, aber jener ist
(nicht) schlecht. Sind diese . . . ?

Lektion 6, page 32

1) ist 2) bin 3) ist 4) ist 5) sind 6) seid 7) sind 8) ist 9) bin 10) ist.

Lektion 6, page 32

1) Er ist kein langsamer Schüler. Ist er ein . . . ? 2) Dezember ist kein kalter
Monat. Ist Dezember . . . ? 3) Wir sind keine reichen Geschäftsmänner. Sind

wir . . . ? 4) Sie sind keine gefährlichen Bullen. Sind sie . . . ? 5) Sie sind
keine hübsche Lehrerin. Sind Sie . . . ? 6) Das ist keine langweilige Arbeit.
Ist das . . . ? 7) Sie sind keine schwierigen Direktoren. Sind sie . . . ? 8) Wir
sind keine glücklichen Leute. Sind wir . . . ? 9) Er ist kein starker Kerl. Ist
er . . . ? 10) Sie haben nicht recht. Haben sie . . . ?

Lektion 6, page 33
1) Er ist ein guter Lehrer und ich auch. 2) Er ist nicht sehr gross und sie
auch nicht. 3) Unsre Schule ist nicht sehr gross und eure auch nicht. 4) Du
bist Student und ich auch. 5) Wir sind nicht in Frankfurt und ihr auch nicht.
6) Sie ist eine gute Studentin und du auch. 7) Du bist Amerikaner(in) und
ich auch. 8) Sie sind keine guten Freunde und ihr auch nicht. 9) Sie haben
recht und wir auch. 10) Wir sind nicht traurig und ihr auch nicht. 11) Diese
Typen sind nicht interessant und jene auch nicht. 12) Diese U-Bahn ist leer
und jene auch. 13) Januar ist kein heisser Monat und Februar auch nicht.
14) Meine Biene ist hübsch und deine auch. 15) Diese Strasse ist nicht
sicher und jene auch nicht.

Lektion 6, page 34
1) Wir sind keine schlechten Sekretare. 2) Sie sind keine glücklichen Kerle.
3) Ihr seid keine guten Krankenschwestern. 4) Sie sind nicht meine guten
Freunde. 5) Die neuen Krankenhäuser sind nicht in der Nähe. 6) Diese
Arbeiten sind nicht schmutzig. 7) Welche Lektionen sind nicht schwierig,
diese oder jene? 8) Diese braunen Stühle sind nicht meine.
9) Diese Probleme sind nicht einfach. 10) Sind wir keine Studentinnen?
11) Ihr seid keine guten Studenten. 12) Die kleinen Kinder sind nicht sehr
hübsch.

Lektion 6, page 34
1) Ich möchte Ihnen Peter vorstellen. 2) Welcher Wagen ist langsam? —
Jener! 3) Ist er ein guter Student? 4) Ja, ich glaube. 5) Sind diese Filme
interessant? 6) Ist das zu viel Arbeit? 7) Danke, es ist genug. 8) Dieses
Buch ist langweilig, aber jenes ist interessant. 9) Gott sei Dank! Diese
Lektion ist leicht. 10) Entschuldigen Sie, bitte! Was bedeutet das? 11)
Welche Hemden sind schmutzig? Jene dort drüben! 12) Er ist ein Bulle!
Das ist schade.

Lektion 7, page 36
1) habe 2) hat 3) habt 4) haben 5) hat 6) hat 7) haben 8) haben 9) hat
10) hat.

Lektion 7, page 38
1) Sie hat nichts. 2) Er hat noch ein Auto(einen Wagen). 3) Ich bin nicht
mehr in Berlin. 4) Es ist noch nicht Mitternacht. 5) Er ist nicht mehr bei

der Arbeit. 6) Niemand ist in der Schule. 7) Wir sind nie zu Hause. 8) Wir haben keine Probleme mehr. 9) Ich bin kein Kind mehr. 10) Sie ist nie bei der Arbeit. 11) Er ist noch kein Doktor. 12) Du bist nicht mehr traurig.

Lektion 7, page 39
1) Hast du etwas? Ich habe nichts. 2) Hat er noch einen Wagen? Er hat keinen Wagen mehr. 3) Bist du noch in Berlin? Ich bin nicht mehr in Berlin. 4) Ist jemand zu Hause? Niemand ist zu Hause. 5) Hat er schon eine neue Biene? Er hat noch keine neue Biene. 6) Ist es schon Mitternacht? Es ist noch nicht Mitternacht. 7) Haben wir immer Schwierigkeiten? Wir haben nie Schwierigkeiten. 8) Haben Sie noch eine Arbeit? Ich habe keine Arbeit mehr. 9) Ist er immer bei der Arbeit? Er ist nie bei der Arbeit. 10) Ist jemand in der Schule? Niemand ist in der Schule.

Lektion 7, page 39
1) Ich habe eine schwarze Katze 2) einen schweren Tisch 3) ein neues Telefon 4) einen neuen Kugelschreiber 5) einen starken Mann 6) meinen alten Wagen 7) einen reichen Typ 8) eine braune Schachtel 9) den kleinen Schlüssel 10) den grünen Aschenbecher 11) einen schwarzen Schuh 12) rote Schuhe 13) ein enges Hemd 14) einen braunen Stiefel 15) einen weissen Regenmantel 16) den grünen Hut 17) einen interessanten Freund 18) einen langweiligen Bruder 19) blaue Augen 20) einen roten Mund.

Lektion 7, page 40
1) Der Schüler hat (k)einen guten Lehrer. 2) Ich habe (keine) Schwierig-keiten. 3) ich habe (k)einen guten Job. 4) Das Zimmer hat (k)eine niedrige Decke. 5) Die Woche hat (nicht) acht Tage. 6) Wir haben (k)einen kalten Sommer. 7) Der Park hat (k)einen grossen See. 8) Ich habe (k)eine schwarze Katze. 9) Frau Schmidt hat (k)einen neuen Hund. 10) Sie haben (du hast) (k)einen schönen Hut.

Lektion 7, page 40
1) ein grosses. Die Zimmer haben grosse Fenster. 2) einen neuen. Die Direktoren haben neue Wagen. 3) eine schöne, einen schönen. Die Kinder haben schöne Katzen und schöne Hunde. 4) einen kleinen, grosse. Die Parks haben kleine Seen und grosse Bäume. 5) keinen, kein. Wir haben keine Wagen und keine Fahrräder. 6) einen neuen. Meine Bienen haben neue Freunde. 7) einen schweren. Wir haben schwere Köpfe. 8) schwarzes, einen weissen, einen roten. Die Casanovas haben schwarze Hemden, weisse Schlipse, und rote Anzüge.

Lektion 8, page 44
1) wartest. Wartest du . . . ? 2) schneit, regnet. Schneit und regnet es? 3) bedeutet. Bedeutet sie dir . . . ? 4) finde. Finde ich es? 5) antwortet.

Antwortet er . . .? 6) hören. Hört ihr . . .? 7) bedeutet. Bedeutet dieser
Film etwas? 8) arbeitet. Arbeitet ihr . . .? 9) finden. Finden Sie . . .?
10) antwortet. Antwortet er . . .? 11) antworten. Antworten wir . . .?
12) findet. Findet ihr . . .? 13) warten (wartet). Warten(wartet) sie . . .?
14) arbeitest. Arbeitest du . . .?

Lektion 8, page 45
1) wiederhole. Wiederhole ich . . .? 2) tut. Tut es . . .? 3) macht. Macht
das etwas? 4) verstehe. Verstehe ich etwas? 5) sprecht. Sprecht ihr . . .?
6) gehst. Gehe ich . . .? 7) fragt, antworten. Fragt ihr, antworten wir?
8) kommen. Kommen Sie . . .? 9) bleibe. Bleibe ich . . .? 10) glaube, ist.
Glaube ich, er . . .? 11) studiert. Studiert ihr . . .? 12) gehen. Gehen wir
. . .? 13) geht. Geht es . . .? 14) hasse. Hasse ich . . .? 15) malocht. Malocht
er . . .? 16) hast. Habe ich . . .? 17) zeigt. Zeigt das Kino . . .? 18) lehrt,
lernen. Lehrt der Lehrer, und lernen die Schüler? 19) kommst. Kommst du
. . .? 20) rauche. Rauche ich gewöhnlich . . .? 21) kommt. Kommt ihr
. . .? 22) schneit. Schneit es . . .? 23) zeige. Zeige ich mein . . .? 24)
glaubt. Glaubt er etwas? 25) bleiben. Bleiben sie . . .?

Lektion 8, page 46
1) brichst 2) sieht 3) lest 4) kann 5) schläfst 6) triffst 7) trägst 8) fangen
(fängt) 9) fährst 10) nimmst 11) geben 12) stiehlst 13) schlägt 14) rätst
15) isst 16) stirbt 17) fangen 18) empfiehlt (empfehlen) 19) will 20) hilft
21) befiehlt 22) wird 23) brätst 24) wäscht (waschen) 25) entlässt 26) ist
27) tue 28) wirft.

Lektion 8, page 47
1) Ich lerne seit Mai deutsch. 2) Er arbeitet jeden Tag schwer. 3) Kommst
du morgen? 4) Sie lesen jetzt. 5) Sie spricht seit zwei Stunden. 6) Studiert
sie? 7) Es regnet und schneit. 8) Wir essen, aber dieses Zeug ist schlecht.
9) Lernst du Englisch? 10) Ich arbeite nur am Morgen. 11) Wer ist an der
Reihe? 12) Weiss sie, wo sie ist? 13) Liebt sie den Schuft? 14) Gott sei
Dank! Ich arbeite Samstag nicht. 15) Ich warte seit heute mittag auf dich.
16) Ich verstehe nicht: er ist verrückt nach dieser Biene. 17) Sie liest nur
gute Bücher. 18) Stelle ich zu viele Fragen? 19) Ich arbeite viel, aber du
faulenzst. 20) Er nimmt jeden Tag die U-Bahn. 21) Kennst du meine
kleine Schwester? 22) Ich beginne jeden Tag am Mittag. 23) Warum hilfst
du nicht? 24) Sprichst du deutsch? 25) Er spricht immer so langsam.

Lektion 9, page 50
1) Wen fragst du? 2) Wer ist zu Hause? 3) Was esst ihr? 4) Was ist gut?
5) Wen siehst du? 6) Wer ist im Büro? 7) Wen siehst du im Moment nicht?
8) Was bestellst du? 9) Wer schläft den ganzen Tag? 10) Was schmeckt sehr gut?

11) Wen triffst du? 12) Was liest sie? 13) Was hat deine Schwester? 14) Wen siehst du? 15) Auf wen wartest du?

Lektion 9, page 51
1) Ich denke, dass sie jeden Tag arbeitet. 2) Ich denke, dass meine Schwester zu Hause ist. 3) Ich denke, dass er das Buch liest. 4) Ich denke, dass niemand zu Hause bleibt. 5) Ich denke, dass der Bahnhof in der Nähe ist.

Lektion 9, page 52
1) Ich weisse nicht, wer kommt. 2) Er ist dick, weil er Brot liebt. 3) Ich denke, dass er bei der Arbeit ist. 4) Es ist schade, dass du zu spät bist. 5) Ich hoffe, dass er pünktlich kommt. 6) Ich kann nicht warten, weil ich in Eile bin. 7) Denkst du, dass er Amerikaner ist? 8) Ich frage, was du liest. 9) Natürlich weiss ich, dass du seit März hier bist. 10) Bist du müde, weil du viel arbeitest? 11) Ich schlafe den ganzen Tag, weil ich in Ferien bin. 12) Kannst du Peter sagen, dass seine Biene wartet? 13) Er fährt einen schnellen Wagen, weil er immer in Eile ist. 14) Er hofft, dass du nicht zu spät bist. 15) Ich lerne deutsch, weil ich nach München gehen möchte. 16) Ich kaufe diesen Regenmantel nicht, weil er teuer ist. 17) Es tut mir leid, ich weiss nicht, wo der Bahnhof ist. 18) Ich bin an der Reihe. 19) Er ist spät, weil er zu Fuss kommt. 20) Ich weiss mehr oder weniger, wer er ist 21) Denkst du, dass er ein Schuft ist? 22) Das ist das Restaurant, wo wir immer essen. 23) Weisst du, wieviel Kinder sie hat? 24) Ich möchte wissen, wann sie zu Hause ist. 25) Ich muss sagen, dass ich verrückt nach Musik bin.

Lektion 9, page 53
1) eine 2) einen 3) — 4) — 5) — 6) einen 7) eine 8) — 9) einen 10) — 11) ein 12) — 13) — 14) ein.

Lektion 9, page 54
1) Wenn ich viel Zeit habe, komme ich. 2) Wenn der Direktor nicht im Büro ist, arbeite ich nicht. 3) Wenn ich kein Geld habe, bleibe ich zu Hause. 4) Wenn der Lehrer gut ist, lerne ich viel. 5) Wenn das Wetter schön ist, gehe ich spazieren. 6) Wenn ich mit der U-Bahn fahre, komme ich pünktlich. 7) Wenn ich Ferien habe, lese ich viel. 8) Wenn mein Hemd schmutzig ist, wasche ich es.

Lektion 9, page 55
1) Wenn ich müde bin, gehe ich schlafen. 2) Wenn das Wetter schlecht ist, bleibe ich zu Hause. 3) Wenn der Doktor Zeit hat, kommt er. 4) Wenn das Kleid teuer ist, kaufst du es? 5) Wenn das Zimmer gross ist, nehme ich es.

Lektion 9, page 55

1) Wenn der Kellner kommt, bestelle ich (k)ein Steak. 2) Wenn das Kleid billig ist, kauft sie es (nicht). 3) Wenn ich Zeit habe, gehe ich (nicht) zu Fuss. 4) Wenn die Sekretärin im Büro ist, arbeitet sie (nicht). 5) Wenn ich Geld habe, gehen wir (nicht) einkaufen. 6) Wenn wir reich sind, fahren wir (nicht) nach Hawaii. 7) Wenn ich in Eile bin, nehme ich (nicht) den Bus. 8) Wenn sie viel trinkt, ist sie (nicht) blau. 9) Wenn ich einen Bullen sehe, bin ich (nicht) glücklich. 10) Wenn einer von beiden gehen muss, geht er (nicht). 11) Wenn die Flasche leer ist, kaufe ich (k)eine neue. 12) Wenn der Kurs interessant ist, lernen wir (nicht) viel. 13) Wenn es Sommer ist, nimmt er (keine) Ferien. 14) Wenn es mir gleich ist, sage ich etwas (nichts). 15) Wenn sie einen schweren Kopf hat, nimmt sie (k)ein Aspirin.

Lektion 10, page 57

1) dem Kind 2) der Frau 3) den Freunden 4) dem Mann und der Frau 5) dem Kellner 6) dem Freund 7) den Kindern 8) der Freundin 9) dem Lehrer oder der Lehrerin 9) dem Doktor und der Krankenschwester.

Lektion 10, page 58

1) dem 2) dem 3) dem 4) den 5) dem 6) dem 7) der 8) dem 9) dem 10) dem 11) dem 12) dem 13) der 14) dem, dem.

Lektion 10, page 59

1) Ich will gut deutsch sprechen. 2) Sie essen oft am Abend im Restaurant. 3) Er kommt selten pünktlich. 4) Wir trinken manchmal Kaffee bei der Arbeit. 5) Der Lehrer stellt den Schülern von Zeit zu Zeit Fragen. 6) Ich gebe meinem Freund ein Buch. 7) Sie sagen immer alles ihren Eltern. 8) Ich möchte der Musik zuhören. 9) Sonntag zeigen wir den Kindern einen Disney-Film. 10) Er kommt endlich. 11) Ich zeige den Freunden mein neues Haus. 12) Wir fahren im Januar nach Berlin. 13) Heute komme ich mit der U-Bahn. 14) Manchmal hilft er seiner Mutter.

Lektion 10, page 60

1) Dieser grosse gelbe Wagen gehört meinem reichen Boss. 2) Wenn du Lamm bestellst, bestelle ich Fisch. 3) Ich habe Lust auf ein kaltes Getränk. 4) Wollen Sie Ihr Steak durchbraten oder blutig? 5) Wieviel kostet ein Kaffee hier? 6) Wenn das Restaurant teuer ist, nehme ich nur Pommes Frites. 7) Gehört diese graue Katze deiner kleinen Schwester. 8) Sie essen seit Montag Fisch. 9) Ich bin im Begriff zu gehen. 10) Er ist allein, deshalb ist er traurig. 11) Ich hoffe, dass dieser schlechte Salat kostenlos ist. 12) Ich kann nicht mehr essen, weil ich satt bin. 13) Ich muss sagen, dass Ihr Nachtisch sehr gut schmeckt. 14) Wenn du Zeit hast, kannst du deinem Bruder helfen. 15) Mein Wagen geht nicht, ich muss zu Fuss gehen. 16) Was

für einen Wagen fahren Sie? 17) Wenn du willst, wasche ich den Wagen.
18) Wenn du den Bus nimmst, kommst du zu spät. 19) Wenn er sein
Mädchen schlägt, geht sie. 20) Ich gehe schlafen, weil ich müde bin. 21)
Worauf haben Sie Lust? 22) Im Moment bin ich nicht hungrig. 23) Wenn
ich meinen neuen Wagen noch nicht habe, gehst du allein. 24) Empfehlen
Sie dieses Buch oder jenes? 25) Wenn es regnet, gehe ich nicht.

Lektion 10, page 61

1) meinem kleinen 2) ihrem neuen 3) dem alten Herrn 4) dem hübschen
5) den kleinen Kindern 6) dem jungen 7) meinem guten 8) seiner neuen
9) seinen schlechten Schülern(seinem schlechten Schüler) 10) ihrem, ihrer
11) ihrem neuen 12) dem alten 13) dem 14) ihrem.

Lektion 11, page 64

1) Morgen stehe ich früh auf. 2) Sie nimmt nicht zu, obwohl sie viel isst.
3) Ich höre auf, weil die Arbeit schmutzig ist. 4) Sie gibt viel Geld aus.
5) Wir gehen am Freitagabend aus. 6) Der Bus kommt um zehn Uhr an.
7) Stehen Sie früh auf? 8) Sie sieht immer gut aus. 9) Setzen Sie die
Arbeiten fort? 10) Wenn du weggehst, bin ich traurig. 11) Was schlägst
du für das Wochenende vor? 12) Er prüft immer sein Geld nach.

Lektion 11, page 65

1) weg. It's late, I'm leaving. 2) an. It depends on my girlfriend. 3) ab. It
depends on my friend. 4) aus. This house is too old, I'm moving out. 5)
auf. I don't get up early. 6) zu. You aren't listening. 7) zu. She admits that
I'm right. 8) vor. What do you suggest? 9) zu. If you eat too much, you'll
gain weight. 10) an. When does the film start? 11) auf. I'm stopping
because I'm tired. 12) aus. He spends a lot of money. 13) ein. Who are you
hiring? 14) herein. She always takes him in. 15) aus. We're taking off our
sweaters because it's hot. 16) frei. They're releasing the bastard. 17) durch.
If he doesn't learn, he'll fail. 18) an. I'll call you tomorrow. 19) auf. The
sun rises at five. 20) fort. When are we continuing the lesson? 21) an. She's
been looking at her friend for a long time. 22) an. He's lighting his pipe.
23) an. If it rains, I'll put on my raincoat. 24) weh. My tooth hurts. 25) gut.
A glass of whisky's always a relief. 26) zustande. He doesn't manage
anything. 27) vor. I prefer coffee. 28) nach. He's checking the bill.

Lektion 11, page 66

1) Wann gehst du weg? 2) Er gibt viel Geld aus. 3) Er zündet seine Pfeife an.
4) Er fängt um acht Uhr an und hört um halb sechs auf. 5) Er zieht seinen Anzug
aus. 6) Er zieht aus. 7) Das kommt auf meinen Vater an (hängt von meinem
Vater ab). 8) Tut dein Kopf weh? 9) Ich rufe dich heute abend an. 10) Ich
hoffe, dass die Polizei den Schuft festnimmt. 11) Du musst zugeben, dass sie

nett ist. 12) Er legt seine Biene immer herein. 13) Ich denke, dass sie meinen Freund einstellen. 14) Seit wann nimmt sie ab? 15) Ziehen Sie Kaffee oder Tee vor? 16) Er packt seine Kleidung ein. 17) Er bringt nichts zustande. 18) Was hast du für das Wochenende vor? 19) Auf wen kommt es an? (Von wem hängt es ab?) 20) Wen stellen sie ein? 21) Morgen abend gehe ich aus. 22) Warum legst du auf? 23) Ich möchte die Lektion fortsetzen. 24) Sie sieht glücklich aus. 25) Warum legst du sie herein? 26) Wann fängt das Abendessen an? 27) Sie zieht ihr sexy Kleid an. 28) Ich wache immer am Mittag auf.

Lektion 12, page 69
1) dem 2) einem 3) dem 4) dem 5) der 6) dem 7) der 8) einem 9) der 10) wem

Lektion 12, page 70
1) den 2) einen, eine 3) wen 4) meine 5) den 6) die 7) das 8) den, den 9) seine 10) seine 11) die 12) meine 13) den 14) wen

Lektion 12, page 72
1) Ja, er muss soviel Geld ausgeben. Nein, er braucht nicht soviel Geld auszugeben. 2) Ja, ich kann morgen abend kommen. Nein, ich kann nicht . . . 3) Ja, er muss mit seiner Freundin sprechen. Nein, er braucht nicht mit seiner Freundin zu sprechen. 4) Ja, du kannst (Nein, du kannst nicht) mit meinem Wagen fahren. 5) Ja, sie kann (Nein, sie kann nicht) englisch (sprechen). 6) Ja, du musst früh aufstehen. Nein, du brauchst nicht früh aufzustehen. 7) Ja, man muss hier Trinkgeld geben. Nein, man braucht hier kein Trinkgeld zu geben. 8) Ja, das kann (Nein, das kann nicht) vorkommen. 9) Ja, man kann (Nein, man kann nicht) so dumm sein. 10) Ja, ich muss (Nein, ich muss hier nicht) aussteigen. 11) Ja, Sie können (Nein, Sie können nicht) die Lektion fortsetzen. 12) Ja, Sie müssen sofort einziehen. Nein, Sie brauchen nicht sofort einzuziehen. 13) Ja, wir können (Nein, wir können nicht) hören. 14) Ja, die Bullen müssen den Mann freilassen. Nein, die Bullen brauchen den Mann nicht freizulassen./Nein, die Bullen müssen (dürfen) den Mann nicht freilassen. 15) Ja, Sie können (Nein, Sie können nicht) die Arbeit zurückweisen.

Lektion 12, page 73
1) Ich muss mit der Sekretärin sprechen, sie kommt nicht oft pünktlich. 2) Man muss verstehen, dass unregelmässige Verben nicht leicht zu lernen sind. 3) Ich kann dir nicht helfen, weil ich meine Hausaufgabe mache. 4) Wir können zu Fuss ins Restaurant gehen. 5) Wir müssen um Mitternacht spazierengehen. 6) Du brauchst es nicht jetzt zu machen. 7) Kannst du deutsch (sprechen)? 8) Ich brauche nicht zu gehen. 9) Kannst du es

machen? 10) Ich muss mit der U-Bahn zum Büro fahren. 11) Sie kann sehr gut englisch (sprechen). 12) Ich muss meinen Vater fragen. 13) Wir müssen heute nachmittag mit dem Lehrer sprechen. 14) Ich weiss nicht, ob er seine Frau liebt oder nicht. 15) Sie ist mit einem blöden Mann verheiratet. 16) Ich denke, dass er ledig ist, weil er bei seiner Mutter wohnt. 17) Du kannst es einem Verwandten, deiner Tante, zum Beispiel, geben. 18) Ich verstehe nicht, warum er gegen ihre Geschwister ist. 19) Meine Schwiegermutter geht um vier Uhr weg; Gott sei Dank! 20) Ich bin gegen diese Idee, obwohl es gerecht ist. 21) Sie geht immer ohne ihren Ehemann aus. 22) Er ruft immer um Mitternacht an; das ist zu spät. 23) Es tut gut, wieder zu Hause zu sein. 24) Wann kommen wir bei seinen Eltern an? 25) Kannst du, bitte, die Zeitung aufnehmen? 26) Sie sucht immer schöne Kleidung aus.

Lektion 13, page 76

1) Ja, sie kennt ihn seit Januar. 2) Ja, er bekommt ihn durch ihn. 3) Ja, er ist für sie. 4) Ja, sie kommt heute ohne ihn. 5) Er bekommt ihn morgen. 6) Ja, sie ist für mich. 7) Ja, ich verstehe Sie. 8) Ja, es ist für uns. 9) Ja, ihr könnt uns morgen anrufen. 10) Ja, wir können euch hören.

Lektion 13, page 77

1) ihn 2) er, sie 3) es 4) ihn 5) sie 6) sie 7) ihn 8) es, ihn 9) sie, sie 10) ihn 11) ihn 12) uns 13) euch 14) ihn 15) uns 16) ihn 17) euch 18) uns 19) sie 20) ihn 21) es 22) sie 23) sie 24) es 25) sie 26) ihn.

Lektion 13, page 78

1) Du musst jeden Morgen dein Bett machen. 2) Die Menge wartet auf die Direktoren. 3) Ist dein Schlafzimmer oben oder unten? 4) Deine Antwort ist richtig, aber seine ist falsch. 5) Sind Sie (bist du, seid ihr) sicher, dass seine Geschichte wahr ist? 6) Ich denke nicht, dass diese Geschichte wahr ist. 7) Ist es für ihn? 8) Sie arbeitet ganztags, obwohl sie fünf Kinder hat. 9) Es ist verschieden von meinem (meiner, meinen). 10) Du kannst den Aufzug nehmen, wenn du in Eile bist. 11) Du musst zugeben, dass jener Pelzmantel sehr teuer ist. 12) Es ist zu dumm, aber ihr Kleid ist das gleiche wie mein(e)s. 13) Wann geht die Sonne im Sommer auf? 14) Warum hörst du deinen Freunden nie zu, wenn sie etwas vorschlagen. 15) Sie ist dumm, sie denkt, dass ihr Diamant echt ist. 16) Wenn deine Schwiegermutter hier wohnt, ziehe ich aus. 17) Es kostet nicht viel, es ist wirklich billig. 18) Ich bin seit ungefähr einer Woche hier. 19) Essen Sie jeden Morgen Eier mit Speck? 20) Bedienen Sie sich, wenn Sie nicht auf das Dienstmädchen warten können. 21) Wenn der Film nicht spannend ist, gehe ich vorher weg. 22) Nehmen Sie sich Zeit, ich bin nicht in Eile. 23) Wenn seine Arbeit nachlässig ist, entlassen wir ihn. 24) Kannst du mir zehn Mark leihen (pumpen)? 25) Es tut mir leid, aber wir machen jetzt zu (schliessen jetzt).

26) Euer Wohnzimmer gefällt mir. 27) Ich kann dich (Sie, euch) nicht gut sehen und sie auch nicht. 28) Wer kennt sie?

Lektion 14, page 84
1) Sie sprechen oft mit ihm. 2) Er gehört ihm. 3) Ich erzähle sie ihnen.
4) Er zeigt sie ihnen. 5) Sie zeigen sie ihnen. 6) Ich leihe ihn ihm. 7) Ich habe ihn noch nicht lange. 8) Es tut ihm leid. 9) Es geht ihr gut. 10) Wir schreiben ihn euch. 11) Er hilft ihnen nie. 12) Gefällt sie dir? 13) Er erklärt sie ihnen. 14) Es gehört ihr. 15) Er zeigt ihn mir. 16) Ich komme mit ihr und ohne ihn. 17) Können Sie ihr helfen? 18) Sie fragen ihn, und er antwortet ihnen. 19) Sie folgen ihm. 20) Geht es ihm gut? 21) Es tut ihr leid, dass . . . 22) Er spricht mit ihm und mit ihr. 23) Er erzählt von ihnen. 24) Ich fahre mit ihr in die Stadt. 25) Er arbeitet mit ihnen. 26) Sie gefallen ihm.

Lektion 14, page 85
1) Wann brauchen Sie den Wagen? Ich brauche ihn Montag. 2) Wem gehört jenes Feuerzeug? Es gehört ihr. 3) Mit wem kommst du? Ich komme mit ihm. 4) Ich möchte es ihm geben. 5) Der Boss verreist den ganzen Monat. 6) Wieviel kostet eine Hin- und Rückfahrkarte? 7) Geben Sie mir einen Scheck, und ich gebe Ihnen das Geld. 8) Ich bin sicher, dass das Fahrrad dir gehört. 9) Wir können sie nur einmal pro Woche sehen. 10) Du musst mir alles erzählen. 11) Du darfst ihm nichts sagen (erzählen). 12) Können Sie mir etwas Geld leihen? 13) Vielleicht kennst du ihn besser. 14) Ist der Kies für mich. Ja, er ist für dich (Sie, euch). 15) Ich habe kein Bargeld bei mir. 16) Jeder Film mit diesem Schauspieler ist ausgezeichnet. 17) Von Zeit zu Zeit schreibt sie mir einen Brief. 18) Für wen reserviert er das Zimmer? 19) Diese Puppe gehört meiner kleinen Schwester. 20) Warten Sie seit ein Uhr auf mich? 21) Wenn das Wasser niedrig ist, kann man nicht schwimmen. 22) Ich denke, dass das Restaurant um Mitternacht schliesst. 23) Mein Bruder ist sehr nett, aber nicht sehr helle. 24) Kommt es auf Sie an? (Hängt es von Ihnen ab?) Nein, es kommt nicht auf mich allein an (Nein, es hängt nicht von mir allein ab). 25) Nimmst du die Wohnung? Ja, ich nehme sie. 26) Warum sind Sie gegen ihn? 27) Gefällt Ihnen dieses Buch? 28) Du musst einen neuen Badeanzug kaufen.

Lektion 15, page 89
1) soll 2) möchte 3) willst 4) darfst 5) will (wollen) 6) möchten 7) wollt 8) soll 9) sollst 10) will, darf 11) müsst 12) soll 13) möchtet 14) willst 15) möchte 16) dürfen, darf 17) will 18) möchtest.

Lektion 15, page 89
1) Du kannst morgen nicht kommen. 2) Ich möchte keinen neuen Wagen.

3) Er will es nicht machen. 4) Ich kann diese Arbeit nicht machen. 5) Du darfst deine Beine nicht auf den Tisch legen. 6) Du kannst nicht in mein Zimmer kommen. 7) Sie will kein neues Kleid kaufen. 8) Wir möchten nicht früh nach Hause gehen. 9) Du sollst diese Arbeit schnell beenden. 10) Soll ich dich heute nacht (abend) anrufen?

Lektion 15, page 90
1) Due darfst hier nicht rauchen. 2) Ich möchte in diesem See schwimmen. 3) Muss ich morgen kommen? 4) Soll ich Samstag kommen? 5) Er möchte ihr helfen, aber er kann nicht. 6) Du sollst Samstag arbeiten. 7) Sie müssen viel Geld machen, um jenes Auto zu kaufen. 8) Kann ich Ihnen seine Geschichte erzählen? 9) Ich darf es dir nicht sagen. 10) Ich möchte Weihnachten kommen. 11) Wenn ich es tun muss, tue ich es. (Wenn ich es machen muss, mache ich es.) 12) Möchten Sie meine Zigarette anzünden? 13) Das muss falsch sein. 14) Kannst du ihn verstehen? 15) Ich möchte mit dir kommen. 16) Kann ich das Fenster öffnen? 17) Die Kinder dürfen schwimmen gehen. 18) Du sollst mir jetzt zuhören. 19) Niemand kann immer gewinnen. 20) Sie dürfen nicht in diesem See schwimmen. 21) Sei (seien Sie, seid) nicht unglücklich, ich gehe mit dir (Ihnen, euch)! 22) Sprich (sprecht, sprechen Sie) mit ihm über die Geschichte! 23) Steig (steigt, steigen Sie) noch nicht aus. 24) Warten wir bis fünf Uhr auf sie! 25) Gehen wir ins Kino! 26) Gehen wir Silvester aus! 27) Vergiss (vergesst, vergessen Sie) es nicht!

Lektion 15, page 92
1) im. Wo arbeiten Sie jeden Morgen! 2) dem, zum. Wohin fahren Sie jeden Morgen mit dem Bus? 3) ins. Wohin gehen Sie jetzt? 4) am. Wo steht der alte Mann den ganzen Tag? 5) ans. Wohin geht die alte Dame? 6) am. Wo ist Peter gerade? 7) ans. Wohin geht er? 8) der, dem. Wo steht der Stuhl? 9) die, den. Wohin stellt sie den Stuhl? 10) im. Wo ist der Whisky? 11) ins. Wohin bringt er den Whisky? 12) der. Wo ist mein Sohn jeden Morgen? 13) die. Wohin geht ihr Sohn auch? 14) die. Wohin fahre ich morgen? 15) der. Wo wohnt meine Freundin? 16) dem. Wo liegen vier Bücher? 17) den. Wohin legt die Sekretärin die Bücher? 18) die. Wohin hängen wir das Bild sofort? 19) im, der. Wo hängt ein schönes Bild? 20) dem. Wo sitzt der kleine Hund? 21) den. Wohin setzt das Kind seinen Hund? 22) im. Wo sitzt meine Freundin schon? 23) den. Wohin steige ich schnell? 24) der. Wo studieren alle meine Freunde? 25) zur. Wohin geht er zweimal pro Woche? 26) die. Wohin gehen die Studenten? 27) der. Wo stehen viele Wagen? 28) die. Wohin stellt er seinen Wagen?

Lektion 16, page 94
1) den, dem. Welchen Mann kenne ich? 2) den, der. Welchen Bus nehmen wir? 3) die, die. Welche Frau ist das? 4) die. Welche Leute sind Amerikaner?

5) dem, der. Mit welchem Wagen fahre ich? 6) der, dem. Welcher Student ist sehr helle? 7) der, den. Welcher Zug ist das? 8) ins, das. In welches Kino gehe ich? 9) das, dem. Welches Buch ist das? 10) die, die. Welche Person kann es behalten? 11) der, die. Welcher Frau soll ich helfen? 12) den, dem. Welchen Schuft können die Bullen nicht mehr finden? 13) der, den. Welcher Mann bekommt viel Geld? 14) die, die. Welche Lektion ist nicht schwierig? 15) die, der. Welche Frau ist sehr reich? 16) den, der. Welchen Studenten frage ich? 17) die, der. Welche U-Bahn ist sehr alt? 18) dem, den. Welchem Mann schreibt sie?

Lektion 16, page 95
1) Ja, ich warte auf ihn. 2) Ja ich warte darauf. 3) Ja, er spricht über sie. 5) Ja, wir sprechen darüber. 5) Ja, sie kommt mit ihr. 6) Ja, ich komme damit. 7) Ja, ich sitze neben ihm. 8) Ja, er steht daneben. 9) Ja, es ist dafür. 10) Ja, er ist für sie.

Lektion 16, page 96
1) Das ist der Mann, mit dem Mary verheiratet ist. 2) Wer ist die Frau, auf die du seit heute morgen wartest? 3) Das Buch, das ich jetzt lese, ist sehr spannend. 4) Die Katze, mit der die Kinder spielen, ist meine. 5) Der Schauspieler, den du hasst, ist in diesem Film. 6) Der Pullover, den du anziehst, ist zu schmutzig. 7) Das sind die Freunde, die mit mir verreisen. 8) Das Mädchen, das sehr müde aussieht, geht jede Nacht aus. 9) Der Kerl, den sie liebt, ist Rechtsanwalt. 10) Dinge, die jeden Tag vorkommen, sind nicht sehr interessant. 11) Ich helfe der Sekretärin, die die Arbeit nicht allein machen kann. 12) Sie schreibt dem Mann, den sie seit einer Woche kennt.

Lektion 16, page 96
1) Worüber spricht er? Er spricht darüber. 2) Über wen sprechen wir? Wir sprechen über ihn. 3) Auf wen warten sie? Sie warten auf ihn. 4) Worauf warte ich immer noch? Ich warte immer noch darauf. 5) Für wen ist dieser Preis? Er ist für ihn. 6) Wofür ist das Geld? Es ist dafür. 7) Womit kommen sie? Sie kommen damit. 8) Mit wem kommt sie immer zum Rendezvous? Sie kommt immer mit ihr. 9) Zwischen wem sitze ich? Ich sitze zwischen ihnen. 10) Wozwischen steht er? Er steht dazwischen. 11) Womit sind wir fertig? Wir sind damit fertig. 12) Worauf liegt die junge Katze? Sie liegt darauf. 13) Wogegen ist der Lehrer? Er ist dagegen. 14) Gegen wen bin ich? Ich bin gegen sie.

Lektion 16, page 97
1) in 2) nach 3) an 4) an 5) auf 6) zu 7) in 8) auf, zu 9) in, zu 10) an, in.

Lektion 16, page 98

1) Gehen wir zuerst auf den Markt! Wohin gehen wir zuerst? 2) Viele Kinder spielen auf der Strasse. Wo spielen viele Kinder? 3) Wenn du Brot brauchst, musst du zum Bäcker gehen. Wohin muss ich gehen, wenn ich Brot brauche? 4) Trinken wir ein grosses Bier im Hofbräuhaus. Wo trinken wir ein . . . ? 5) Dieses Jahr möchte ich nach Heidelberg fahren? Wohin möchtest du dieses Jahr fahren? 6) Du kannst auf der Post telephonieren. Wo kann ich telephonieren? 7) Ich habe Zahnschmerzen, ich muss zum Zahnarzt gehen. Wohin musst du gehen? 8) Er muss jetzt zum Bahnhof gehen? Wohin muss er jetzt gehen? 9) Sie sind diesen Monat an der See. Wo sind sie diesen Monat? 10) Er geht heute nachmittag auf die Bank. Wohin geht er heute nachmittag?

Lektion 16, page 98

1) der 2) die 3) der 4) den 5) das (ins) 6) das (ans) 7) dem (am) 8) die 9) den 10) dem 11) den 12) dem 13) der (zur) 14) die 15) meinem 16) dem (am) 17) die, die 18) der

Lektion 16, page 99

1) Wir sind sechs. 2) In diesem Zimmer stehen (sind) drei Stühle. 3) Viele Kinder spielen im Park. 4) In diesem Büro arbeiten sieben Sekretärinnen. 5) Eine(r) von uns kann nicht kommen.

Lektion 16, page 100

1) Bleiben wir zu Hause, es ist zu kalt. 2) Es ist ziemlich heiss hier im Sommer. 3) Es ist selbstverständlich, dass Sie arbeiten, wenn Sie im Büro sind. 4) Es scheint, dass er sie sehr liebt. 5) Es ist wichtig, dass du mich heute abend anrufst. 6) Ist es möglich, dass ich die Arbeit morgen beende? 7) Es kommt vor, dass die Flugzeuge nach Frankfurt ein wenig spät sind. 8) Ich bin gern in den Bergen, wenn es schneit. 9) Es ist sicher, dass mein Boss nicht hier ist. 10) Es scheint mir, dass sie unrecht haben. 11) Es gibt immer viele Touristen in dieser Stadt. 12) Gibt es viel zu tun? 13) Gibt es Probleme mit dieser Lektion? 14) Es gibt ein nettes Restaurant in diesem Dorf. 15) Es gibt mehrere Tabletten gegen Zahnschmerzen. 16) Was gibt es zu sehen? 17) In diesem Ort gibt es nichts zu tun. 18) Gibt es viel Schnee im Winter? 19) Kommst du mit der U-Bahn oder mit dem Bus? 20) Ich muss nach dem Frühstück weggehen. 21) Es ist nicht sicher, dass er bei seiner Familie bleibt. 22) Es ist unmöglich, dass ich nach dem Mittagessen komme. 23) Es kommt vor, dass fünfzig Leute am Mittag hier sind. 24) Es kommt nie vor, dass ich etwas vergesse. 25) Es ist selbstverständlich, dass du mit deinem neuen Freund kommst. 26) Sogar im Januar ist es ziemlich warm hier. 27) In diesem Restaurant sind nur vier Leute. 28) Ein Mann, den ich nicht kenne, ist am Telefon.

Lektion 17, page 102

1) schneller, der schnellste, am schnellsten, 2) grösser, der grösste, am grössten, 3) kälter, der kälteste, am kältesten, 4) sorgfältiger, der sorgfältigste, am sorgfältigsten, 5) interessanter, der interessanteste, am interessantesten 6) langsamer, der langsamste, am langsamsten 7) leichter, der leichteste, am leichtesten 8) höher, der höchste, am höchsten 9) wärmer, der wärmste, am wärmsten 10) schwieriger, der schwierigste, am schwierigsten, 11) länger, der längste, am längsten 12) kürzer, der kürzeste, am kürzesten

Lektion 17, page 103

1) Er ist jünger als seine Schwester. 2) Dieser Winter ist nicht so kalt wie der letzte. 3) Dein Wagen ist genau so schnell wie meiner. 4) Er ist so faul, dass sein Lehrer nicht sehr glücklich ist. 5) Ich hoffe, dass ich einen besseren Doktor finde. 6) Wer ist älter, dein Vater oder deine Mutter? 7) Mein Vater ist älter als meine Mutter. 8) Sie sieht älter aus als er. 9) Ich muss ein Kleid finden, das nicht länger als mein Mantel ist. 10) Entschuldigen Sie, aber ich kann nicht früher kommen. 11) Viele Leute sind netter in den Ferien als bei der Arbeit. 12) Kuchen schmeckt mir besser als Brot. 13) Im Winter sind die Nächte länger als im Sommer. 14) Er ist mein bester Freund. 15) Wir müssen ein billigeres Restaurant finden. 16) *Love Story* ist der traurigste Film, den ich kenne. 17) Ich hofte, dass es interessanter wird. I8) Er ist so reich, dass er so viel Geld ausgeben kann wie er will. 19) Warten wir, bis es sonniger ist. 20) Dieser See ist nicht so tief wie du denkst.

Lektion 17, page 103

1) am längsten 2) am kürzesten 3) am längsten 4) am schönsten 5) am besten 6) am schlechtesten 7) am interessantesten 8) am schnellsten.

Lektion 17, page 104

1) die grösste 2) der wichtigste 3) das kälteste 4) ältester 5) jüngste 6) modernsten 7) grösster 8) beste 9) höchsten 10) meisten 11) interessanteste 12) ältester, jüngster 13) schwierigste.

Lektion 17, page 104

1) jünger als 2) höher als 3) sorgfältiger als 4) schöneres als 5) später 6) unordentlicher als 7) besser als 8) kälter als 9) wärmeren 10) weniger als 11) schneller 12) bessere 13) ärmer als 14) früher, besser.

Lektion 17, page 106

1) guter. Er ist kein . . . . 2) gut, Sie spielt nicht . . . . 3) sorgfältig. Er arbeitet nicht . . . . 4) sorgfältige. Das ist keine . . . . 5) schnelles, schönes. Ich möchte nicht gern . . . . 6) zweite. Heute ist nicht . . . . 7) fünfundzwanzigsten. Weihnachten ist nicht . . . . 8) zweite. Claudia ist nicht . . . . 9) erster.

Peter ist nicht . . . . 10) glücklich. Sie sieht nicht . . . . 11) beschäftigter, beschäftigt. Er ist kein sehr . . . . auch nicht sehr beschäftigt. 12) fleissige. Sie ist keine . . . . 13) neuesten. Sie kommt nicht . . . . 14) besten. Ich will nicht . . . . 15) zweiten. Er zieht seinen zweiten Sohn nicht . . . . 16) ersten. Sie ist nicht . . . . 17) viertes. Sein viertes Buch ist nicht . . . . 18) schwierigste. Das ist nicht . . . . 19) grösste. Er ist nicht . . . . 20) höchste. Das ist nicht . . . . 21) jüngsten. Peter ist nicht . . . . 22) neuesten. Ich will seinen neuesten Film nicht . . . . 23) spannenderes. Ich kenne kein . . . . 24) schnelleren. Ich möchte keinen . . . . 25) wärmeren. Ich brauche keinen . . . . zu kaufen. 26) kälteste. Januar ist nicht . . . . 27) schönsten. Dieses Bild ist nicht . . . . 28) schlechteren. Ich kenne keinen . . . .

Lektion 17, page 107
1) Gehst du gern ins Kino? 2) Ich trinke lieber Whisky als Bier. 3) Die Übungen werden immer schwerer. 4) Ich lese am liebsten Romane. 5) Er arbeitet immer weniger. 6) Was mich betrifft, schwimme ich lieber im Meer. 7) Im Grossen und Ganzen arbeite ich gern mit ihm. 8) Was machst du gern in deinen Ferien? 9) Ich gehe am liebsten in den Bergen spazieren. 10) Sie fährt lieber Ski. 11) Ich fahre am liebsten ein sehr schnelles Auto. 12) Gehen Sie lieber ins Kino als ins Theater? 13) Sie faulenzt gern. 14) Er fährt immer schneller.

Lektion 18, page 110
1) meines Vaters 2) dieser 3) meiner 4) der, meines Direktors 5) eines reichen Mannes 6) des Mädchens 7) dieser 8) Peters, seines Bruders 9) meiner jüngsten 10) eines interessanten Schriftstellers 11) dieses Restaurants.

Lektion 18, page 111
1) der, seines Bruders 2) seines hohen Alters, 3) der 4) eines Monats 5) des starken Regens 6) des nächsten Urlaubs 7) eines wichtigen Anrufs 8) seines Fiebers 9) meines Vaters 10) seines Sonnenbrandes 11) eines sehr reichen Mannes 12) dieses Schülers 13) eines grossen Fehlers 14) ihres jüngsten Kindes 15) dieser 16) dieser.

Lektion 18, page 112
1) Wem helfe ich gern. Ich helfe ihm gern. 2) Wessen Zimmer ist das? Das ist sein Zimmer. 3) Wem gefällt dieses Stück sehr. Es gefällt ihm sehr. 4) Wen nimmt man fest? Man nimmt ihn fest. 5) Wessen Frau ist das? Das ist seine Frau. 6) Wen sehe ich? Ich sehe sie. 7) Wer kommt morgen. Sie kommt morgen. 8) Wem schreibt sie einen Brief? Sie schreibt ihm einen Brief. 9) Wessen Fleischer ist das? Das ist ihr Fleischer. 10) Auf wen warten wir? Wir warten auf sie.

Lektion 18, page 113

1) Ja, ich habe einen. Nein, ich habe keinen. 2) Ja, ich verstehe etwas. Nein, ich verstehe nichts. 3) Ja, er hat schon eins. Nein, er hat noch keins. 4) Ja, Sie können etwas für mich tun. Nein, Sie können nichts für mich tun. 5) Ja, sie hat welche. Nein, sie hat keine. 6) Ja, ich lerne etwas bei diesem Lehrer. Nein, ich lerne nichts bei diesem Lehrer. 7) Ja, ich habe einen. Nein, ich habe keinen. 8) Ja, es gibt etwas zu sehen. Nein, es gibt nichts zu sehen. 9) Ja, ich habe etwas. Nein, ich habe keinen. 10) Ja, ich kann etwas verstehen. Nein, ich kann nichts verstehen.

Lektion 19, page 114

1) Wessen Geschenk trägst du? 2) Sie hat die gleiche Grösse wie ihre Schwester. 3) Gehen wir zuerst in die Damenabteilung. 4) Wenn die Pelzmäntel im Sonderangebot sind, kaufe ich einen. 5) Ich bin erschöpft, aber es war der Mühe wert. 6) Es würde mich nicht wundern, ihn trotz seines Fiebers zu sehen. 7) Er ist so wohlhabend, dass er nicht zu arbeiten braucht. 8) Die Summe ist höher als erwartet. 9) Die Herrenabteilung ist im dritten Stock. 10) Ich bin einundzwanzig (Jahre alt). 11) Wann? Je früher desto besser. 12) Ich komme während des Wochenendes. 13) Im Grossen und Ganzen ist dieser Supermarkt ziemlich billig. 14) Bald sind alle diese Kleider im Ausverkauf. 15) Er sieht mich absichtlich nicht. 16) Ich muss alle 14 Tage zum Doktor (gehen). 17) Ich rufe dich an, sobald ich ankomme. 18) Die Verabredung ist für den fünften März. 19) In 14 Tagen muss ich eine Prüfung machen. 20) Verbinden Sie mich, bitte, mit der Sekretärin meines Vaters. 21) Ich habe nur noch zwei Minuten. 22) Es tut mir leid, ich habe keine Ideen mehr. 23) Ich bin noch nicht fertig. 24) Wessen Wagen ist der schnellste? 25) Es ist seine Biene die ihn so nervös macht. 26) Sie dürfen im Zimmer des Direktors nicht rauchen.

Lektion 19, page 116

1) Er wird nächsten Jahr kommen. 2) Sehr wahrscheinlich wird er durchfallen. 3) Sie wird ihn heiraten. 4) Er wird sehr erfolgreich sein. 5) Die Polizisten werden ihn festnehmen. 6) Der Zug wird morgen ankommen. 7) Du wirst links abbiegen müssen. 8) Ich werde ins Museum gehen. 9) An diesem Bahnhof werden wir aussteigen. 10) Ich werde bald aufhören. 11) Sie wird ihm einen Brief schreiben. 12) Er wird seiner Mutter helfen. 13) Ihr werdet zu spät kommen. 14) Du wirst es nicht wissen.

Lextion 19, page 117

1) Im Sommer gibt (wird) es viele Touristen hier (geben). 2) Sie heiratet (wird) in 14 Tagen (heiraten). 3) Ich spreche (werde) nicht mit ihm (sprechen). 4) Wenn ich viel esse, nehme (werde) ich zu (zunehmen). 5) Wir ziehen (werden) nächsten Monat aus (ausziehen). 6) Es ist sicher, dass sie sich scheiden lassen (werden). 7) Morgen besichtigen (werden) wir die

wichtigsten Gebäude dieser Stadt (besichtigen). 8) Wenn ich das Diplom bekomme, bin (werde) ich sehr glücklich (sein). 9) Dieses Stück wird ein Reinfall sein. 10) Ich gehe (werde) nach München (gehen) wenn du möchtest. 11) Wann hörst (wirst) du mir zu (zuhören)? 12) Wir müssen (werden) bald eine Verabredung treffen (müssen). 15) Weihnachten fahre (werde) ich ski (skifahren). 14) Morgen früh stehe (werde) ich früher als du auf (aufstehen). 15) Wenn ich müde bin, gehe (werde) ich schlafen (gehen). 16) Wenn die Wohnung gross ist, nehme (werde) ich sie vom ersten des Monats an (nehmen). 17) Wir kommen (werden) nicht Weihnachten, sondern Ostern (kommen). 18) Sie schliessen (werden) nächste Woche die Damenabteilung (schliessen). 19) Du trinkst (wirst) diesen Wein auch lieber (trinken). 20) Er verkauft (wird) seinen alten Wagen (verkaufen) und kauft einen neuen (kaufen). 21) Ich rufe (werde) dich Montag an (anrufen). 22) Er weiss (wird) es nicht (wissen).

Lektion 19, page 118
1) Nein, er ist noch nicht verheiratet. Nein, er wird noch nicht verheiratet sein. 2) Nein, ich habe (werde) keine Zeit mehr (haben). 3) Nein, wir verstehen (werden) nichts (verstehen). 4) Nein, niemand ist (wird) im Büro (sein). 5) Er ist (wird) noch nicht auf der Bank (sein). 6) Nein, er hat (wird) noch keinen Job (haben). 7) Nein, wir müssen (werden) noch nicht links abliegen (müssen). 8) Er kommt (wird) nie zurück (zurückkommen). 9) Nein, er spricht (wird) noch nicht deutsch (sprechen). 10) Er lernt (wird) nicht mehr englisch (lernen). 11) Man kann (wird) nichts für sie tun (können). 12) Niemand will (wird) mir helfen (wollen).

Lektion 19, page 119
1) Ich warte seit drei Uhr auf sie. 2) Wie lange bist du in dieser langweiligen Stadt? 3) Er lernt seit einem halben Jahr deutsch. 4) Wir fahren seit einem Tag. 5) Seit heute mittag besichtigt sie das Museum. 6) Arbeitest du seit heute morgen? 7) Ich höre den ganzen Nachmittag Musik. 8) Ist sie seit Ostern hier? 9) Ich schreibe ihm morgen. 10) Er wohnt seit März hier.

Lektion 20, page 123
1) Er hat mich nicht gesehen. 2) Er hat den Film noch nicht gesehen. 3) Sie haben noch keine Ferien genommen. 4) Wir haben nichts gesucht. 5) Du hast nicht mehr hier gearbeitet. 6) Ich habe kein Geld mehr gehabt. 7) Ihr habt niemanden eingeladen. 8) Er hat es nie gesagt.

Lektion 20, page 124
1) Die Sonne hat den ganzen Tag geschienen. Hat die Sonne . . . ? 2) Er hat auf dem Platz dort gesessen. Hat er . . . ? 3) Ich habe etwas verstanden. Hast du etwas . . . ? 4) Er hat ein gutes Buch gelesen. Hat er . . . ? 5) Sie haben das Papier weggeworfen. Haben Sie . . . ? 6) Sie hat ein hübsches Kleid

getragen. Hat sie . . . ? 7) Er hat nichts gemacht. Hat er etwas . . . ? 8) Ich habe Sie angerufen. Haben Sie mich . . . ? 9) Sie hat sicher gewusst, wo ihr Mann arbeitet. Hat sie . . . ? 10) Er hat ihr einen Rechtsanwalt empfohlen. Hat er ihr . . . ? 11) Er hat lange geschlafen. Hat er . . . ? 12) Wir haben den Bus genommen. Habt ihr . . . ? 13) Sie hat nie die Tür zugemacht. Hat sie je . . . ? 14) Er hat sich rasiert. Hat er sich . . . ? 15) Der Fahrer hat den Wagen gewaschen. Hat der Fahrer . . . ? 16) Du hast das Licht angemacht. Habe ich . . . ? 17) Er hat das Geschenk zerbrochen. Hat er . . . ? 18) Man hat ihren Diamanten gestohlen. Hat man . . . ? 19) Ich habe nicht viel Geld bekommen. Hast du . . . ? 20) Er hat der alten Frau geholfen. Hat er . . . ? 21) Ich habe ihm Geld geliehen, weil er keins hat. Hast du . . . ? 22) Ich habe das Fleisch mit dem grossen Messer geschnitten. Hast du . . . ? 23) Er hat gern Whisky getrunken. Hat er . . . ? 24) Sie hat ihm geschworen, bei ihm zu bleiben. Hat sie . . . ? 25) Der Film hat um 6 begonnen und um 8 aufgehört. Hat der Film . . . ? 26) Er hat sehr schnell gesprochen. Hat er . . . ? 27) Er hat es gekonnt. Hat er . . . ? 28) Ich habe ihr einen Brief pro Woche geschrieben. Hast du . . . ?

Lektion 20, page 125

1) Ich habe diesen Film nie gesehen. 2) Ich habe dieses Museum nie besucht. 3) Er ist nie durchgefallen. 4) Sie hat ihn nie gefragt. 5) Wir haben nie einen Fehler gemacht. 6) Ich habe Sie nie getroffen. 7) Ich habe nie jemanden geschlagen. 8) Ihr habt mir nie geholfen. 9) Ich habe diesen Roman nie gelesen. 10) Sie haben nie zu viel getrunken.

Lektion 20, page 127

1) Was hast du gestern gemacht? 2) Vor einer Stunde hat er viel gegessen. 3) Letzte Woche hat er mir ein Geschenk gegeben. 4) Gestern hat es gegossen. 5) Vor einem Augenblick hat der Regen aufgehört. 6) Ich hoffe, dass es nicht wehgetan hat. 7) Was hat er zugegeben? 8) Er hat nie einen Fehler gemacht. (Er hat sich nie geirrt) 9) Wie hast du sie gefunden? 10) Was hast du deinem Bruder vorgeschlagen? 11) Letzte Nacht habe ich einen Alptraum gehabt. 12) Er hat schon sein Gepäck ausgepackt. 13) Heute Morgen hat er mir eine Zeitung gebracht. 14) Warum hast du ihn geschlagen? 15) Vor zwei Wochen hat sie alle seine Briefe zerrissen. 16) Wo hast du ihn getroffen? 17) Essen Sie gern gebratenes Hammelfleisch? 18) Ich bin sicher, dass ich dein Paket nicht bekommen habe. 19) Ich habe es gewusst. Ich habe recht gehabt! 20) Ich verstehe nicht, warum du ihr nicht geholfen hast. 21) Letzte Woche haben sie den Schuft gefangen. 22) Er hat seinen Regenmantel angezogen. 23) Was hast du gedacht? 24) Er hat in der Klemme gesessen. 25) Du hast Glück gehabt. 26) Ich habe ihn erst vor zwei Tagen gesehen. 27) Warum hast du die Tür geschlossen? 28) Hat er es geschworen?

Lektion 21, page 131

1) Ich bin in Berlin gewesen. 2) Das Buch ist auf den Boden gefallen. 3) Ich bin eine Woche hier geblieben. 4) Er ist sehr weit geschwommen. 5) Ist er eingetreten? 6) Wo sind Sie umgestiegen? 7) Wann ist der Zug angekommen? 8) Er ist von New York nach Hamburg geflogen. 9) Er ist Ingenieur geworden. 10) Ich bin mit dem Bus gefahren. 11) Wo bist du gewesen? 12) Was ist passiert? 13) Es ist mir nicht gelungen. 14) Er ist hinter den anderen Studenten zurückgeblieben.

Lektion 21, page 132

1) ist 2) hat 3) hat 4) sind 5) ist 6) hat 7) bin 8) hat 9) ist 10) hat 11) bin 12) ist 13) hat 14) ist 15) ist 16) bin 17) hat 18) sind 19) hast 20) sind 21) sind 22) habe 23) hat (haben) 24) ist 25) haben 26) ist 27) ist 28) hat.

Lektion 21, page 133

1) Ich bin eine Stunde lang dort gewesen. 2) Ich habe ihn vor einem Moment gesehen. 3) Einer von sechs ist durchgefallen. 4) In jenem Park habe ich Angst gehabt. 5) Ich hoffe, dass er aufgeholt hat. 6) Er hat mir eine Falle gestellt. 7) Er hat die schmutzige Arbeit nicht gemacht. 8) Wir sind letzte Woche umgezogen. 9) Warum hat sie ihren Mantel nicht ausgezogen? 10) Ich bin seit einem Monat hier. 11) Wohin ist sie nachher gegangen? 12) Er ist schon eingetreten. 13) Hat er dich betrogen? 14) Wen hast du im Kino getroffen? (Wem bist du . . . begegnet?) 15) Sie sind ihm ins Kino gefolgt. 16) Ist es dir gelungen, es zu tun? 17) Wie gewöhnlich ist er eingeschlafen. 18) Ich bin vor einer Stunde angekommen. 19) Ich habe es vorgehabt. 20) Weiss sie, was aus ihm geworden ist? 21) Ich bin sehr stolz auf ihn gewesen. 22) Er ist vor drei Jahren gestorben. 23) Ich habe dich sofort angerufen. 24) Ich bin im Januar ausgezogen. 25) Dann habe ich mich umgezogen. 26) Er ist, wie gewöhnlich, um 8 Uhr gekommen. 27) Sie haben gestern den neuen Direktor gewählt. 28) Ist es dir gelungen, reich zu werden?

Lektion 22, page 139

1) bin, gegangen. ging. 2) haben, gearbeitet. arbeiteten 3) hat, getroffen. traf. 4) hat getrunken. trank. 5) hat, geholfen. half. 6) bin, gewesen. war. 7) hat, umgezogen. zog. 8) habe, verstanden. verstand. 9) sind, gekommen. kamen. 10) hat, geschlagen. schlug. 11) hast, begonnen. begann. 12) habe, gesessen. sass. 13) hat, geschrieben. schrieb.

Lektion 22, page 140

1) besuchte, assen 2) verbot, erlaubte 3) liess, traute 4) trafen, war 5) kritisierte, lobte 6) flüsterte, konnte 7) fand, sagte 8) fuhr, kannte 9) las, vorbereitete 10) ging aus, aussah 11) fiel, schien 12) übertrieb,

wusste, glaubte 13) mochte, half 14) schlief, lag 15) sprachen, zuhörte
16) half, sah, hatte 17) gewann, kämpfte 18) begegnete, feierten 19) flog,
fuhr 20) schnitt, dachte 21) trug, heiratete 22) verdiente, studierte.

Lektion 22, page 141
1) Als er eintrat, sah ich fern und mein Mann las die Zeitung. 2) Was tat
deine Frau, als du heute morgen weggingst? 3) Worüber spracht ihr, als ich
euch sah? 4) Woran dachtest du, als er das sagte? 5) Als der Krieg anfing,
lebten wir in Europa. 6) Als sie im Café sassen, kam der Kellner an ihren
Tisch und brachte die Speisekarte. 7) Ich machte diese Erfahrung, als ich
für ihn arbeitete. 8) Während sie den Kuchen schnitt, nahmen die Gäste
Platz. 9) Als er sie verliess, begann sie zu weinen. 10) Ich tat es, weil ich es
musste. 11) Es schneite, als wir in Ferien waren. 12) Als wir die Lektion
beendeten, stellte der Lehrer eine schwere Frage. 13) Er holte die anderen
auf, weil er viel studierte. 14) Ich weinte, während sie lachte. 15) Ich traf
ihn, weil wir die gleiche U-Bahn nahmen. 16) Als ich ihm sein Frühstück
brachte, schlief er noch. 17) Ich wachte auf, als ich diesen Alptraum hatte.
18) Ich war so hungrig, dass ich einen Apfel stahl. 19) Fuhren Sie, als es
passierte? 20) Wir hatten Gäste, als wir diesen schrecklichen Streit hatten.
21) Ich bemerkte den Fehler, als ich die Rechnung nachprüfte. 22) Ich gab
ihm ein grosses Trinkgeld, weil er mein ganzes Gepäck trug. 23) Er wusch
seinen Wagen, während sie die Hausarbeit machte. 24) Die Polizei fing ihn,
als er in Ferien war. 25) Ich schlug es ihr vor, weil sie mich fragte.

Lektion 23, page 146
1) er ginge, würde gehen 2) du nähmest, würdest nehmen 3) ich käme,
würde kommen 4) sie führen, würden fahren 5) ihr zeigtet, würdet zeigen
6) sie fände, würde finden 7) es schiene, würde scheinen 8) du gäbest,
würdest geben 9) er nähme, würde nehmen 10) er ässe, würde essen 11) wir
ässen, würden essen 12) du vergässest, würdest vergessen 13) wir hülfen,
würden helfen 14) er träfe, würde treffen 15) sie gäben, würden geben
16) er liesse, würde lassen.

Lektion 23, page 147
1) Wenn ich müde wäre, ginge ich schlafen. 2) Wenn das Wetter schlecht
wäre, bliebe ich zu Hause. 3) hätte, käme 4) wäre, nähme 5) übertriebe,
sagte 6) wäre, wäre 7) sähe, würde 8) liebte, täte 9) kämest, freute
10) schneite, führen 11) empfählest, nähme 12) hätte, ginge 13) käme,
bliebe 14) schneite, führe.

Lektion 23, page 147
1) hätte, führe 2) käme, ware 3) belögest, spräche 4) traute, schwiege
5) langweilte, ginge . . . aus 6) kämet, könntet 7) verdiente, brauchte
8) machte, verböte 9) schriebe, kaufte 10) wären, lernten 11) liehe, hälfe
12) wolltest, könntest 13) wäre, gäbe 14) sähe, sagte.

Lektion 23, page 148

1) Wenn ich mehr Zeit hätte (habe), besuchte (besuche) ich dich. 2) Wenn du deutsch sprächest (sprichst), gingest (gehst) du nach Deutschland? 3) Wenn du könntest (kannst), würdest (hilfst) du mir helfen. 4) Wenn der Film ein Reinfall wäre (ist), sähen (sehen) wir ihn nicht. 5) Wenn du geradeaus gingest (gehst), fändest (findest) du das Gebäude. 6) Wenn sie fleissig lernten (lernen), bekämen (bekommen) sie ihre Diplome. 7) Wenn sie nicht kommen könnte (kann), riefe (ruft) sie dich an. 8) Wenn wir heute abend nicht arbeiten müssten (müssen), gingen (gehen) wir tanzen. 9) Wenn das Buch dir gehörte (gehört), liehest (leihst) du es mir? 10) Wenn du jeden Tag zu spät kämest, (kommst), feuerte (feuert) dich dein Boss? 11) Wenn du nach Berlin gingest (gehst), besuchtest (besuchst) du die Mauer? 12) Wenn er nicht so schüchtern wäre (ist), küsste (küsst) er seine Biene. 13) Wenn jener Pelzmantel im Ausverkauf wäre (ist), kaufte (kauft) sie ihn. 14) Wenn du es machen könntest (kannst), machtest (machst) du es? 15) Wenn er dir alles erzählte (erzählt), glaubtest (glaubst) du ihm nicht. 16) Wenn ich die Frau meines Lebens heute träfe (treffe), heiratete (heirate) ich sie morgen. 17) Wenn ich müsste (muss), pumpte (pumpe) ich mir das Geld von ihm. 18) Wenn du Afrika gern hättest (hast), zögest (ziehst) du dorthin? 19) Wenn er dich schlüge (schlägst) verliessest (verlässt) du ihn? 20) Wenn du einen Job suchtest (suchst), kauftest (kaufst) du die Morgenzeitungen? 21) Wenn du mit dem Wagen führest (fährst), müsstest (musst) du sorgfältig fahren. 22) Wenn er sie nicht liebte (liebt), lebte (lebt) er nicht mit ihr. 23) Sogar, wenn du mir die Wahrheit sagtest (sagst), glaubte (glaube) ich dir nicht mehr. 24) Wenn du zum Zahnarzt gingest (gehst), nähmest (nimmst) du vorher eine Tablette. 25) Wenn du die Nase voll hättest (hast), hörtest (hörst) du auf? 26) Wenn es sonnig wäre (ist), gingen (gehen) wir spazieren.

Lektion 24, page 150

1) zu essen 2) uns zu helfen 3) rechtzeitig anzukommen 4) fernzusehen 5) lange zu schlafen 6) öfter geschrieben 7) besser ausgesehen 8) alle herein -zulegen 9) jedes Wochenende gekommen 10) allein zu sein.

Lektion 24, page 152

1) a) die b) der c) die d) deren e) deren f) der 2) a) dem b) dessen c) den d) der e) den f) dessen 3) a) die b) deren c) die d) denen e) denen f) die 4) a) dem b) dessen c) das d) dessen e) das f) das 5) a) deren b) die c) denen d) denen e) die f) deren.

Lektion 24, page 153

1) Er sah aus dem Fenster, während er sprach. 2) ein weinendes Baby 3) ein gut gehendes Geschäft 4) die scheinende Sonne 5) Der Boss mag Angestellte nicht, die im Büro schlafen. 6) ein aufregender Film 7) Viele Leute beklagen sich über die steigenden Preise. 8) die fallenden Blätter

9) Er sieht sich die Kinder an, die im Meer schwimmen. 10) die in der Ecke tanzenden Mädchen 11) ein brennendes Haus 12) ein schmerzender Zahn 13) Ich hasse diese ermüdende Arbeit 14) Ich mag Leute nicht, die die ganze Zeit schreien. 15) ein wohlhabender Mann 16) Bevor er ging, küsste er sie. 17) Du darfst nicht zu viel sprechen, während du fährst. 18) Nachdem ich dieses Buch gelesen habe, schreibe ich meinen Freunden darüber.

Lektion 24, page 154
1) bittet 2) fragt, nach 3) bitte, um 4) fragt 5) fragt, nach 6) bittet 7) bitte, um 8) fragt 9) Worum bittet 10) Wonach fragt.

Lektion 24, page 155
1) Er fragt sie, ob sie verheiratet ist. 2) Sie fragt sie, ob sie schon gegessen haben. 3) Er fragt, ob sie schon wieder ausgehen will. 4) Sie fragt mich, wo ich gestern abend gewesen bin. 5) Sie fragt ihn, ob ihm der schöne Sportwagen gehört. 6) Ich weiss nicht, ob ich dir das Geld zurückgegeben habe. 7) Sie möchte wissen, ob sie ihm helfen kann. 8) Er fragt sie, wer von ihnen heute zu spät gekommen ist. 9) Sie fragen, ob sie ins Kino gehen dürfen. 10) Sie fragen ihn, ob ihm diese Musik gefällt. 11) Ich frage dich, ob du es mir erzählen willst. 12) Er fragt sie, ob sie ihn heiraten will.

Lektion 24, page 155
1) Er hat mich gefragt, ob ich dich gestern abend gesehen habe. 2) Ich kannte die Stadt nicht, deshalb fragte ich den ersten Mann, den ich sah, nach dem Bahnhof. 3) Du bittest immer deine Freunde um Zigaretten. 4) Ich habe ihn nur gebeten, mir 5 Mark zu leihen. 5) Wonach hast du ihn gefragt? (Worum hast du ihn gebeten)? 6) Sie hat ihren Boss um einen besseren Job gebeten. 7) Er hat mich nach der Zeit gefragt. 8) Ich bitte sie um ein Rendezvous. 9) Ich habe ihn um Feuer gebeten. 10) Darf ich Sie um eine Zigarette bitten? 11) Darf ich Sie bitten, das Fenster zu schliessen. 12) Der Tourist fragte die Frau nach der Post. 13) Sie fragte nach meinem Vater. 14) Können Sie Judy, deren Arbeit nachlässig ist, bitten, in mein Büro zu kommen. 15) Obwohl er sie schon mehrere Male darum gebeten hat, bittet er sie noch einmal um eine Verabredung. 16) Sie fragte mich, warum ich so stolz auf meine Tochter war.

Lektion 25, page 158
1) Ich dachte, ich führe morgen ab. 2) Er dachte, er müsste es bald machen. 3) Sie dachte, er wollte sie heiraten. 4) Wenn ich genug Geld hätte, kaufte ich dieses Haus. 5) Ich dachte, dass er es machen müsste. 6) Wir dachten, dass es regnen würde. 7) Wir hofften, dass sie auch käme. 8) Du dachtest, sie würde dir alles glauben. 9) Wenn du wolltest, könntest du das Examen bestehen. 10) Sie dachten, dass ich sie nicht sähe. 11) Ich glaubte, dass er es allein machen könnte. 12) Wenn er nicht käme, wäre ich ihm böse. 13) Er dachte, dass er durchfiele.

Lektion 25, page 158

1) Ich dachte (denke), sie würde (fragt) mich noch einmal fragen. 2) Sie hoffte (hofft), er würde (heiratet) sie heiraten. 3) Sie dachte (denkt), er liebte (liebt) sie mehr. 4) Wenn ich allein wäre (bin), versuchte (versuche) ich, interessante Leute kennenzulernen. 5) Wenn er mir einen Streich spielte (spielt), legte (lege) ich ihn auch herein. 6) Sie dachte (denkt), er versuchte (versucht) sie betrügen. 7) Ich dachte (denke), der Mörder wäre (ist) im Gefängnis. 8) Wenn jemand deinen Freund erschösse (erschiesst), brächtest (bringst) du ihn um die Ecke? 9) Ich dachte (denke), der Mörder sei (ist) aus dem Gefängnis geflohen. 10) Wir alle glaubten (glauben), die Preise würden (werden) sinken. 11) Der Kandidat dachte (denkt), sie würden (wählen) ihn wählen. 12) Wenn du Haschisch rauchtest (rauchst), versuchte (versuche) ich es auch. 13) Er sagte (sagt) er käme (kommt) rechtzeitig. 14) Der Direktor dachte (denkt) ich vergässe (vergesse) es. 15) Wenn sie das wüsste (weiss), ginge (geht) sie nicht mit ihm aus. 16) Er sagte (sagt), wir würden (werden) von ihm hören.

Lektion 25, page 160

1) Soll ich ihn anrufen? 2) Ich sollte mit ihr tanzen gehen. 3) Du solltest diesen Unsinn verhindern. 4) Er tut so, als wäre er sehr reich. 5) Er sollte langsamer sprechen. 6) Als ob er es nicht wüsste! 7) Sie sollte mit ihrer hübschen Schwester kommen. 8) Er kam zurück, als ob nichts ihm Sorgen machen könnte. 9) Er sollte das nicht sagen. 10) Ich sollte auch dorthin gehen.

Lektion 25, page 160

1) Ihr solltet Ihr (k)einen Vorschlag machen. 2) Er sollte seinen Eltern (nicht) die Wahrheit sagen. 3) Du solltest (nicht) versuchen, ihn zu überreden. 4) Sie sollte (nicht) zum Doktor gehen. 5) Wir sollten diesen Kandidaten (nicht) wählen. 6) Sie sollten den Schuft (nicht) laufen lassen. 7) Ihr solltet ihm (nicht) sagen, was ihr von ihm haltet. 8) Ich sollte sie (nicht) heute anrufen. 9) Du solltest es ihr (nicht) sagen. 10) Sie sollte auch (nicht) kommen. 11) Ihr solltet es (nicht) noch einmal versuchen. 12) Er sollte es (nicht) übersetzen. 13) Sie sollte (nicht) daran denken. 14) Sie sollten es (nicht) wissen. 15) Ich sollte (k)ein Zimmer reservieren. 16) Man sollte es (nicht) tun.

Lektion 25, page 161

1) Sie sprechen nie miteinander. 2) Sie hassen einander. 3) Sie leben nahe beieinander. 4) Der kleine Junge und das kleine Mädchen spielen immer miteinander. 5) Sie denken immer aneinander. 6) Wir wohnen nicht weit voneinander. 7) Sie kommen nacheinander herein. 8) Sie kämpften gegeneinander.

Lektion 25, page 161
1) Er hat noch nicht angerufen. 2) Er hat noch keine Freundin gefunden.
3) Sie ist nicht mehr in Berlin. 4) Der Direktor hat keinen Mercedes mehr.
5) Wir haben noch kein Examen gemacht. 6) Sie haben noch nicht gesagt,
dass sie mitkommen.

Lession 26, page 164
1) Ich brauchte am Wochenende nicht zu arbeiten. 2) Du hättest mich nicht
anrufen sollen. 3) Du solltest ihn auch nicht einladen. 4) Wir brauchten
nicht zweimal pro Woche auf die Bank zu gehen. 5) Wir brauchten nicht
viel Kies für das Auto zu bezahlen. 6) Sie hätten nicht mehr arbeiten müssen.
7) Ich brauchte mich nicht über sie zu beklagen. 8) Sie hätte nicht netter zu
ihm sein sollen. 9) Wir brauchten nicht gegeneinander zu kämpfen. 10) Ich
hätte meiner Frau kein Geburtstagsgeschenk geben sollen.

Lektion 26, page 164
1) Ich musste (werde) früh schlafen gehen (müssen). 2) Du musstest (wirst)
es gleich machen (müssen). 3) Sie mussten (werden) mich zuerst fragen
(müssen). 4) Sie musste (wird) ihn heute abend anrufen (müssen). 5) Du
musstest (wirst) mir von deiner Reise erzählen (müssen). 6) Ich musste
(werde) auf ihn warten (müssen). 7) Ihr musstet (werdet) dem Lehrer
zuhören (müssen). 8) Er musste (wird) eine bessere Arbeit finden (müssen).
9) Wir mussten (werden) versuchen (müssen), bessere Noten zu bekommen.
10) Sie mussten (werden) gegen die Gewerkschaft kämpfen (müssen).

Lektion 26, page 165
1) Er sagte, er musste sie verlassen. 2) Die Kinder durften nicht spät
aufbleiben. 3) Er hätte dir zuhören sollen. 4) Du hättest schneller
arbeiten sollen. 5) Die Bullen mussten ihn festnehmen. 6) Der Journalist
musste einen Artikel über den neuen Kandidaten schreiben. 7) Wir hätten
auf den Bus warten sollen. 8) Warum ist er nicht gekommen? Er muss
nicht in München sein. 9) Ich habe ihn lange nicht gesehen, er muss wieder
im Gefängnis sein. 10) Sie sagte, sie musste abnehmen. 11) Ich musste
diese Arbeit zuerst beenden. 12) Er hätte mir ein Beispiel geben sollen.
13) Du solltest im Dunkeln keine Angst haben. 14) Er sollte einen Mantel
tragen. 15) Ich hätte jenes Gemälde kaufen sollen. 16) Vor dem Empfang
musste ich zum Friseur gehen. 17) Die Strassen waren nass. Es muss
geregnet haben. 18) Sie hätten ihm kein Schmiergeld geben sollen. 19) Er
sollte nicht um einen goldenen Handschlag bitten. 20) Er ist so komisch,
er muss Haschisch geraucht haben. 21) Ich musste gestern nicht gehen
(brauchte nicht . . . zu gehen). 22) Musstest du ihm das erzählen) 23) Ihr
Baby hätte gestern geboren werden sollen. 24) Was in aller Welt hätten wir
tun sollen? 25) Er ist nicht zu Hause, er muss in seinem Büro sein. 26) Er
durfte nicht mit uns an die See fahren. 27) Wir brauchten gestern die

Prüfung nicht zu machen. 28) Ich musste ihm sagen, dass ich die Nase voll hatte.

Lektion 26, page 166

1) Danke, ich habe gerade ein Getränk gehabt. 2) Ich ass gerade, als er mich anrief. 3) Ich lese gerade Ihren Brief. 4) Wir sind gerade von dort gekommen 5) Ist er gerade weggegangen? 6) Er ist gerade aus dem Gefängnis geflohen. 7) Ich sehe gerade den Film, den du empfohlen hast. 8) Ich habe gerade fünf Pfund abgenommen. 9) Er ist gerade dort. 10) Ich dachte gerade an dich, als ich deinen Brief bekam. 11) Er ist gerade angekommen. 12) Wir sahen gerade fern, als meine Mutter eintrat. 13) Wir haben gerade unsere Prüfungen bestanden. 14) Stören Sie mich nicht; ich mache gerade meine Hausaufgaben. 15) Hat er gerade davon gehört. 16) Die Bullen haben ihn gerade gefangen. 17) Ich schlief gerade, als das Haus Feuer fing.

Lektion 26, page 167

1) Er hat es mir (nicht) gesagt. 2) Ich habe (keine) Zeit. 3) Wenn ich es bekäme, wäre ich (nicht) froh. 4) Wir sind schon einmal (noch nie) hier gewesen. 5) Ich verstehe sie (nicht) gut. 6) Das ist (nicht) alles, was ich von ihm bekommen habe. 7) Ich weiss (nicht), wohin er gefahren ist. 8) Ich habe deinen Kugelschreiber (nicht) genommen. 9) Ich habe (k)eine Wohnung gefunden. 10) Du hättest (nicht) kommen sollen. 11) Ich sollte es (nicht) sofort tun. 12) Er hat jemanden (niemanden) hereingelegt.

Lektion 26, page 167

1) Ich musste es machen, nicht wahr? 2) Wusstest du, was er machen wollte? 3) Wir werden einander lieben, nicht wahr? 4) Er hat sie nicht geheiratet, hoffe ich. Doch, er hat sie geheiratet. 5) Du solltest ihr helfen, nicht wahr? 6) Was hat er gewollt? 7) Ich frage mich, was er tut. 8) Jetzt weiss ich, was ich hätte tun sollen. 9) Sie sieht gut aus, nicht wahr? 10) Sie hat eine hübsche Figur, nicht wahr? 11) Wenn du wüsstest, was ich weiss, würdest du ihr nicht trauen. 12) Natürlich habe ich gesagt, was ich sagen musste. 13) Er hat sie allein gelassen, nicht wahr? 14) Du fährst nicht, nicht wahr? Doch, ich fahre. 15) Er ist nicht Ihr Freund, nicht wahr? — Doch, er ist mein Freund. 16) Du hast sie nicht betrogen, nicht wahr? — Doch, ich habe sie betrogen.

Lektion 26, page 168

1) Bald wird es früher dunkel. 2) Können Sie es, bitte, wiederholen. Ich habe es nicht kapiert. 3) Ich hoffe, dass ich nächsten Monat mehr Geld verdiene. 4) Wenn du nicht schweigst, wirst du dein Fett abbekommen. 5) Bist du gestern oder heute morgen dort angekommen? 6) Wenn du nach Deutschland fährst, kannst du mir etwas deutschen Wein beschaffen. 7) Ich muss es zwanzig Mal versucht haben, aber ich habe keine Verbindung mit

ihr bekommen. 8) Wo hat er sich die schöne Jacke beschafft. 9) Ich denke, du solltest versuchen, dieses Jahr dein Diplom zu bekommen. 10) Könntest du es mir erklären; ich kapiere es nicht.

Lektion 27, page 170
1) Als sie kam, war es schon dunkel geworden. 2) Als sie diesen Job zurückwies, hatte sie schon einen anderen angenommen. 3) Sie glaubte ihm nicht, weil er ihr nicht immer die Wahrheit gesagt hatte. 4) Ich tanzte nicht, weil meine Beine wehtaten. 5) Der Dieb rannte, weil er die Bullen erblickt hatte. 6) Sie antwortete nicht, weil sie eingeschlafen war. 7) Er hatte Angst, weil ihm jemand gefolgt war. 8) Als wir geschwommen waren, gingen wir essen. 9) Nachdem er seine Zigarette angezündet hatte, gab er sie ihr. 10) Ich dachte, er hatte es euch schon gesagt.

Lektion 27, page 171
1) Er war schon angekommen, als ich in den Bahnhof ging. 2) Er las das Buch, dass mir gut gefallen hatte. 3) spielte, gehört hatten. 4) wusste, gekannt hattest 5) half, gebeten hattest 6) anriefst, war schlafen gegangen 7) wollte, hatte aufgehängt 8) rief, gesehen hatte 9) glaubte, belogen hatte 10) war, vergessen hatte 11) gratulierte, hatte bestanden 12) tanzte, hatte getrunken 13) empfahl, hatte gefunden 14) war aufgestanden, weckte 15) bat, war abgebogen 16) eintrat, war eingeschlafen 17) gelesen hatte, musste 18) stellte . . . vor, gekommen war 19) verstanden hatte, wollte, sagte 20) trug, gekauft hatte.

Lektion 27, page 172
1) Wann wird er hier sein? 2) Ich weiss nicht, wann er angekommen ist. 3) Wenn ich ihn sehe, sage ich es ihm. 4) Als ich ihn sah, sagte ich es ihm. 5) Können Sie mir sagen, wann der Film anfängt? 6) Ich möchte wissen, wann er seine Prüfung macht. 7) Als er sechzig (Jahre alt) war, trat er in den Ruhestand. 8) Sie weiss nicht, wann sie den Job bekommt. 9) Wann werden Sie in den Ruhestand treten? 10) Wenn ich die See sehe, bin ich glücklich. 11) Als er mir drohte, wurde ich wütend. 12) Als ich den Brief bekam, las ich ihn sofort. 13) Wann wird dieser Job frei sein. 14) Jedes Mal, wenn ich ihn sehe, sprechen wir über Musik. 15) Sie war schon ausgegangen, als ich anrief. 16) Hat er dir gesagt, was passiert war? 17) Ich weiss nicht, wann ich es machen kann. 18) Als ich nach Hause kam, war er eingeschlafen. 19) Jedes Mal, wenn ich ihn sehe, sieht er sehr müde aus. 20) Wann hast du ihn getroffen?

Lektion 28, page 174
1) Wenn ich Zeit hätte (gehabt hätte), käme (wäre) ich (gekommen). 2) Wenn der Direktor nicht im Büro wäre (gewesen wäre), arbeitete (hätte) ich nicht (gearbeitet). 3) Wenn ich kein Geld hätte (gehabt hätte), bliebe (wäre)

ich zu Hause (geblieben). 4) Wenn das Wetter schön wäre (gewesen wäre), ginge (wäre) ich spazieren (spazierengegangen). 5) Wenn ich mit der U-Bahn führe (gefahren wäre), käme (wäre) ich pünktlich (gekommen). 6) Wenn ich Ferien hätte (gehäbt hätte), läse (hätte) ich viel (gelesen). 7) Wenn mein Hemd schmutzig wäre (gewesen wäre), würde (hätte) ich es waschen (gewaschen). 8) Wenn ich müde wäre (gewesen wäre), ginge (wäre) ich schlafen (gegangen). 9) Wenn ich einen schweren Kopf hätte (gehabt hätte), nähme (hätte) ich ein Aspirin (genommen). 10) Wenn es mir gleich wäre (gewesen wäre), sagte (hätte) ich nichts (gesagt).

Lektion 28, page 175

1) sieht, wird. sähe, würde. gesehen hätte, wäre . . . geworden. 2) empfiehlst, nehme. empfählest, nähme. empfohlen hättest, hätte . . . genommen. 3) willst, kannst. wolltest, könntest, gewollt hättest, hättest . . . gekonnt. 4) schneit, fahren. schneite, führen. geschneit hätte, wären . . . gefahren. 5) liebt, tut, liebte, täte. geliebt hätte, hätte . . . getan. 6) leiht, hilft. liehe, würde . . . helfen. geliehen hätte, hätte . . . geholfen. 7) schreibt, kaufe. schriebe, kaufte. geschrieben hätte, hätte . . . gekauft. 8) macht, verbiete. machte, verböte, gemacht hätte, hätte . . . verboten. 9) sind, lernen, wären, lernten. gewesen wären, hätten . . . gelernt. 10) langweilt, geht . . . aus. langweilte, ginge . . . aus. gelangweilt hätte, wäre . . . ausgegangen. 11) traut, schweigt. traute, schwiege. getraut hätte, hätte . . . geschwiegen. 12) belügst, spreche. belögest, spräche. belogen hättest, hätte . . . gesprochen. 13) kommt, bin. käme, wäre. gekommen wäre, wäre . . . gewesen. 14) hat, fahren. hätte, führen. gehabt hätte, wären . . . gefahren. 15) kommt, feuere. käme, feuerte. gekommen wäre, hätte . . . gefeuert. 16) regnet, gehen . . . spazieren. regnete, gingen . . . spazieren. geregnet hätte, wären . . . spazierengegangen. 17) wird, verliert. würde, verlöre. geworden wäre, hätte . . . verloren. 18) rauchst, bist. rauchtest, wärst. geraucht hättest, wärst . . . gewesen. 19) durchfalle, mache. durchfiele, machte. durchgefallen wäre, hätte . . . gemacht. 20) schreibst, antworte. schriebest, antwortete. geschrieben hättest, hätte . . . geantwortet. 21) bittet, gebe. bäte, gäbe. gebeten hätte, hätte . . . gegeben. 22) wohnt, besuche. wohnte, besuchte. gewohnt hätte, hätte . . . besucht. 23) suchst, findest. suchtest, fändest. gesucht hättest, hättest . . . gefunden. 24) einlädt, lade . . . ein. einlüde, lüde . . . ein. eingeladen hätte, hätte . . . eingeladen. 25) muss, tue. müsste, täte. gemusst hätte, hätte . . . getan. 26) weiss, sage. wüsste, sagte. gewusst hätte, hätte . . . gesagt.

Lektion 28, page 176

1) Wenn du Sonntag hättest arbeiten müssen, hättest du gearbeitet? 2) Wenn du es hättest tun können, hättest du es getan? 3) Wenn du es tun könntest, würdest du es tun? 4) Wenn sie ihn hätte verlassen müssen, hätte sie ihn verlassen. 5) Wenn ich ihn daran hätte hindern können, hätte ich ihn daran gehindert. 6) Wenn ich das Spiel hätte gewinnen wollen, hätte ich es

gewonnen. 7) Wenn sie ihn hätte gehen lassen müssen, hätte sie ihn gehen lassen. 8) Wenn er sie hätte heiraten wollen, hätte er sie heiraten können. 9) Wenn ich mit euch hätte gehen dürfen, wäre ich mit euch gegangen. 10) Wenn wir die Prüfungen hätten bestehen wollen, hätten wir sie bestanden. 11) Wenn er es hätte machen müssen, hätte er es gemacht. 12) Wenn der Doktor etwas hätte tun können, hätte er es getan. 13) Wenn ich mir ein neues Kleid hätte machen lassen, wäre ich auf die Party gegangen. 14) Wenn die Kinder an den Strand hätten gehen dürfen, wären sie gegangen. 15) Wenn sie hätten anrufen können, hätten sie angerufen. 16) Wenn du mit mir hättest sprechen wollen, hättest du mit mir sprechen können.

Lektion 28, page 178

1) Wenn ich eine Lösung gefunden hätte (fände, finde), wäre (wäre, bin) ich glücklicher gewesen. 2) Wenn ich gewonnen hätte (gewänne, gewinne), hätte (bekäme, bekomme) ich einen Preis bekommen. 3) Wenn ich diese Wohnung gekauft hätte (kaufte, kaufe), hättest (könntest, kannst) du bei mir wohnen können. 4) Wenn du dich besser gefühlt hättest (fühl(te)st), wärst (kämst, kommst) du mit uns gekommen? 5) Wenn wir den Bus früher genommen hätten (nähmen, nehmen), wären (kämen . . . an, kommen . . . an) wir pünktlich angekommen. 6) Wenn er langsamer gefahren wäre, (führe, fahrt) hätte (hätte, hat) er keinen Unfall gehabt. 7) Wenn die Polizei dem Mörder mit dem Auto gefolgt wäre (folgt(e)), hätte (würde . . . fangen, fängt) sie ihn gefangen. 8) Wenn es nicht so lächerlich gewesen wäre (wäre, ist), hätte (glaubte, glaube) ich es geglaubt. 9) Wenn ich die Nase voll gehabt hätte (hätte, habe), hätte (hörte . . . auf, höre . . . auf) ich aufgehört. 10) Wenn es sonnig gewesen wäre (wäre, ist), wären (gingen, gehen . . . spazieren) wir spazieren gegangen. 11) Wenn ich sie lieber gehabt hätte (hätte, habe), wäre (zöge, ziehe) ich in ihre Wohnung gezogen. 12) Wenn ich es gemusst hätte (müsste, muss), hätte (borgte, borge) ich das Geld von ihm geborgt. 13) Wenn du einen Job gesucht hättest (suchtest, suchst), hättest (würdest . . . kaufen, kaufst) du die Morgenzeitungen gekauft? 14) Sogar, wenn du mir die Wahrheit gesagt hättest (sagtest, sagst), hätte (würde . . . glauben, glaube) ich dir nicht geglaubt. 15) Wenn er nicht so schüchtern gewesen wäre (wäre, ist), hätte (küsste, küsst) er sie. 16) Wenn er fleissig studiert hätte (studierte, studiert), hätte (bekame, geküsst, bekommt) er seine Diplome bekommen. 17) Wenn der Film ein Reinfall gewesen wäre (wäre, ist), hätte (verlöre, verliert) er sein ganzes Geld verloren. 18) Wenn der Pelzmantel im Ausverkauf gewesen wäre (wäre, ist), hätte (kaufte, kaufe) ich ihn gekauft. 19) Wenn sie nicht hätte kommen können (könnte, kann), hätte (liesse, lässt) sie es euch wissen lassen. 20) Wenn wir heute abend nicht hätten arbeiten müssen (müssten, müssen), wären (gingen, gehen) wir tanzen gegangen. 21) Wenn du geradeaus gegangen wärst (gingst, gehst), hättest (fändest, findest) du die Kirche gefunden. 22) Wenn du deutsch gesprochen hättest (sprächst, sprichst),

wärst (führst, fährst) du nach Deutschland gefahren. 23) Wenn ich es gesucht hätte (suchte, suche), hätte (fände, finde) ich es gefunden. 24) Wenn er listig genug gewesen wäre (wäre, ist), hätte (überredete, überredet) er ihn überredet. 25) Wenn du ihn zuerst gesehen hättest (sähest, siehst), hättest (sprächst, sprichst) du mit ihm gesprochen? 26) Wenn es nicht geregnet hätte (regnete, regnet), wären (wären, sind) wir nicht zu Hause gewesen. 27) Wenn du deinen Regenschirm nicht verloren hättest (verlörest, verlierst), wären (würden, werden) wir nicht nass geworden.

Lektion 29, page 182
1) sich. Wer fühlt sich gut? 2) sich. Warum muss sie sich beeilen. 3) sich. Wo waschen sie sich? 4) dir. Was wäschst du dir? 5) mir. Wer putzt sich die Zähne? 6) uns. Wann können wir uns ausschlafen? 7) uns. Worum streitet ihr euch? 8) sich. Hat sie sich je verspätet? 9) sich. Wer schämt sich nicht? 10) mich. Worauf freust du dich? 11) sich. Würde er sich wundern? 12) dir. Was kämme ich mir? 13) sich. Worüber freut sie sich? 14) sich. Was erfüllt sich nicht? 15) sich. Was hat sich verbessert? 16) sich. Wann verloben sie sich? 17) sich. Wer hat sich geirrt? 18) uns. Was für einen Film seht ihr euch an? 19) sich. Über wen regt er sich auf? 20) mich. Mit wem verstehst du dich? 21) mich. Warum ziehst du dich aus? 22) sich. Wofür macht sie sich fertig? 23) euch. Wofür interessieren wir uns? 24) uns. Bei wem entschuldigt ihr euch? 25) sich. Wann lassen sie sich scheiden? 26) mir. Um wen machst du dir Sorgen? 27) mich. Wohin setzt du dich? 28) euch. Woran erinnern wir uns?

Lesson 29, page 183
1) Beeilen wir uns! 2) Ich ziehe mich gerade an. 3) Wofür interessierst du dich? 4) Ich rasierte mich, während sie sich umzog. 5) Wenn er sich entschied, würden wir uns nicht länger Sorgen machen müssen. 6) Wir könnten weggehen, wenn sie sich jetzt fertigmachte. 7) Wenn wir jetzt heirateten, liessen wir uns morgen scheiden. 8) Reg dich nicht auf! (Regt euch/Regen Sie sich nicht auf!) 9) Was würdest du dir aussuchen? 10) Alle Träume erfüllen sich nicht. 11) Die Lage wird sich verbessern. 12) Ich freue mich auf deine Geburtstagsparty. 13) Jedes Mal, wenn sie sich streiten, wird er wütend. 14) Nehmen Sie sich Zeit! (Nimm dir/Nehmt euch Zeit!) 15) Sonntags schlafe ich mich aus, und montags verschlafe ich mich. 16) Worüber beklagt er sich? 17) Du wirst dich an sein Benehmen gewöhnen. 18) Heute nacht will ich mich amüsieren. 19) Er erkältete sich, als wir in den Bergen waren. 20) Zuerst zankten sie sich, und dann floh er. 21) Erinnerst du dich an ihn? 22) Ich brach mir ein Bein, als wir den Unfall hatten. 23) Entschuldige dich! (Entschudigt euch! Entschuldigen sie sich!) 24) Verabreden wir uns für Montag. 25) Ich verlief mich, als ich vom Bahnhof zurückkam. 26) Ich muss mich ein paar Minuten lang auf mein Bett legen. 27) Er versteht sich gut mit seiner Frau. 28) Ich frage mich, ob mein Übersetzung richtig ist.

Lektion 30, page 185

1) Sie hat sich mit ihrem neuen Kamm gekämmt. Womit hat sie sich gekämmt? 2) Ich habe mir am Morgen und am Abend die Zähne geputzt. Wann hast du dir die Zähne geputzt. 3) Er hat sich immer mit seiner Frau gestritten. Mit wem hat er sich immer gestritten? 4) Sie hat sich wieder verspätet, weil sie sich verschlafen hat. Warum hat sie sich wieder verspätet? 5) Wir haben uns schlecht gefühlt. Wer hat sich schlecht gefühlt? 6) Der Junge hat sich schon rasiert. Hat sich der Junge schon rasiert? 7) Er hat sich beim Direktor über seine Sekretärin beklagt. Über wen hat er sich beim Direktor beklagt? 8) Er hat sich Zeit genommen. Wer hat sich Zeit genommen? 9) Wir haben uns in einer Diskothek amüsiert. Wo habt ihr euch amüsiert? 10) Ich habe mich für Blues interessiert. Wofür hast du dich interessiert? 11) Sie haben sich für nächste Woche verabredet. Für wann haben sie sich verabredet? 12) Sie haben sich um einen Sitzplatz gezankt. Wer hat sich um einen Sitzplatz gezankt? 13) Wir haben uns gut mit unseren Kollegen verstanden. Mit wem habt ihr euch gut verstanden? 14) Die alte Dame hat sich in den grossen Sessel gesetzt. Welche Dame hat sich in den grossen Sessel gesetzt? 15) Wenn er sich ärgerte, stritten sie sich. Wann stritten sie sich? 16) Du hast dich immer im Januar erkältet. Wann hast du dich erkältet? 17) Sie haben sich das Stück angesehen. Was haben sie sich angesehen? 18) Wir haben uns Zeit nehmen können. Wer hat sich Zeit nehmen können?

Lektion 30, page 186

1) Kannst du dir vorstellen, dass sie in Ohnmacht gefallen ist? 2) Es tut mir leid, ich hatte Unrecht. 3) Die Lage hat sich zeitweilig verschlechtert. 4) Wenn du dich gebessert hättest, wäre die Mutter sehr froh gewesen. 5) Harry hat sich wieder verlaufen. 6) Putzen Sie sich die Zähne mit einer harten Zahnbürste? 7) So gut wie alle haben sich für die Unterhaltung interessiert. 8) Du solltest dich schämen, diesen Klatsch ernst zu nehmen. 9) Wenn ich mir Zeit nähme, kämen wir nie dort an. 10) Wenn sie wieder wie die Katze um den heissen Brei schleicht, werde ich wütend. 11) Legen wir uns ins Gras, um uns auszuruhen. 12) Wenn das Bier abgestanden ist, musst du dich darüber beklagen. 13) Wenn dieser Plan Wirklichkeit geworden wäre, wäre ich in Ohnmacht gefallen. 14) Ich kann mich nicht an den neuen Wagen gewöhnen. 15) Freust du dich auf deine nächsten Ferien? 16) Schau! Das Restaurant in jenem Wolkenkratzer dreht sich. 17) Du hättest dich entschuldigen sollen. 18) Ich schneide mich, wenn ich mich schnell rasieren will. 19) Wenn du dir Zeit nähmest, wäre deine Arbeit besser. 20) Hast du dich mit ihr verabredet? 21) Schämst du dich nicht? 22) Wenn ich mich beeilt hätte, wäre ich nicht zu spät gekommen. 23) Stell dir vor, was du machen könntest, wenn du gute Verbindungen hättest. 24) Hör auf, dir um ihn Sorgen zu machen! 25) Wenn sie ihn fingen, würde er versuchen zu fliehen. 26) Verloben wir uns! 27) Fürchten Sie sich in der Dunkelheit? 28) Sehen Sie sich gern den Mond an?

Lektion 30, page 187

1) Er hat es selbst gemacht. 2) Hast du das Buch für dich (selbst) oder deinen Freund gekauft? 3) Wenn ich es selbst hätte machen können, hätte ich es selbst gemacht. 4) Ich bin erstaunt, dass sie es selbst macht. 5) Hast du den Unfall selbst gesehen? 6) Wir haben das Geschenk selbst gemacht. 7) Sag es ihm selbst! 8) Die alte Dame spricht mit sich selbst. 9) Er hat nur sich selbst gern. 10) Sie fragen ihn selbst. 11) Ich habe das Steak selbst gebraten. 12) Wir hätten es selbst machen können. 13) Ich habe den Brief nicht selbst geschrieben. 14) Du hättest ihn selbst einladen sollen.

Lektion 31, page 190

1) seinen ältesten. 2) einen neuen, meine, ein neues. 3) die junge, ihren alten, ihre alte. 4) den hohen. 5) ein, gutes. 6) dieser neue, wichtige. 7) einen neuen. 8) diese, den höchsten. 9) ein billigeres, einen neuen. 10) unsere kleinen, grosse. 11) der, den besten, die beste.

Lektion 31, page 190

1) Wir haben einen schönen, blauen Wagen gekauft. 2) Unsere neue Wohnung sollte wenigstens drei grosse Zimmer haben. 3) Meine jüngste Tochter und mein jüngster Sohn sehen sich einen interessanten Film an. 4) Letztes Jahr haben wir einen sehr langen und kalten Winter gehabt. 5) Ich möchte einen süssen, heissen Tee trinken. 6) Wir haben einen riesigen Baum, schöne Blumen, einen kleinen Garten und einen sauberen Hof gesehen. 7) Wir sind durch einen grossen Park, einen dunklen Wald und hohes Gras gegangen. 8) Ich gebe dir ein neues Stück Seife, ein sauberes Handtuch und eine neue Zahnbürste. 9) Du brauchst eine warme Decke, ein weiches Kissen und ein weisses Laken. 10) Sie hat ein gelbes Hemd, einen braunen Anzug, einen schwarzen Schlips, ein grünes Kleid, einen blauen Mantel und schwarze Schuhe gekauft. 11) Weihnachten hat sie mir ein interessantes Buch, einen roten Schal und eine schöne Pfeife geschenkt.

Lektion 31, page 191

1) Das schöne Haus gehört dem jungen Mann, der mit seiner hübschen Frau und ihren beiden Kindern in dem ersten Stock wohnt. 2) In dem neuen Supermarkt gibt man den ersten Kunden eine kleine Flasche Whisky. 3) Wir helfen dem jungen Engländer, der netten Amerikanerin, dem braunen Italiener, dem charmanten Franzosen und den reizenden Japanerinnen deutsch zu lernen. 4) Der gute Lehrer antwortet den guten Schülern sowie den schlechten. 5) Ich gebe dem freundlichen Arzt und der netten Krankenschwester ein kleines Geschenk.

Lektion 31, page 192

1) Er ist der jüngste Bruder seiner zweiten Frau. 2) Ist das der Wagen deines Vaters, deines Onkels, deiner Tante oder des Herrn von nebenan. 3) Das ist

Peters Frau. 4) Trotz des schlechten und kalten Wetters fuhren wir zu der Gartenparty unserer neuen Freunde. 5) Wegen einer sehr schlechten Note hat er das schwere Examen nicht bestanden. 6) Ist das das Büro des neuen Ingenieurs, des ersten Direktors oder der alten Sekretärin. 7) Während meiner nächsten Sommerferien fahre ich mit dem grossen Wagen meines älteren Bruders durch Europa.

Lektion 31, page 193
1) Als ich ein Kind war, wollte ich immer ein grosser Gangster werden. 2) Das sind die grossen Kinder meines Kumpels. 3) Wenn ich meiner Schwester hätte helfen können, hätte ich ihr geholfen. 4) Als ich ihn traf, trug er einen weissen Anzug, ein weisses Hemd und einen schwarzen Schlips. 5) Ich habe den kleinen Kindern ein paar Bonbons gegeben. 6) Er sitzt zwischen einem schweren Stuhl und einem altmodischen Schreibtisch. 7) Ich streite nicht mit kleinen Jungen. 8) Ich brauche den Brief binnen einer halben Stunde. 9) Trotz der heissen Sonne spielten wir ein ermüdendes Spiel. 10) Während der langweiligen Unterhaltung schliefen viele Leute ein. 11) Mein bester Freund ist gegen deine gute Idee. 12) Ich hätte nichts gegen ein Glas kaltes deutsches Bier. 13) Ich traue diesem falschen Schuft nicht. 14) Ich habe einen schweren Unfall mit dem Wagen meines Bruders gehabt. 15) Er versucht, ein kleines Geschäft in diesem alten Haus zu eröffnen. 16) Er hat seinen jungen, fleissigen und sorgfältigen Arbeiter gefeuert. 17) Der erfolglose Schriftsteller wohnt in einem kleinen, billigen Zimmer. 18) Ich verstehe keins von den Bildern dieses Malers. 19) Die Birne der grossen Lampe in unserem gemütlichen Wohnzimmer ist kaputt. 20) Die Polizei hat den jungen Mann, der den echten Diamanten der reichen Dame gestohlen hatte, festgenommen. 21) Wenn gute Freunde in ein anderes Land ziehen, versuche ich, sie jeden Sommer zu besuchen. 22) Junge Leute kümmern sich oft nicht um alte Leute. 23) Er hat seine neue Armbanduhr und seinen teuren Kugelschreiber verloren. 24) Ich werde wütend, wenn ich ein langweiliges Buch lese oder einen schlechten Film sehe. 25) Ist das der Wagen dieses oder jenes Mannes. 26) Er bekommt viel Geld für die schönen, kleinen Dinge, die er in seinem kleinen Zimmer im siebten Stock macht.

Lektion 32, page 197
1) Als ich den Alptraum hatte, hatte ich Angst. 2) Ich stehe immer früh auf. 3) Isst du gerade? Isst du immer so früh? 4) Ich hörte Radio, als ich nicht schlafen konnte. 5) Wir haben ihn letzte Woche in den Bergen getroffen. 6) Trafst du sie, als ihr an der See wart. 7) Dieses Stück wird wegen seines Regisseurs ein Reinfall sein. 8) Ist sie heute morgen hier gewesen? 9) Was taten Sie, als ich anrief? 10) Ich wurde wütend, anstatt ihr zu vergeben. 11) Als das kleine Mädchen mit seiner Puppe spielte, zerbrach es sie. 12) Sind Sie je in München gewesen? Ja, ich bin letzte Woche dort gewesen. 13) Werden sie ihn feuern, weil er in der Gewerkschaft ist. 14) Sie haben

gestreikt, um mehr Geld zu verdienen. 15) Ich bin um 10 Uhr dort. 16)
Jeden Sommer fahren wir in den Süden. 17) Hast du ihre dumme Unterhaltung gehört? 18) Ich kenne sie seit zwei Jahren. 19) Sie ist gestern auf das
Land gefahren. 20) Ich werde vor dir aufstehen. 21) Ich wurde wütend, als
er das Buch zerriss. 22) Gehst du heute abend mit uns? 23) Warum hast du
ihm nicht geholfen? 24) Sie wartet seit heute mittag auf ihn. 25) Was werde
ich machen? 26) Ich bin früher einmal pro Jahr ins Ausland gefahren. 27) Ich
bin es nicht gewohnt, deutsches Essen zu essen. (Ich bin deutsches Essen
nicht gewohnt.) 28) Wird sie mir je verzeihen?

Lektion 32, page 198

1) Wenn ich Zeit hätte (gehabt hätte), führe (wäre) ich in die Berge (gefahren).
2) Wenn ich eine Lösung fände (gefunden hätte), wäre ich glücklich (gewesen).
3) Wenn ich das Geld bekäme (bekommen hätte), liehe ich dir etwas. (hätte
. . . geliehen). 4) Wenn ich ihn träfe (getroffen hätte), entschuldigte (hätte)
ich mich bei ihm (entschuldigt). 5) Wenn ich könnte (gekonnt hätte), machte
(hätte) ich es (gemacht). 6) Wenn du es wolltest (gewollt hättest), könntest
(hättest) du es machen (können). 7) Wenn ich den Ring verlöre (verloren
hätte), wäre ich sehr traurig (gewesen). 8) Wenn ich sie besser kennen würde
(gekannt hätte), fragte (hätte) ich sie (gefragt). 9) Wenn du nicht allein
gehen wolltest (hättest wollen), ginge (wäre) ich mit (mitgegangen). 10) Wenn
er mit ihr spräche (gesprochen hätte), würde (wäre) er rot (geworden).
11) Wenn die Sonne nicht schiene (geschienen hätte), bliebe (wäre) ich zu
Hause (geblieben). 12) Wenn er nicht sorgfältiger arbeitete (gearbeitet hätte),
feuerte (hätte) ich ihn (gefeuert). 13) Wenn du mir versprächest zu schweigen
(versprochen hättest), sagte (hätte) ich es dir (gesagt). 14) Wenn Sie es ihm
erzählten (erzählt hätten), traute (hätte) ich Ihnen nicht mehr (getraut).

Lektion 32, page 198

1) Wenn er zu spät käme, würde ich nicht warten. 2) Wenn sie nicht kommen
kann, ruft sie dich an. 3) Wenn ich allein gewesen wäre, wäre ich schlafen
gegangen. 4) Wenn ich es hätte machen müssen, hätte ich es gemacht. 5)
Wenn ich nicht arbeiten muss, spiele ich mit den Kindern. 6) Wenn du es
nicht zustandebringst, helfe ich dir. 7) Wenn er es mir erzählt hätte, hätte ich
eine Lösung gewusst. 8) Wenn der Gangster den Bullen hätte töten müssen,
hätte er es getan. 9) Wenn sie die Preise erhöhen, verlieren sie viel Geld. 10)
Wenn du den Film gesehen hättest, hättest du auch geweint. 11) Wenn er
diesen Kampf verlöre, gäbe er diesen Sport auf.

Lektion 32, page 199

1) Müssen wir jetzt gehen? Ja, wir müssen jetzt gehen, 2) Du hättest es ihr
sagen sollen. 3) Du hättest es mir nicht zu sagen brauchen. 4) Glaubst du
wirklich, ich hätte es ihr sagen sollen. 5) Obwohl es mich freut, Sie zu sehen,
muss ich jetzt gehen. 6) Du sollst es unbedingt machen. 7) Er muss lachen,

während jener Lehrer spricht. 8) Ich hätte gestern fast jene alte Uhr gekauft.
9) Sie glaubt nicht, dass ich es machen kann. 10) Er hätte dir die Wahrheit
sagen sollen. 11) Ich arbeite hier seit einem Jahr. 12) Wie konntest du soviel
trinken? 13) Du musst es jetzt machen. Ich musste es gestern machen.
14) Letzte Woche brauchten wir nicht zu arbeiten. 15) Er durfte nicht mit
uns gehen. 16) Darf ich Ihnen eine Frage stellen. 17) Er ist nicht gekommen,
er muss krank gewesen sein. 18) Ich kann meinen Regenschirm nicht finden,
ich muss ihn verloren haben. 19) Sie kann noch nicht fertig sein. 20) Sie
hätten nicht heiraten sollen. 21) Du darfst diesen Pullover nicht waschen.
22) Ich war enttäuscht, da er nicht mit uns verreisen konnte. 23) Wie hätte
ich es machen sollen? 24) Er brauchte nicht so früh zu gehen. 25) Er denkt,
er kann sich nicht irren. 26) Du sprichst seit einer Stunde. 27) Gott sei
Dank! Ich muss es nicht allein machen. 28) Arbeitetet ihr, während wir
assen?